DATE DUE

PIONEER WRITER

Louisa Atkinson
(Mitchell Library, State Library of NSW)

PIONEER WRITER

*The life of Louisa Atkinson: novelist,
journalist, naturalist*

PATRICIA CLARKE

ALLEN & UNWIN

Sydney   Wellington   London   Boston

By the same author

The Governesses. Letters from the Colonies 1862–1882 (1985, paperback edition 1989)

A Colonial Woman. The Life and Times of Mary Braidwood Mowle 1827–1857 (1986)

Pen Portraits. Women Writers and Journalists in Nineteenth Century Australia (1988)

First published in 1990
Allen & Unwin Australia Pty Ltd
An Unwin Hyman company
8 Napier Street, North Sydney, NSW 2059 Australia

Allen & Unwin New Zealand Limited
75 Ghuznee Street, Wellington, New Zealand

Unwin Hyman Limited
15–17 Broadwick Street, London WIV 1FP England

Unwin Hyman Inc.
955 Massachusetts Avenue, Cambridge MA 02139 USA

National Library of Australia
Cataloguing-in-Publication entry:

Clarke, Patricia.
  Pioneer writer.

  Bibliography.
  Includes index.
  ISBN 0 04 442267 9.

  1. Atkinson, Louisa, 1834–1872—Biography.
  2. Novelists, Australian—19th century—
  Biography. 3. Women novelists, Australian
  —19th century—Biography. I. Title.

A823.1

Set in 11/12 pt Palatino by Graphicraft Typesetters Ltd, Hong Kong
Printed by South Wind Production Singapore Private Limited

Publication assisted by the
Australia Council, the Australian
Government's arts funding
and advisory body.

Contents

Illustrations

Acronyms

AONSW	Archives Office of New South Wales
AVC	A Voice From the Country
HRA	Historical Records of Australia
ISN	*Illustrated Sydney News*
ML	*Mitchell Library*
NLA	National Library of Australia
RAHS	Royal Australian Historical Society
SH	*Sydney Herald* (before 1 August 1942)
SM	*Sydney Mail*
SMH	*Sydney Morning Herald* (after 1 August 1842)

Acknowledgements

My thanks are due to the late Miss Janet Cosh, the only direct descendant of Louisa Atkinson, for her very generous help while I was researching this book. On my numerous visits to her home at Moss Vale, she could not have been more hospitable and helpful in providing information and allowing me to see the material relevant to Louisa Atkinson that she retained. The thanks of all people interested in preserving our early history are due to her for the donations of material about Louisa Atkinson, including many of her drawings and paintings, that she has made over the past twenty or thirty years to the Mitchell Library. I saw Janet Cosh for the last time in September 1989, just after I had completed the writing of this book. She expressed great pleasure at its forthcoming publication. Unfortunately she died suddenly at the age of 88 on 22 October 1989.

At various times in researching this book I was dismayed at the lack of personal material concerning Louisa Atkinson. Although there is some correspondence in the Mitchell Library, the collection includes only six letters written by Louisa Atkinson—one to a servant, three to her solicitors, one to Rev. William Branwhite Clarke and one to Mrs Sarah Woolls. Obviously, this is only the remnant of what must have been a voluminous correspondence, both personal and connected with Louisa's work as a plant collector. There are more letters to Louisa Atkinson but these too are a haphazard and small part of what must have been many hundreds of letters.

Being concerned at the absence of personal letters, I thought that tracing Louisa Atkinson's relatives might bring to light some previously overlooked correspondence. In this regard I am particularly grateful to Dr Marion Amies for alerting me to the existence of a descendant of Louisa Atkinson's eldest sister, Charlotte Elizabeth NcNeilly. From this first contact with Mrs Essie Whiteman of Springwood, I gradually came in contact with many other descendants of this branch of the family and I wish to thank among these

Enid Canning, Georges Hall, New South Wales; Charlotte Drevermann, South Belmont, New South Wales; Neil McCormack, Loftus, New South Wales; Essie Whiteman, Springwood, New South Wales; E.C. Mason, Mosman, New South Wales and genealogical expert, Jan Gow, Auckland, New Zealand, who invited me to a gathering of descendants of the Atkinson, McNeilly, Garlick, Newcombe, Farraher, MacDonald, Fraser and Millikin families, held at Narwee Public School in October 1988. It was at this gathering that I first met many of these descendants. After many false starts I traced descendants of Louisa Atkinson's brother to Perth and I am grateful to James Burnet Atkinson, Bentley, Western Australia for his kind assistance. I also wish to thank descendants of Louisa Atkinson's uncle, John Atkinson, particularly James Fellows, Sydney, and Joyce and James Atkinson, Wattle Glen, Victoria. Although these contacts did not lead me to the hoped-for long lost bundle of letters or similar treasures, I did gain invaluable family information from them all.

The circumstance of Louisa Atkinson's early death militated against the survival of direct family records, information and tradition. Unfortunately there was a similar situation in her husband's family, as the family of James Calvert's only brother died out without leaving descendants. I am grateful to his sister's descendants, Dr Adrian Dawson, Hamilton, New South Wales, and Mrs Nan Dawson, Paddington, New South Wales, for their assistance with information on this side of the family.

I found two communications of Louisa Atkinson's in official institutions—one a letter to Baron von Mueller in the National Herbarium, Melbourne, and the other a communication to William Macleay in the Macleay Museum, University of Sydney. I thank Doris Sinkora at the National Herbarium, Melbourne, and Julian Holland at the Macleay Museum for their assistance in locating these items and for other help. I am grateful to Dr Gerhard Bagan, University of Kiel, Professor Johannes Voigt, University of Stuttgart and Université Louis Pasteur, Strasbourg for their investigations concerning the possible location of material of Louisa Atkinson's overseas.

I thank the staff in the Petherick Room of the National Library, Canberra, particularly Jean James, and in the newspaper and microfilm room, particularly Bill Tully; the staff of the Mitchell library, particularly Janet Anderson, who located invaluable material in the Berry papers; the staff of the Archives Authority of New South Wales, both at the Rocks and Kingswood; Mrs Patricia Bofinger, Bathurst District Historical Society; Mrs J. Ralph and members of the Berrima District Historical Society; Marion McCarthy and members of the Yass Historical Society; Rachel Roxburgh, Moss Vale, author of a history of Throsby Park; Max Thompson, author of a biography of William Woolls; Mrs J. Smail, author of a booklet on Louisa Atkinson at Kurrajong; Ken Snell, music expert; Dr Marjorie Jacobs, RAHS Archives Officer; Shirley McGlynn, who undertook research; Marcie Muir, Kensington Gardens, South Australia; Elizabeth Plimer, Lindfield, New South Wales; Victor Crittenden, Cook, Australian Capital Territory; Tim White, Deakin, Australian Capital Territory; Penny Pemberton, Australian Capital Territory; Lillyan MacDonald, Research Secretary, Society of Australian Genealogists; Mr Palazzi, Warden All Saints, Sutton Forest, New South Wales; Tim Fisher, Australian National Gallery, Australian Capital Territory; Rev. N.J. Pilcher, St Peter's, Richmond, New South Wales; Mrs Kathleen Cape, Rose Bay, New South Wales; Mrs Judy Bartram, Neutral Bay, New South Wales; Mrs J. Selkirk-Provis, Mosman, New South Wales.

When visiting places where Louisa Atkinson lived I received great assistance for which I am very grateful from David Sherbon, Oldbury, Helen Castle Roche, Cavan West, Les Hewitt, Cavan, and Mrs Mitchell, Swanton. My husband, Hugh, was as usual very forbearing in accompanying me on my researches and I thank him for the great interest he has taken in the project.

This book was researched with the assistance of a Special Purpose Grant from the Literature Board of the Australia Council. This was a great help with travel and research expenses and the acquiring of photographs and I express my appreciation to the Board.

Author's note

Except in quotations, I have used the usually accepted present spelling for place names, rather than the sometimes different nineteenth-century spelling used by Louisa Atkinson.

Misprints were frequent in Louisa Atkinson's newspaper articles and novels, probably caused by compositors misreading her handwritten copy. In her novels the names of people are often spelt differently in different episodes and punctuation is haphazard. Botanical terms were particularly prone to mistakes. At the end of 'The Cataract Coal Mine' (*Sydney Morning Herald*, 6 October 1870) she corrected no less than three misprints of botanical terms that had occurred in her previous article 'Wallaby Rocks' but usually she allowed the mistakes to go without comment. Where misprints are glaring, I have made minimal changes.

1

Searching for Louisa Atkinson

I searched for Louisa Atkinson in the green paddocks at Sutton Forest, on the southern tablelands of New South Wales, 140 kilometres south from Sydney. In 1820 Governor Lachlan Macquarie, passing through the district on an exploratory expedition to the south, wrote in his journal that the country resembled 'a fine extensive pleasure ground in England'. On his return journey he named 'this rich and beautiful tract of country' Sutton Forest after Charles Manners Sutton, the Speaker of the House of Commons.[1]

Specifically I searched for Louisa at Oldbury, a distinctive two-storey sandstone English-style farmhouse, built about 160 years ago in the lee of Mt Gingenbullen on Oldbury estate at Sutton Forest. In the grounds lavender, phlox and other old-fashioned flowers grow profusely. A driveway circles a green lawn in the centre of which stands an enormous golden cypress, its lower branches, in its old age, supported by wooden props. Elms along the creek date from the time of James Atkinson, Louisa's father, who settled at Oldbury soon after Governor Macquarie named the district. After years of neglect Oldbury, classified by the National Trust, is being restored to its original state, a solid plain building with neither verandahs nor balconies. Extraneous additions have been removed, layers of paint have been scraped from the cedar woodwork, wallpaper stripped from walls and picture windows replaced with deepset small square-paned ones of the original design. Appropriately a painting by English painter John Glover hangs on a wall. Here in 1834 Louisa was born and spent the first years of her life, and to it she returned on many occasions during her short life. At Oldbury she developed her love of plants, animals and birds, she absorbed information for her nature columns published in city newspapers, she gained inspiration for her

1

This watercolour of Oldbury, Sutton Forest looking from Mt Gingenbullen was painted by Louisa Atkinson. She was born here in 1834 in a two-storey house built from local sandstone by her father in about 1830. (Mitchell Library, State Library of NSW)

drawings of flora and fauna, and the farm and country life she observed around her provided a background for her novels.

I searched for Louisa at Swanton, the overseer's cottage of four spartan rooms on the other side of Mt Gingenbullen, where she died so suddenly. Swanton, until recently a dilapidated ruin, is no longer part of the Oldbury estate. When she lived there its porch was covered in climbing plants and around it chickens, ducklings and angora goats flourished and bees buzzed around the beehive.

I searched in the graveyard of All Saints Anglican Church, Sutton Forest, where, among the graves of notable early families, unknown convicts, child victims of epidemics, young soldiers of the military guard at Berrima and victims of bushrangers and highway robbers, Louisa lies buried.

A few kilometres from Sutton Forest at Moss Vale, Louisa's only descendant, Janet Cosh, until her death in October 1989, lived amid towering trees. She fed flocks of magpies and currawongs so used to regular meals that they filled the air with their raucous demands if she was a little late. One spring she finished a letter to me thus: 'The bush is flowering wonderfully. I wish Louisa was here.'[2]

At Kurrajong Heights, about 70 kilometres west of Sydney, Louisa lived as an adult in a house called Fernhurst, 'a beautifully situated cottage',[3] where the gully, lush with ferns near her home, was known as 'Miss Atkinson's gully'.[4] Kurrajong was the scene of her greatest endeavours in plant collecting and in publicising the beauty of the Australian bush. Though frail and delicate in constitution, she gained strength in the pure mountain air. For many hours she would ride over rock-strewn, precipitous tracks, along narrow ridges and through dense fern gullies, on botanising trips as far as Mount Tomah to the west and Wiseman's Ferry to the north-east.

Places are important, but to unravel Louisa's life legal papers, untouched for nearly 150 years, proved just as vital. Under layers of black dust, they held the secrets of the extraordinary legal battles that dominated her childhood and moulded her attitude to life, leaving her with an underlying, but only partially expressed belief, in women's independence. Although blurred in expression, she demonstrated in her own life the right of a woman to study natural science, to write for newspapers and to write novels, all unusual pursuits for a woman in mid-nineteenth century Australia.

Louisa Atkinson was born at Oldbury less than 50 years after the arrival of the First Fleet at Botany Bay. Although regarded as good country, Sutton Forest was connected by only a cart track to Picton on the road to Sydney. When Louisa was born the European population of New South Wales was little more than 60 000 people and she was one of only about 12 000 of European descent who were Australian-born. New South Wales was still a frontier society. Convicts transported from England, Ireland and Scotland provided most of the labour on farms and in Sydney, the only town of any size. Law and order was roughly administered by floggings and assignment to chain gangs. Bushrangers, often escaped convicts, roamed freely in parts of the countryside. Conflicts between the Aborigines and the white settlers were sometimes bloody, but more often they developed into a war of attrition through the dislocation of the lives of Aborigines and their insidious destruction through disease.

3

Louisa Atkinson painted this watercolour of Oldbury Mill. She spent the first years of her life at the Atkinson family home at Oldbury and returned there on many occasions. (Janet Cosh)

Louisa grew up familiar with convicts and bushrangers and during her lifetime she witnessed the virtual disappearance of the Aboriginal race from the areas she knew. She saw the end of the convict era and the start of the mass arrival of free settlers. She lived through the enormous social changes and excitement of the gold rushes of the 1850s, she observed the operation of large sheep and cattle properties and later she saw the results of the land acts promoting free selection by small farmers.

Louisa was to write about all these subjects, and also about the animals and birds and plants she loved so much.

It is comparatively easy to document Louisa Atkinson's life, although in this there are gaps because so much material has been lost. It is harder to grasp and describe the details of her character. Some information can be gathered from her novels and there are delightful glimpses of her own life in her writings on natural history. It is obvious she was energetic and determined and had a fine intelligence and disciplined mind. By nature she was cheerful and kindly and had a special radiance that made people, more especially children, remember and recall her. Her life was guided by religion but it was a religion expressed in good works not in dogma.

The closest we can get to an intimate feeling of the person is in a talk given to the Royal Australian Historical Society by Margaret Swann in 1928, some 56 years after Louisa's death.[5] It is an important source because it is based, in part, on information from Henry Selkirk, for many years a councillor of the Royal Australian Historical Society. His mother Emma Selkirk was Louisa's greatest friend, and he himself knew Louisa well in his childhood.

The writer is important too. Margaret Swann, born in 1871, was an uncompromising feminist, interested in any movements that would bring the achievements of women before the public. Her interest in writing about Louisa Atkinson, a woman who achieved so much at a time when the usual role of women was entirely domestic, is obvious.[6]

Henry Selkirk, born in 1857, remembered Louisa Atkinson's 'magnetic personality'. When she visited the Selkirk home it was an occasion for Henry (called Harry by his mother), his sister May, and when they were old enough, his brothers William and Robert, to be out on the road leading down from Kurrajong Heights to Richmond watching for a first sight of their visitor. She would appear, a small, slight woman, her hair a mass of long dark ringlets, her large eyes, greyish in colour, ever alert, dressed in a neat brown holland habit, riding her shaggy pony. They were always delighted to see their mother's friend for everyone came under her spell.

She made regular visits on the third Sunday of every month, weather permitting, when she rode the twenty kilometres down from Kurrajong Heights, across the Hawkesbury River to Richmond to attend St Peter's Anglican Church. First she went to the Selkirk home and after the service spent the rest of the day with Emma Selkirk, her husband, John, a doctor, and their children in their two-storeyed house in March Street. As Louisa arrived the children would race inside to tell their mother, calling, 'Here comes Dianelle', the name Emma Selkirk had given her friend. At other times Emma Selkirk and her children stayed with Louisa at Fernhurst and Oldbury. She 'was wonderfully good to me as a child,' Henry Selkirk said.[7]

The other personal glimpse from Margaret Swann's article is of Louisa Atkinson and Emma Selkirk clambering up and down mountains, over creeks and rocks and fallen trees, adventurously dressed in 'more suitable costumes' than the 'usual long skirts which was the normal dress for women of the day'. This caused 'some twitterings in the ranks of the colonial Mrs Grundy'.

They were both of a happy, cheerful temperament, and cared nought for the gossips, especially when they returned victorious from an expedition bringing new specimens for their own collection, for that of their friend Dr Woolls, or for that 'Prince of Australian Botanists,' Baron von Mueller. In collecting plants they brought not only specimens to press and mount, but roots and seeds which they cultivated in their own gardens, watching and noting their growth and habits.[8]

Another source of information on Louisa Atkinson's character is in the sermon preached by her great friend and fellow botanist William Woolls in 1874, two years after her death. The occasion was the unveiling of a tablet in her honour at St Peter's Church, Richmond. Distinguished people who had been her friends including Bishop Frederic Barker, Anglican Bishop of Sydney, the botanist Baron Frederick von Mueller, the geologist Rev. William B. Clarke and the editor of the *Sydney Morning Herald*, John Fairfax, had arranged for the memorial tablet. Coming from the scientific world, the church and the press, they represented the public aspects of Louisa Atkinson's life—her achievements as a writer and journalist and as an acclaimed amateur botanist, and her uncomplicated and sincere dedication to simple Christian virtues.

Only four months before he preached about Louisa, William Woolls had been ordained at the age of 59 an Anglican clergyman and appointed incumbent of St Peter's, Richmond. Louisa had known him not as a clergyman but as a fellow botanist during the time when he conducted his own school at Parramatta. His sermon, later published, stressed the religious aspects of her life and her talents as a botanist but there are glimpses also of the more private world of this woman who was, Woolls said, 'one of the most interesting of Australia's daughters' and 'one of the most excellent and talented daughters of Australia'.[9]

He spoke of the 'keenness and brilliancy' of her eye, her great powers of observation, her great skill in drawing flowers and animals and her journeys on 'elevated ranges' and in the 'depths of rocky gullies' collecting 'rare and beautiful plants' bringing to notice 'some of the hidden beauties of nature'. But it was his comments on Louisa Atkinson's religious outlook that provide the most detail of the life behind the public figure. Her religion was practical. She conducted Sunday schools, visited the sick, wrote letters, drew up wills for illiterate people and exerted her influence to ensure children were 'kindly and gently treated'. She saw, Woolls said, 'the hand of God in everything' and so had 'little time for the frivolities of life, the variableness of fashion, or pursuits that were unprofitable'. Her religion was 'not of the bigoted or narrow type', she had 'a catholicity of spirit', 'and amiable disposition', there was a 'uniform cheerfulness in her character' and she had 'the singular felicity of passing through life without making any personal enemies'. From a later perspective, her granddaughter wrote of Louisa's religious outlook, 'She had the piety of her time, but was not prim'.[10]

Not surprisingly, considering the context of his remarks, William Woolls's sermon was almost entirely laudatory. The exception was a reference to her having like 'all daughters of Eve' 'failings, peculiarities, and weaknesses'. It is unfortunate that we will never known what he believed these 'failings' were.

Woolls' panegyric for Louisa Atkinson illuminates some aspects of her character, but her life was far more complex. Her roots were in the southern tablelands of New South Wales in the country to the south of Sydney and the background to her life and her writing both more interesting and more complex than William Woolls portrayed.

2

Atkinson is as fat as a pig and as saucy as a New South Wales farmer

Louisa Atkinson was the fourth child of English-born parents, James Atkinson and his wife Charlotte. James Atkinson had been in New South Wales only fourteen years when Louisa was born but in that time had established himself as a remarkably successful and innovative farmer, a self-made man who had friends among the most successful and influential of the Colony's farmers and businessmen, and the author of a widely read and highly regarded practical book on agriculture.

Louisa did not know her father. She was born at Oldbury, Sutton Forest, on 25 February 1834, just two months before his death. Although previously a strong and healthy man, at the time of her birth, when he was 39, he was suffering from the illness that caused his death. Louisa later concluded this was caused by drinking 'impure water on the top of Razorback Mountain',[1] a formidable barrier on the journey between Sydney and Oldbury. It has been speculated that he contracted typhoid fever; according to a contemporary newspaper report he died of an unspecified, 'lingering and painful illness'.[2] The pain must have been severe as when the baby Louisa was carried into his room, James Atkinson, normally a kindly and considerate man, could not bear her crying and ordered that she be removed. She grew up believing that 'probably he never saw me'.[3] Hearing of this rejection did not affect her opinion of her father. In her childhood she heard many stories of his adventurous pioneering life—stories which she was to use in her writing—and it is obvious she admired him greatly.

The deprivation she felt in never knowing her father remained with her, however, to be expressed in her novels through her heroines who are, if not orphans, deprived of at least one parent.

All of these heroines have the qualities of independence, leadership and capability that Louisa Atkinson exhibited in her own life and which developed, at least partly, as a result of growing up without a father.

Her father's death had a profound effect on the life of the Atkinson family. Although Atkinson left a large estate, many vicissitudes, some of them probably a direct result of the strain his death placed on his widow, led to the family living an unsettled life, at times threatened with physical violence and disintegration, sometimes at Oldbury, once escaping in fear to a very isolated outstation, later in Sydney and later still at Kurrajong Heights.

James Atkinson, born at his father's farm at Oldbury, West Kent, had arrived in Australia in 1820. Louisa believed that the family originally came from Yorkshire where they were 'estated and wealthy people'.[4] Nothing is known about her father's boyhood, but it is clear that he learned a great deal about agriculture from his father who in addition to general farming, grew hops. In later life he stated that he 'was bred' in the professions of 'Agriculture and Grazing'.[5] On the evidence of his authorship he was well educated, probably at Counter Hill Academy at Deptford, later the site of the Royal Naval School. In 1810 at the age of sixteen, either because of the need to earn a living away from the farm, a desire to be independent or perhaps to aid the war effort during the Napoleonic Wars, James Atkinson took a job as a clerk at the Naval Dockyard at Deptford.[6]

Apparently a very sociable man, he made many friends during his years at Deptford. They included two enterprising merchants, Alexander Berry and Edward Wollstonecraft, whose trade links ranged from Spain and Portugal to South America and from the Cape of Good Hope to New South Wales and New Zealand. In 1819 Berry and Wollstonecraft decided to emigrate to Australia. James Atkinson followed, sailing on the *Saracen* in December 1819 with £1000 in money and tools, sufficient capital to allow him to apply for a grant of land in New South Wales.

After his arrival in Sydney in May 1820, he stayed with his friend Edward Wollstonecraft at the cottage Wollstonecraft had erected on the north shore of Sydney Harbour. Wollstonecraft had obtained a grant of 202 hectares on the north shore of Port Jackson and had named the cottage he built there the Crow's Nest because of its elevated and commanding position.[7] The Sydney north shore suburbs of Crows Nest and Wollstonecraft commemorate Wollstonecraft's early association with the area. Wollstonecraft wrote to Berry, who was on business in England, about Atkinson's arrival:

I was not a little surprised a few weeks since by the unexpected appearance of our Friend James Atkinson who arrived here in the Saracen after a pleasant but rather protracted voyage. He is in excellent health.

His views are, as you may suppose, solely Agricultural, and he comes provided with good recommendations and cash sufficient for his purpose and a good store of implements of husbandry. I have however advised him to delay making his choice of land for at least six months and in the meantime to make himself acquainted by personal inspection with every part of the Colony which is known.

He has taken up his residence with me until he is determined on that head and will fill up, in some degree, the blank which your absence leaves in our society.[8]

Within a year of his arrival, Atkinson had received land grants and although he continued to work for another year in Sydney he took possession of 324 hectares which he named Oldbury, and an adjoining 283 hectares, which he named Mereworth. The land was at Sutton Forest, 140 kilometres south of Sydney.

Life was going well for James Atkinson, as Wollstonecraft reported on 9 June 1821 in a letter to his sister in England.

Atkinson is as fat as a Pig—and as saucy as a New South Wales Farmer—he still however remembers his Greenwich friends and altho he writes a whole Packet of letters himself desires his best wishes to yourself & the Pickerings & Wilkins Families and (as the style [?] goes) to all enquiring friends.[9]

Soon after Atkinson began living at Oldbury, his grant was increased to 809 hectares and he began his successful career as a farmer. He took up residence at Oldbury in 1822 with his younger brother John Atkinson, aged twenty-four, who had arrived in Sydney on the *Mariner*. The following year John was promised a grant of 809 hectares, adjoining his brother's land on the north. He took over the name of Mereworth for his land and James Atkinson's combined grants became known as Oldbury.[10]

At Oldbury James Atkinson lived at first in a bark hut built from materials found on his property.[11] Then he followed a pattern of development he was later to advocate in his book *An Account of the State of Agriculture and Grazing in New South Wales* by building a dairy, a piggery, a shed for farm equipment and huts for the convicts assigned to him.[12] He built his convict huts at Oldbury on the western slopes of Mt Gingenbullen, a striking 800-metre high feature of the Oldbury estate.

Soon after he moved to Oldbury, James Atkinson ventured into the largely unexplored country between Sutton Forest and the

This illustration entitled 'An exploring party' appeared in James Atkinson's book on farming in New South Wales published in 1826. Atkinson was among the first settlers to penetrate the wild Shoalhaven gorges. (*An Account of Farming and Grazing in New South Wales*)

coast on exploring trips in search of land to pasture his cattle and to visit his friends Berry and Wollstonecraft at their large land grant on the south coast of New South Wales near the mouth of the Shoalhaven River. In later years stories about her father's adventurous journeys into unknown country became part of Atkinson family legend and were to provide a rich source of material for Louisa's articles and novels. As a result of his journeys down the gorges of the Shoalhaven, Atkinson established a cattle station at Budgong on Bugong Creek, a tributary of the Shoalhaven River.

By 1825 Atkinson was established among the leading farmers and landholders in New South Wales. Although referred to as 'our plain plodding friend' by Alexander Berry,[13] he was a most innovative farmer with a pride in his achievements that made him a match for the highest in the land. He was one of the landholders who formed the prestigious Agricultural Society of New South Wales, the principal aim of which was to raise the quality of wool produced in the Colony by importing pure merino sheep from England.

On 7 February 1825 with his farm well established and holding a substantial position in the Colony, James Atkinson sailed for England on the ship, the *Mangles*, captained by John Coghill, who was to feature later in James' life. James' journey was probably precipitated by the death of his mother in 1824 and the wish to see his aged father. Also, at the age of 31, and well established in the Colony, he almost certainly had in mind the possibility of finding a suitable wife in England. Another reason for the trip was to look at Saxon merino sheep in Germany with a view to importing some.

In the preface to his book, *An Account of Agriculture and Grazing in New South Wales*, which he completed while staying at his father's farm in Kent and which was published in London in 1826, he said he had written it because he had received so many inquiries regarding prospects in New South Wales. He had drawn on his experience 'and somewhat successful practice, as a Settler'. Written in a straightforward manner, the book contained practical information and advice on all aspects of settlement. It included advice on methods of clearing and improving lands, breeding and grazing livestock, erecting buildings, the system of employing convicts, the cost of labour, and the method of applying for grants of land.

It is obvious that Louisa Atkinson inherited some of her ability to observe and describe scenery and natural phenomena from her father, and there are resemblances in style between father and daughter, as in the inclusion of useful or educational information in the midst of descriptive writing.

In mid-1826 after he had completed writing his book, James Atkinson accompanied by Charles Macarthur, a Royal Naval lieutenant and a nephew of Australia's famous pioneer pastoralist and politician, John Macarthur, toured Saxony to study sheep farming. At the end of that year they made arrangements to travel back to Sydney together on the *Cumberland*, which carried several members of the interrelated King and Macarthur families: Harriet, wife of Admiral Phillip Parker King, and four of their sons, and her brother Robert Copland Lethbridge and his wife Mary, who was Admiral King's youngest sister. Also aboard was Charlotte Waring, who had been engaged in England by Harriet King to become governess to the children of her sister and brother-in-law, Anna Maria and Hannibal Hawkins Macarthur.[14] This was the woman James Atkinson was to marry.

3

She must be mistress of her own actions

Charlotte Waring, born in London on 13 March 1796, was a small, woman, only 156 cm in height, of 'particularly handsome and brilliant' appearance with 'full large black eyes, black hair which curled naturally and fine features'.[1] At 30, she was at an age when women of the time were either married or considered unmarriageable. A well-educated woman of very decided character, she was used to leading an independent life.

As she grew up Louisa Atkinson absorbed information about her mother's antecedents that may have had a romantic hue. Just before she died Louisa wrote down these views in the form of notes for her daughter. Above the notes she drew a decorative coloured illustration of the names Warrenne and Waring. She wrote that her mother was descended from the Norman William de Warrenne, who had reached England with William the Conqueror and who became the first Earl of Surrey. The name had been anglicised to Waring some 200 years previously. Her mother's grandfather, Louisa wrote, was Thomas Waring, a man of property who lived in great style. He had married the widow of the heir to the title of Lord Saye and Sele. One of his six sons, Albert, married Elizabeth Turner, a girl of 'exquisite beauty and small stature', seventeen at the time of the marriage. Albert Waring was 'of handsome appearance', his hair was naturally curly and he was of 'good height and slender figure'. They had four daughters, Elizabeth Waring dying after the birth of the fourth child. The third daughter, Louisa's mother Charlotte Waring, was about twenty months when her mother died.[2]

Soon after his wife's death Albert Waring met with an accident, which resulted in him becoming a permanent invalid. According to his daughter's death certificate he was a barrister but apparently had sufficient means to keep his family in some style without practising law, 'a man of fortune' Louisa believed. He lived in London amusing himself, 'rearing pet birds and animals and drawing for which he had a great talent'. Charlotte Waring was reared by an aunt. According to Louisa, and there is other evidence to support this, her mother grew up a prodigy:

> At 2 years of age she could read well and professed throughout her life brilliant talents and great clearness of mind. No words could too highly paint her excellence and worth. Warm in disposition and affections she was too marked a character not to meet with persons to whom her uprightness and courage made her obnoxious...[3]

At the age of about ten Charlotte was sent to a school in Kent that was apparently a very superior one. Apart from being instructed 'in the general branches of polite female education', she was taught music, drawing and French by masters of some distinction. They included 'the celebrated Mr Glover'—John Glover, landscape painter, at that time President of the Society of Painters in Water-Colours, later to become famous in Australia. At school Charlotte attained 'considerable celebrity' for 'diligence and talent in her several studies'.[4]

Although Charlotte Waring was born into an affluent family, it is likely that she had no prospect of an inheritance. Her father had remarried and had a son. Like the legions of other educated, unmarried, middle-class women at the time—there was a marked surplus of women in the British population in the nineteenth century—she became a governess. Unlike some other women who aspired to positions as governesses, Charlotte Waring's academic qualifications and her aptitude and enthusiasm for teaching gained her positions in families of some wealth and standing.

Immediately after leaving school, at the age of about fifteen she was engaged as a governess in the family of John Lochner, of London and Enfield, to superintend and educate three children, the eldest then eight, at a salary of £50 a year. The arrangement allowed her to continue her own education. She studied music, drawing, Italian and French under distinguished teachers. After about four years she left the Lochner family to take a position as governess in the family of Thomas Trafford of Trafford Park, Lancashire where she was in charge of the education of five children, the eldest fifteen, without any assistance from masters. She stayed there about two years at £70 a year until she was forced to resign because of ill health.[5]

A story she wrote later relates to this time spent in the north of England; it also conveys her love of 'botanizing':

During a sojourn which I made in the north of England some years ago, I was very fond of rambling about in the woods, or forests; which consist chiefly of fir trees; and are here called mosses. Probably, from the numerous mosses of every shade and variety, which clothe the ground: while the trees are frequently covered with beautiful lichens. There is also an endless variety of beautiful little plants, and wild native fruits; such as the wortleberry; the bilberry; the English cranberry &c. Some of these curiosities I delighted to draw; others I dried, and thus made a pleasing addition to my herbal. I will draw you a little sprig of the cranberry. It is a pretty little plant, and trails along the ground. The flower is very much the form and colour of the autumnal cyclamen; and the berry is about the size of a pea; and the color of a ripe apricot.

In one of these botanizing excursions, I saw a beetle of a large size; and beautiful purple color: apparently in great pain; and unable to walk...I was never so fortunate as to find a dead purple beetle; and you know my dear children I am unwilling to destroy life.[6]

Charlotte's interest in animals and birds and in 'botanizing' and her ability to draw and paint was inherited from her father and she was to pass on these interests to her children.

In her own account of her career, Charlotte said she left the Trafford family when she was about 21 and shortly after was engaged to teach the children of Hannibal Macarthur in New South Wales. In fact she was 30 when she sailed for Sydney, suggesting that either her illness persisted for nearly nine years or that she was employed in other unspecified governessing positions. Perhaps, in the economic depression and social upheaval that followed the end of the Napoleonic wars, she was, like many thousands of other women of genteel background, desperate for a position, or perhaps she wanted a more challenging and adventurous life. From the marked independence of character she showed throughout her life, she may have absorbed some of the emerging ideas on the right of women to an independent life. Deciding to take a position half way around the world in New South Wales was a courageous step. The 24 women who applied for the position when it was first advertised in London—in a vague manner with the destination omitted—all withdrew their applications when they found it involved travelling to distant New South Wales.[7] Charlotte agreed to take the position at the very high salary of £100 per year.[8]

When she first engaged Charlotte Waring, Harriet King told her husband that she was 'about 30' and 'highly recommended'. Within a short time her favourable opinion had changed and she wrote to her husband:

I am very much disappointed in Miss Waring the Governess, she is very different from what she ought to be, or we expected. We had

Charlotte Waring arrived in New South Wales early in 1827 and soon after married James Atkinson. This watercolour is believed to have been painted by her daughter Charlotte Elizabeth. It one of a set of four comprising Charlotte and three of her children, the missing child being Charlotte Elizabeth. (Mitchell Library, State Library of NSW)

not been 2 hours on board, before I saw she was flirting with Mr Atkinson, and ere 10 days were over she was engaged to him. She came around in the ship from London but altogether, it was about 3 weeks acquaintance. Her conduct is far from what I could wish otherwise, as she does not act with propriety. I have spoken to her, and represented how vexed Hannibal & Maria will be, but she told me, it should not interfere with her engagement with them, but she must be mistress of her own actions.[9]

Harriet King's chagrin at the prospect of a highly competent governess being lost to the family may have coloured her views about Charlotte Waring's behaviour. Her letter also expresses the shock of one sure of her superior position over a woman employed as governess. Charlotte Waring did not see herself in the role of a compliant governess; she was not a woman prepared to be dominated.

After the *Cumberland* arrived in Sydney Charlotte Waring took up her position with the Hannibal Macarthur family at The Vineyard. Her pupils were Elizabeth, aged eleven, (who later married Philip Gidley King, MLC) Anna, ten (later married to Captain John Wickham, Government Resident at Brisbane) and Kate, eight (later married to Queensland pioneer Patrick Leslie). Harriet King must have had some hope that Charlotte would remain as governess, as she reported to her husband that James Atkinson's ardour appeared to have cooled.[10] This was not so, however. Early in April Atkinson arrived at The Vineyard to take Charlotte to Sydney to stay with Elizabeth Wollstonecraft, who had joined her brother Edward and Alexander Berry at Crow's Nest.

Alexander Berry wrote to Edward Wollstonecraft in 1827:

> Atkinson is now in Sydney, & has brought his intended to reside for a few days with Miss W. I must say I *never* saw a lady whose *manners* were less to my taste, nor do I think less fitted for our plain plodding friend—the grossest levity![11]

A week later in a letter about James Atkinson's plans to gain more land, he was more sanguine about the coming marriage:

> There has lately come out an order that no more large farms, particularly for grazing, shall be permitted to be granted either on the coast, or on the banks of navigable rivers—*Our Jim* says that this regulation originated in his own suggestions,—& that he produced as an illustration the large tract occupied by Darcy Wentworth at Illawarra—& *no doubt*, although he denies it the tract occupied by B & W—Shoal Haven.—He *wished* me to furnish him any sketches of the coast in my possession—*Our Jim* may explore the coast for himself.— His intended has been living with your sister for the last 10 days.—No doubt according to the doctrine of contrasts & contraries it will be an excellent match.[12]

As Charlotte Waring's visit stretched from 'a few days' to over ten, it would be surprising if the two women—and Berry—did not talk about the Wollstonecrafts' aunt, Mary Wollstonecraft Godwin, the famous eighteenth century 'mother' of feminism. It is likely that the independent-minded Charlotte Waring agreed with many of Mary Wollstonecraft's views on the right of women to education and to an independent life.

After her stay at Crow's Nest Charlotte Waring returned to the Macarthurs, staying with them in all seven months. Mrs King,

This watercolour of Oldbury is believed to have been painted by Charlotte Atkinson. As a student in England she had been taught painting by the famous water colourist John Glover. (Mitchell Library, State Library of NSW)

reporting her departure, wrote, 'she behaved very ill and gave herself many airs'.[13] Shortly after she left the Macarthurs, on 29 September 1827, Charlotte married James Atkinson and the couple went to live at Oldbury in the simple farmhouse Atkinson had built. Charlotte described this house in 'The History of the Swallows', in which she told the story of two swallows, Rapid and Lightning, who 'In the spring of 1829' while searching for a place to build a nest:

> accidently flew into the verandah of a rustic little white cottage, whose pillars overgrown and shaded by sweetbriar, greatly charmed the little wanderers: who chanted many a merry lay, as they skimmed to and fro; now mounting high in the air; and again, diving into the furthermost corner of the verandah. Nor were these excursions made, with a view to pleasure only; the quick eyes of the little strangers, were examining every nook; in the hopes that further search would prove unnecessary: by their being enabled to build a warm and snug little nest, on one of the numerous ledges, formed by the rough materials of which the roof was composed.
> ...the lady who inhabited the white cottage (the parlor of which opened into the verandah) sat busying herself with her needle; while her darling baby lay wrapt in soft slumber, in her little cot...
> When fatigued by their frequent rambles in search of building materials, the little birds were accustomed to alight on the window of a sleeping apartment, which opened into the verandah.[14]

Asked by one of listening children 'Did it really happen?' the storyteller replied, 'It is quite true, my dear. And really happened, just as I have described'. The baby Charlotte Atkinson referred to in this story was her first child, Charlotte Elizabeth, born at Oldbury on 22 July 1828.

The domestic scene described in this story was probably typical of Charlotte Atkinson's life over the next six years as her husband worked at improving and extending his farming enterprises and carrying out his role as a public figure. They had three more children: Jane Emily (known as Emily) born on 6 June 1830; James John Oldbury born on 7 April 1832; and Caroline Louisa Waring (known as Louisa) born on 25 February 1834.

During these years Oldbury increased in size to 1117 hectares and James Atkinson continued to introduce innovative farming practices. When William Edward Riley, son of pioneer merchant and pastoralist Alexander Riley, travelled through the country to the south-west of Sydney in 1830, he noted James Atkinson's farm at Oldbury 'prettily situated and some excellent land, farm in high order, about 200 acres cleared, has yielded some large crops of wheat. Mr Atkinson has succeeded in distilling some very good spirit and has some quantity by him—has a tolerably good garden and the country about here being very thinly and prettily wooded'.[15]

On 9 October 1828 James Atkinson sent Sir John Jamison, President of the Agricultural Society of New South Wales, his latest publication *On the Expediency and Necessity of Enouraging Distilling and Brewing from Grain in New South Wales*. It was so popular a second edition appeared the next year, in which he replied to criticisms in newspapers by editors who, he said, 'treated the Author as if he were a public writer, or author by profession, rather than what he is—a humble farmer, who makes no pretensions to literary merit'. (Atkinson made these sort of comments more than once, but his writing had the great merit of simplicity.) The pamphlet argued for a relaxation of the law so that farmers could use grain they could not sell for distilling. By this means 'the Farmer would be enabled to adopt a proper rotation of crops, and cultivate barley, rye, oats, peas etc, and consume them upon his own farm'; it would also save large sums in importing spirits and malt liquors.

Apart from his agricultural pursuits, James Atkinson replaced the simple timber house at Oldbury with a much larger one built of local sandstone which still stands today. It is an unusual design for an Australian country homestead, resembling English farmhouses in the north of England and the Cotswolds. There are no verandahs or balconies at the front or sides. A flight of stone steps leads to the portico entrance, which opens to the raised ground floor. Under this there are extensive cellars. The stairs in the entrance hall lead up to three bedrooms at the front and others at the back under a sloping roof. With its pleasing straightforward style, panelled doors and windows and numerous bedrooms, Oldbury would have been an inviting place to stay. While James Atkinson was alive there was probably a stream of visitors.

After James Atkinson was appointed a magistrate,[16] in June 1827 he sat regularly on the Sutton Forest Court of Petty Sessions. The offenders he dealt with were mainly convicts assigned to properties in the district. In 1834, at the height of his success as a leader of the community and as a farmer, James Atkinson contracted a fatal illness. He died in the prime of his life, 'a gentleman of great energy and considerable talent'.[17] In the *Sydney Gazette* he was described as 'a gentleman of considerable literary attainments, and, as a practical agriculturalist, was, we believe, second to none in the Colony. His death is deeply lamented by a numerous circle of relatives and friends'.[18]

In his will James Atkinson left to his 'dearly beloved wife' the whole of his personal property and all his real estate, to be held by her during her life, or as long as she remained a widow, the proceeds to be applied by her in the education and maintenance of the children. After her death the whole of the property was to be equally divided among the children, as soon as they all attained 21 years, with the exception of the estate of Oldbury which with all additions was to descend undivided to his son. He also provided that if Charlotte should marry again she was entitled to the sum of £1000 out of his personal property for her sole use and benefit, the remainder of the personal property and all the real estate being held in trust by the executors for the use and maintenance of the children until they all reached 21 years.

James Atkinson had made his will on 25 October 1831, two and a half years before his death. He named as his executors his wife Charlotte Atkinson and his friends John Coghill, now a landowner at Kirkham, and Alexander Berry and Edward Wollstonecraft of Sydney. Edward Wollstonecraft had died in 1832 after a lengthy illness, leaving Charlotte Atkinson to deal with John Coghill and Alexander Berry as the other executors. It was to take many years of costly legal battles before James Atkinson's seemingly simple will was finally settled.

The success of James Atkinson as a farmer is apparent from the inventory made at Oldbury after his death. His livestock included about 3000 sheep, of which 49 were Merino ewes, and about 200 cattle, including 53 stud heifers. In addition there was a comfortable, generously stocked home. The goods listed were valued at £3517/7/4.[19] Together with the value of his land at Oldbury, his invested money, his cattle station at Budgong, land on the Wollondilly River and other land at Belanglo, James Atkinson had left a considerable estate, a tribute to his enterprise and success in New South Wales.

The inventory was signed on 5 July 1834 by Charlotte Atkinson and George Bruce Barton, a farmer at Belanglo. Barton, originally from Kent in England, was said to have been a friend of James Atkinson[20]. He appears to have been engaged by Charlotte Atkinson to manage the Oldbury property following the death of her husband.

With the loss of her husband and the problems she faced in the aftermath of this tragedy, Charlotte did not have her youngest child, Louisa, baptised until 15 October 1834, when the baby was eight months old. She arranged by correspondence for one of her former pupils in London, a daughter of Mr and Mrs Lochner of Mecklenburg Square, to be Louisa's godmother.[21]

4

A widow lady and her family took refuge at her cattle station

Louisa Atkinson's early years were spent in an atmosphere of family crisis. Her own birth, followed so closely by her father's death, appear to have combined to place an unbearable strain on her mother, revealed in some of her actions. To add to Charlotte Atkinson's personal stress were the difficulties of managing a large property, the running of outstations, the control of convict labour and the handling of negotiations with the executors of her husband's will. Despite her friendship with Berry's wife, the former Elizabeth Wollstonecraft, from the start she found the executors difficult to deal with and soon began to suspect they were not handling the estate in the best interests of her children.[1]

Her problems in running Oldbury were made worse by a notorious breakdown of law and order in the Berrima district. Attacks on homesteads and on travellers by bushrangers were almost daily occurrences. Among the victims were the Rev. John Vincent, rector of Sutton Forest, Bong Bong and Mittagong, who was assailed by bushrangers in 1836,[2] and John G. Colyer, whose property, Colyersleigh, was attacked three times. Colyer attributed the prevalence of bushrangers to the convenient hiding places in the hills and gullies at Belanglo and other places where convict shepherds and stockmen were friendly with the bushrangers.[3]

Her various difficulties apparently led Charlotte Atkinson to decide to marry again, but she was later bitterly to regret her choice. Following James's death, George Bruce Barton had been employed either directly by Charlotte Atkinson or by the executors of Atkinson's will as superintendent of Oldbury.[4] Although his name does not appear on the shipping list, he almost certainly arrived in New South Wales on 1 May 1832 on the *Sir William Wallace*, possibly listed as Miller, since this was his trade. Being from Kent it is possible he had known James Atkinson in England and his emigration may have been arranged by Atkinson, who had a flour mill at Oldbury.

A very frightening episode, which occurred on 30 January 1836 when she was threatened with flogging and shooting by bushrangers, probably precipitated Charlotte's decision that she needed a protector. The closeness of her relationship to Barton at this stage is obvious from the incident, from which she emerges as a woman of enterprise, disregarding the conventions of the time, to accompany Barton alone on a journey by horseback to visit both their sheep stations to the north-west. An account of what must have been an extremely terrifying experience for Charlotte Atkinson during which both she and Barton came close to being killed appeared in the form of a statement sworn by George Barton:

George Bruce Barting [sic] states that he left Oldbury on the morning of the 30th ult., to visit his farm at Belangola [sic] and some of Mrs Atkinson's sheep stations in that neighbourhood; he had proceeded about ten (10) miles, when, in going down a steep mountain, at the time leading two horses, he was suddenly stopped by two bushrangers who sprung from behind a rock close to him, presenting, the one a double-barreled percussion gun, and the other a pistol, close to his head, and in the most diabolical language ordered him to stop. This order he complied with; they then told him to turn his horses loose, this he refused to do; then to take his jacket off, this was done, deponent thinking they intended to take it. The deponent's money was next demanded; this he gave them to the amount of 21s. The man who acted as leader, told the man with the gun to keep it levelled at the deponent, and to fire directly he gave the order. He then took deponent's hankerchief from his neck, and proceeded to tie him to a tree; this he would not submit to until persuaded by Mrs Atkinson, who was with deponent at the time, deponent still thinking the bushrangers only meant to detain him. The leader then tore out the back of the deponent's waistcoat and shirt, and told the other bushranger, who still kept his gun presented at deponent, to give him the cat. He immediately gave the leader an uncommonly thick stockman's whip, very short in the thong, made of green hide, and exceedingly heavy. The bushranger, a very strong man, then began to lash the deponent's back with all his strength, in the most deliberate manner; and in answer to deponent, who asked how many stripes he was to expect? replied thirty, about which number were inflicted. The rascal then said he would give deponent ten minutes' rest, and then ten minutes more punishment; this through the intercession of Mrs Atkinson was not inflicted, but he directed Mrs Atkinson to untie deponent, which she did. The bushranger then brandished his whip over Mrs Atkinson's head with one hand, and holding a large pistol close to her face with the other, declared, although he never had struck a woman, he had a good mind to serve her as deponent had been served, as she allowed *her men to be treated so very bad in her establishment;* this she denied, and defied him to name any man that could complain; he said he did not have his information from her servants, but from a Gentleman, a Mr Munn (who is the son of the professor of that name in Edinburgh); the leader then told deponent that he was not the only one that was served in that manner, as he considered it his duty to go around and flog all the Gentlemen so that they might know what punishment was, this he repeated twice; deponent was then ordered to return; the bushranger declaring deponent should be shot if he attempted to proceed on his journey; deponent further states, that within these *last twelve months,* his own and Mrs Atkinson's stations have been robbed at least ten times, and he believes by the *same party;* that the bushrangers are constantly shooting a bullock when they want meat, taking of the same as much as they require, leaving the remainder to spoil; that the shepherds are constantly loosing [sic] their shoes and clothes, and that, although some of the stations are twenty-five miles distant, they are obliged to be rationed weekly as the huts are constantly being ransacked by bushrangers; deponent feels satisfied there was one, if not more of the party that stopped him that did not show themselves; one of whom was called Simmons.[5]

Barton later stated that another of the bushrangers involved in this assault was Lynch, who was to reappear in Barton's life during the following years with devastating results.

Barton's statement was reported in the *Sydney Herald* and its contents would have been widely known in the Sutton Forest and Berrima district. This very public account of what could be interpreted as a close relationship between Barton and Charlotte Atkinson may have precipitated their marriage.

Just over a month after the flogging episode, on 3 March 1836, George Bruce Barton and Charlotte Atkinson, having applied for a special licence, were married in the chapel of All Saints, Sutton Forest.[6] Following the marriage the executors of the Atkinson estate let Oldbury to George Barton at £400 per year, allowing him a sum for the maintenance of his step-children (this sum had amounted to £600 by 1 December 1839).[7] Charlotte's marriage changed her legal position drastically; from being the custodian of Oldbury, she became merely the wife of the lessor.

The day immediately following Charlotte's marriage to Barton, the lawlessness endemic among the convicts in the district came to a head with the murder of one of those assigned to Oldbury. Two convicts, John Lynch and John Williamson, were charged with murder and sent to prison on Cockatoo Island, Sydney, to await trial. George Barton was to be the principal witness for the prosecution, and was called to Sydney to give evidence.

That Lynch and Williamson were subsequently aquitted was at least partly due to the fact that Barton was unable to take the stand. The *Sydney Herald* later claimed that Lynch's extraordinarily brutal series of subsequent murders would never have occurred had Barton given evidence against him at his first trial. Barton had appeared in the witness box apparently so drunk that he was incapable of giving evidence. He was fined £50 for contempt of court. Defence witnesses claimed Barton was mentally and physically ill. Barton wanted to appeal but was told that the contempt was committed in the presence of a Judge, who had power at once to decide it; and 'he (Mr Justice Burton) was determined to check such gross improprieties'.[8]

Barton's excitable mental state, ill health and addiction to drink continued after his return to Oldbury. It later emerged that he did little in running the farm apart from erecting and operating a steam flour mill. Any organisation of farm work was done by Charlotte Barton. She stated later that not only before but after her marriage to George Barton she had to be 'both Father and Mother both with reference to the education and comfort' of her children and in providing them with 'their daily food', because when Barton was intoxicated 'as the fact was for many weeks together and utterly incapable of attending to any business' she 'was obliged to act for him and to endeavour to prevent more confusion arising'.[9]

Charlotte Barton probably regretted her second marriage almost from the day it took place and the three years she spent with Barton must have had a disturbing effect on her children, particularly Louisa. In such a household it must have been difficult for Charlotte Barton to find moments of calm during which to teach her children or to take them on excursions into the bush to impart her own love and knowledge of nature. On a couple of occasions because of the 'multitude' of her duties at Oldbury she had to hire governesses to supplement her own teaching. For Louisa this disturbed period lasted from when she was two to five years old. She would have remembered very little of it directly but it remained a subconscious memory and, doubtless, was the subject of many family discussions. With a step-father who was mentally disturbed and violent, this time probably accentuated the close relationship between Louisa and her mother which survived to the exclusion of other attachments until Charlotte's death.

Charlotte Barton was forced to rely on several assigned convicts to help her keep Oldbury functioning. With Barton too drunk and disinterested to visit the outstations, she herself made several trips to Budgong, extraordinary journeys considering the steep gorges and impenetrable bush she had to traverse, and the other outlying stations in the company of convicts. Barton was later to accuse Charlotte Barton of cohabiting with these convicts. In a sworn statement he said:

> ...she did some time in or about the year of our Lord one thousand eight hundred and thirty eight or one thousand eight hundred and thirty nine leave the Dwelling house of this Deponent with a Convict man named James Barnett assigned to this Deponent and was away with the said Convict for a week or ten days or thereabouts and did on several other occasions commit the same offence with another convict man during these years and the following year and on the said Charlotte Barton's return to Deponent's House after Deponent had retired to rest Deponent refused to admit her to his Bed and remarked to the said Charlotte Barton that he Deponent was not going to keep illegitimate children of Jews and convicts and that Deponent hath never since slept with the said Charlotte Barton and Deponent has every reason to believe that his Wife the said Charlotte Barton has had improper and criminal intercourse with convict men and various other persons.[10]

His lawyer later offered to withdraw these accusations.

Being treated like an interloper in her own home must have had a devastating effect on Charlotte Barton. By 1839 Barton's drunkenness and neglect of the property had become notorious, creating a problem for the executors who decided to terminate his lease and sell the livestock. Charlotte Barton, in a dangerous situation with Barton, also distrusted the executors' motives. Alexander Berry wrote to her on 1 June 1839:

> I have received your letter of yesterday's date and beg to say that it is entirely on account of Mr Barton that I fear for the children's property.
> He is your Husband—his intemperance is known to the whole world and I know from yourself and others that he is a useless idler who neglects his concerns. I believe that he has never once visited the stock at Badjong—some time ago he told me that having been flagellated he was afraid to do so—under these circumstances there is reason to fear that everything will be squandered.—Therefore the step I intend to take is to put the remainder of the property beyond his control. You and Mr Barton have often attributed the anxiety of myself and Capt Coghill to get the property out of Mr Barton's hands to sinister motives this step however will convince you that we are disinterested as the property will then be entirely beyond our control...
> The expense will not be much unless you offer idle opposition — it will be best if you join me and Coghill in one application to the Court but although this might lessen the expense it is not necessary.[11]

The Oldbury sheep, one of the most prized flocks in the Colony in James Atkinson's day, were put up to auction on 1 October

When escaping from her second husband, Charlotte Barton took her children down the precipitous Meryla Pass into the wild gorges of the Shoalhaven River. This engraving of the scene near the Fitzroy Falls illustrates the difficulties of travelling down the mountain and through the dense bush. (*Sydney Mail* 2 December 1871)

1839, but there were no bids. According to Berry there was an impression 'that they could not be good after having been managed for some years by Mr Barton'.[12] On instructions from John Coghill, Charles Throsby, a neighbour, bought the steam flour mill erected at Oldbury by Barton on behalf of the estate. Coghill believed that the flour mill had doubled the annual value of Oldbury and buying it would be greatly to the advantage of the children.[13] Berry told Charlotte Barton he intended taking legal action against Barton for the recovery of money he had gained from selling flour as it was clearly a felony. He raised the question whether Barton should be prosecuted in the civil or criminal court. He continued:

> As you value your own future comfort and the welfare of your children you must exert yourself and look well after him [Barton] in the meantime to prevent his making away with the property—nothing that he may do will surprise me after what he has said of yourself—I consider him ready to deprive your children of their last morsel and I beg of you to recollect that Captn Coghill and myself being mere

strangers cannot have the same strong interest as a Mother in protecting those children.[14]

Two days later he wrote again to tell Charlotte the Oldbury sheep had been sold for sixteen shillings each. He sent the letter with a person he had engaged to supervise the farm and to 'prevent Mr Barton making away with any of the property':

> We understand he means to sell your furniture and pocket the money—you must prevent this for any punishment he might receive for depriving the children of their property would be a poor remedy to them. You must give Notice to all parties that provided one shilling is paid to Mr Barton we shall again make them pay to ourselves.[15]

During the following weeks Charlotte Barton became increasingly frightened by Barton's violent and unpredictable behaviour. She sent off a considerable amount of furniture to Sydney and determined to escape with her children from Oldbury to the Atkinson cattle station at Budgong. Leaving her large, established and comfortable home in the possession of a husband she regarded as a 'raving lunatic' she packed such goods as she could carry onto drays and she and her children set out across the rugged country leading to the coastal escarpment and down Meryla pass, so steep that rough steps had been cut into its side to allow bullocks to descend.

Louisa Atkinson, in delicate health and at five years old the youngest member of the group, was led down the precipitous mountain track to live in a primitive shack on the edge of wild, only partly explored country at Budgong. She may have remembered a few details of their flight and must have heard the story retold many times in the family. She wrote about it in 'Incidents of Australian travel', published twenty-four years later.[16]

The stay at the outstation was planned to be semi-permanent; Charlotte Barton put her writing desk into a pack slung across the back of a bullock and the children took their pet koala. The party consisted of Charlotte Barton, her children Charlotte Elizabeth, eleven, Jane Emily, nine, James, seven, Louisa, five, several servants, probably all convicts apart from Charley, an Aboriginal, and a friend recently arrived from England.

The first twenty-five kilometres were relatively easy going, although even Charlotte must have had considerable problems in keeping such a cavalcade of small children and such quantities of goods moving. The real difficulties began when the party reached Meryla mountain, where they had to make a precipitous descent from the tablelands to the coastal hinterland. Louisa wrote of this descent and subsequent events:

28

The pass had been improved by cutting steps down the face of the rocks, and the oxen, accustomed to such scenes, stumbled down as best they could, while the horses groaned audibly, trembled, and even in some instances sunk powerless on the dangerous declivity, not encouraged by the sight of the gully yawning at the side of the narrow road.

Coaxing, shouting and other exertions of will surmounted this difficulty, and the party proceeded briskly, leading their horses; the pack bullocks and their drivers soon falling into the rear. The nature of the country had entirely changed, the barren sand had given place to vegetable mould; the flowering scrub to a dense semi-tropical thicket; the sun's rays were obscured by the overhanging branches, or fell like mosaic upon the mossgreen stones and ferns. The cabbage-palms stretched their slender stems above the tangled copse and looked up at the face of heaven; the tree ferns, elkshorn and birds-nest ferns revelled in the humid shades. The shreiks of the blue mountain and king parrots gave life to the green wood, and every stream was occupied by frogs which vied with each other in their shrill-toned croaking.

Onward trudged the travellers, hastening to the foot of the mountain where they were to encamp for the night. Darkness gathered round early in that deep narrow vale, where mountains rose abruptly on either side of the creek. Persons who travelled these parts with stock had erected a yard near the little stream on a small level, to secure their cattle in during the night, and near this the party sat them down, after lighting a fire, awaiting the arrival of the tents, provisions and servants, for only the black boy Charley had accompanied them. But total darkness closed above them, and the absentees came not; all ears were strained to catch the first sound of them; conversation had flagged, then ceased.

During this anxious hush the fire had died down—it was a darkness which could be felt—when suddenly appeared a small light, scarcely larger than a spark. 'Charley, what is that?' inquired several tremulous voices.

'Debel, debel, I believe,' returned the lad in a tone as if his teeth were chattering. On came the light, about two feet from the ground.

'Nonsence, Charley; what can it be?'

Charley again hinted the possibility of the presence of his Satanic Majesty—while the little luminous speck crept cautiously onwards towards the horrorstruck group.

'Can it be a bushranger?' whispered the lady. 'I believe so, missus,' returned the aboriginal.

A bushranger with a lighted pipe in his mouth, about to fire upon the helpless victims, rendered visible by the flickering of a tongue of flame in the fire, while darkness concealed him, and goodness knows how many more! All this presented itself to the imaginations. The lady fainted, the young people were panic-struck, Charley equally so. The gentleman who was recently from England, and entirely unused to bush life, although then on his way to inspect a station, prior to entering on possession, entered into the general alarm, but surmounted it so far as to throw some dead branches on the almost expiring fire. A bright blaze shot up, illuminating the surrounding scene—not revealing a band of brigands, but setting the light flickering in a way that bore evidence of its insect origin.

Inspired by new courage, active exertions were made, and a small brown beetle about three inches long captured; the light appeared to be emitted from a pale yellow spot on the under part of the body.

Still the men and the pack bullocks did not arrive; the chill dews of evening were falling, and no tents erected, no supper to refresh and invigorate the weary travellers. There is nothing like sitting in the dark watching, and listening, to provoke or evoke fear. Spite of the bushranger turning out a little beetle, fear held possession of all hearts, when presently was heard the tramping of heavy feet; one of the pack bullocks was running wildly down the mountain, dragging behind him a heavy body.

Again the black was applied to, as being better provided with bush lore, not courage, for he was overpowered by cowardice and superstition. In reply to a volley of questions he expressed an opinion that the bullock had killed his driver, and was dragging his lifeless body behind him. The ghastly suggestion was received in all faith, everyone being too horror-struck to reflect that as the driver was in no way attached to the bullock's harness, he would not be dragged.

On rushed the animal, concealed by the darkness, plunged into the creek, and hurried to the stockyard where it was in the habit of being released from its load. There was a pause, as of death—again were heard hurried feet, and again. The three pack bullocks had assembled at the yard, each dragging something behind them—their loads, suggested some one; and so it proved.

Now came the drivers and related the cause of their detention. A bright fire, warm cup of tea and the snug canopy of the tent, disposed the travellers to acknowledge 'that there is but one step from the sublime to the ridiculous'.

As the family, who formed the greater number of the party, were intending to make rather a lengthy stay when they reached their destination—they had brought with them a very important member of the household, no less a one than a *pet bear*. This rather portly gentlemen had been accommodated with a seat in a pannier, and swung on one side of the pack saddle, while 'to make the balance true', a hamper of earthenware and a writing desk were suspended on the other side.

Whatever were Master Maugie's thoughts on this occasion, he had manifested that philosophy which usually marked his actions and given no expression to them, till he found his bearer descending the steep mountain side. This was too much for any choleric gentleman, who had nerves. Maugie waxed wrath, and stuck his long claws through the wicker-work into the bullock's back, no doubt intending 'to make assurance double sure,' but such a one-sided arrangement did not suit the ox; he began to run, the shaking causing Maugie to roar aloud, much to the horror of the bovine trio, who thereupon ran away, scattering such of their load as was insecure along the road, breaking the fragile, to wit, the earthenware, and releasing the bear, who speedily made his way up a tree. The drivers being unable to coax him down, felled it—a work of some time, trusting to the bullocks keeping the right road, and then had to secrete such of the loads as were scattered about, by which time night had closed in.

The bear, it must be understood, was neither the great polar, nor the Russian black, the Californian brown, or the American grizzly bears, but only a *phascolarctus fuscus*, of leaf-eating habits, not given to hugging its prey, and a drug in the bears-grease market. And thus ends this 'o'er true tale'.

Louisa also referred to this enforced exile at the outstation at Budgong in an article, 'Recollections of the Aborigines'.[17] Illustrating the devotion of Aborigines to 'those who show them kindness', she wrote:

A curious instance of this occurred some years back, and might have led to tragic results.

A widow lady and her family, who had suffered much and had been forced to seek shelter at her cattle station, was one day accosted by a black who had been employed by the police in tracking bushrangers and had formed one of the mounted police force. He wished for a confidential conversation; the lady walked to a short distance from her dwelling, still in sight of her rather anxious family, for the aboriginal in question was not regarded with much confidence.

'Mrs——,' he said, in a mysterious tone, 'you used to have a big house and plenty *jumbucks* (sheep); me bin say where they all gone?'

A reply that those who should have guarded the orphans' property had abused their legal power, excited him to fury; with an oath he exclaimed, referring to one in question, 'I'll shoot him.'

'No, no; that will never do,' was the alarmed reply.

'Bail shoot? I see! make too much noise, I'll spear him.'

Quite satisfied with the prudence of this arrangement, the man explained where he could surprise his victim on a solitary path he occasionally had occasion to traverse.

Much alarmed lest he should carry this murderous intention into effect, but unable to make this zealous sable friend see any moral objection, the lady suggested that she would tell the Governor. This idea was seized upon warmly. 'Yes, tell Mister Gubbener; say Mister Gubbener currajong him—currajong him.' This meant hang.

To appease him it was promised that the Governor would be requested to have the extreme penalty of the law put into force upon the delinquent.

31

The people referred to by Charlotte Barton as 'those who should have guarded the orphans' property' but who had 'abused their legal power' were the executors, Alexander Berry and John Coghill. Berry, meticulous in his duties towards the Atkinson children, had an antipathy towards Charlotte Barton. He had regarded her as strange when he first met her and unsuited to be the wife of his friend, James Atkinson. His opinion had hardened, as did hers of him, into mutual antagonism. Coghill, now a successful farmer at Braidwood, where he was to survive the depression of the 1840s while his neighbours sank into bankruptcy, was also a hard man. The successful carrying out of the provisions of the will required some rapport between Charlotte Barton and the executors, but this was missing from the start. Letters which remain between Coghill and Berry show that they found the task of executing Atkinson's will onerous and worrying. Charlotte thought that they deliberately mismanaged their task to the extent of depriving her children of income and of misappropriating money. In addition Berry and Coghill had differences between themselves on ways to handle the estate.

Stories she wrote later indicate that Charlotte Barton and her children took advantage of their stay at Budgong to explore the country around. In 'Extraordinary sounds' she wrote of a boy, aged about eight years, clearly meant to be her son James: 'I remember a little Gentleman whose name I will not mention, who bravely rode his horse through a deep Salt Water River, while his Mamma was afraid to venture, till this little Gentleman had returned more than once, to re-assure her.'[18]

Another of the children in the story remarks on the 'curious Stones we found on the beach, at Swan Lake', which floated as though made of cork. The narrator explains to the children that they were pumice stones and that Swan Lake appeared to have been the crater of a volcano. In another exchange one of the children mentions a pelican seen at Swan Lake but remarks 'We had a better view of one at St George's Basin'. There are also references to the Wandandian, a salt water river which like St George's Basin overflows without destroying the surrounding vegetation, and to the canoes made by Aborigines out of the bangalee tree.

St George's Basin and Swan Lake are on the coast just south of Jervis Bay. If Charlotte Barton and her children ventured as far from Budgong as this, it would have been a very adventurous journey. As Louisa Atkinson, as well as her mother, was to use this locale in some of her stories, it is probable that the family had friends who lived in this area.

Another of the children in Charlotte Barton's book expresses the wish to spend weeks exploring the mountain ranges. 'I would take my spears and try to spear some of those beautiful birds for Mamma to have stuffed,' he says. His mother replies, 'if it were possible for us to travel by slow stages, about those Mountains, all the way to Wollongong, it would afford us such delight, as well as information. We should find abundance of subjects for our pencils'.[19]

Charlotte and her children lived at Budgong for about seven months from December 1839. Although the accommodation was primitive and supplies of food and other necessities very uncertain, it appears from the stories she and Louisa later wrote that this time provided a welcome refuge from the turmoil of the previous years. Charlotte used the time to teach her children in an atmosphere of calmness, with only the bush around. But the extreme isolation of the station made it impractical as a permanent home. At some stage there were illnesses among the children, and Charlotte incurred a debt, which remained unpaid for some years, to surgeon Kenneth McKenzie of Nerriga, between Braidwood and Jervis Bay.[20]

Problems continued in the administration of Oldbury. In a letter to Coghill, Berry wrote:

> Mr Humphries [Humphery][21] has returned from Oldbury—he reports that he found Barton alone—in charge of the farm confined to his room & semi-insane—he however refuses to give up the sheep which are running about the place without anyone to look after them.
>
> The mother of Mr Atkinson's children is now at Badjong [sic] with her factotum Mr [or Mrs] Ash—she left instructions with Barton not to deliver the sheep notwithstanding the arrangement which took place between you & her—under these circumstances I see no chance of having one shilling for the children's property unless you will send some one to take possession of the sheep & deliver them to Mr Atkinson who is now at Goulburn.[22]

This is a reference to James Atkinson's brother, John, who had apparently agreed to take charge of the sheep for which William Lithgow, the New South Wales auditor-general who had extensive farming interests, had paid over £2000. Cattle sold at the same time raised £452 but the buyer paid only £341 because 55 head were missing from the herd handed over by Barton.[23]

John Atkinson, although closely associated with his brother in their early days in New South Wales, was rarely mentioned after James's death. Legal confusion over land held by the two had been a complication. In 1823 John Atkinson had been promised a grant of 809 hectares adjacent to Oldbury and had taken possession of this land and named it Mereworth. The grant was still not finalised when James Atkinson died. As both brothers were recorded as J. Atkinson, John's 809 hectares were included in James's estate.[24] This caused great confusion—and perhaps a family estrangement —as Charlotte could not finalise her late husband's estate and John, the father of seven children, became financially embarrassed.

John Atkinson, who had been James's partner and, with his wife, a witness at the wedding of James Atkinson and Charlotte Waring, seems to have slipped away from the life of Charlotte and her children. James had not named his brother as one of the executors of his will, John was not a prime promoter of a plan to erect a monument to James, he was not a witness at Charlotte's second marriage and Charlotte did not turn to him for help when she escaped from Barton to flee to the outstation at Budgong.

About the middle of the 1840s, John Atkinson, his wife and children moved to Tumut Plains where Atkinson bought a 29 hectares property. Here the Atkinsons flourished leaving a large number of descendants some on the land in the Tumut district and others in the Riverina.

In 1840 the executors appear to have persuaded George Barton to move away from Oldbury and Charlotte Barton and her children returned there temporarily. During this time at Oldbury, members of the local Aboriginal tribe visited Charlotte and her children, as she relates in 'Anecdotes of the Aborigines of New South Wales':

> The tribe belonging to the neighbourhood where our property is situated, were very much attached to your dear lamented father.
> You know they never mention the name of a deceased person; but they were giving me to understand, the regret and sympathy they felt at his loss. I had the locket with me at the time, with a lock of all our hair in it. I showed this to them, pointing out his (to us) much valued brown curl; when they uttered a piercing cry; and all turned away; holding down their heads a short time: when they looked I saw they were in tears. One of the women stepped aside; and whispered to me 'Bail you show that to blacks ebber any more missus.' This of course I promised to refrain from. I was much surprised and effected [sic] at their manner, having wished to give them pleasure. It was six years after our bereavement.[25]

Soon after the Atkinson family left Oldbury. The executors arranged to lease the estate to Thomas Bott Humphery, and

Charlotte took her children to live in Double Bay, near the city of Sydney. Thus far Louisa had lived in an atmosphere of extraordinary stress but, particularly in the last year or two, she had absorbed a great deal of the knowledge and attitudes of her mother towards the birds and animals, the plants and insects of the bush around her. This was to be an important influence on her life. At that early age she had already gained from her mother the intense interest and joy in observing nature that she was never to lose.

5

I am totally averse to having any connection with such a notable she dragon

Soon after the Atkinson family moved to Sydney, relations between Charlotte Barton and the executors of Oldbury reached a crisis. Alexander Berry had formed such an opinion of Charlotte Barton and his antipathy towards her was such that he had decided she was incapable and unfit to be guardian of her own children. From the time of her flight to Budgong in December 1839 she received no allowance from the executors to keep her children and had supported them by the sale of furniture and other personal assets, by running up debts and by obtaining loans.

This situation could not continue and the case of *Atkinson Versus Barton and Others* was soon before the Equity Court for the first of what were to be innumerable listings over the next six years. The case came before the Court as the Atkinson children—plaintiffs —versus the defendants George Bruce Barton, Charlotte Barton, Alexander Berry and John Coghill. Charlotte Barton's interest in the case was in being appointed guardian of the children—this was not automatically a mother's right[1]—and in getting a sufficient yearly sum from the estate to support and educate them. Barton was a defendant in the case as the husband of the children's mother and their step-father and as the person to whom the executors had leased Oldbury, but from July 1841 Charlotte Barton gained the right to proceed separately from him.[2] The executors, Alexander Berry and John Coghill, were responsible for administering the estate in accordance with the terms of the will. The children's lawyers wanted adequate support awarded to them while they were minors. They also had a duty to ensure that as much of the estate as possible was kept to be divided among them when they became adults, particularly as the chief asset, the Oldbury estate, had been left to the only son, making some accumula-

James Atkinson named his friend from his Greenwich days, Alexander Berry, an executor of his estate. The antagonism which developed between Berry and Atkinson's widow led to many legal battles. (*Reminiscences of Alexander Berry*)

tion of money necessary if there were to be a division among the daughters.

The costs of the preparation of cases and innumerable court appearances, with the children and each of the defendants represented separately, was to be an enormous drain on the estate left by James Atkinson, eventually leaving a much depleted sum to be divided among the children. At a stage when the case still had many years to run, legal costs had reached the then huge sum of £1475.[3]

The case began with a petition from Charlotte Barton to the Chief Justice, Sir James Dowling, on 1 September 1840. In it she reiterated many of her complaints about the administration of James Atkinson's estate by the executors. She blamed them for letting the estate to Barton and its consequent greatly diminished value. She accused them of then letting it to an insolvent, Thomas Bott Humphery, and of being generally responsible for the decrease in value of Oldbury to only £500 from the £6000, which had been its value at the time of James Atkinson's death. She stated that she had no funds whatsoever and she and her children had been for some time past in a state of destitution without sufficient food or clothing. 'Her situation is extremely distressing. She

37

assures me she and the Children are literally starving', her solicitor wrote in the petition.[4]

In another letter she asked to be allowed to rent Oldbury. She offered to pay £550 the first year and £600 a year in subsequent years, which would allow £150 a year to accumulate for each child. In addition she would also educate and maintain them.[5] Her offer was refused. Instead the Master in Equity began an inquiry into whether she was fit to be guardian of her children. It was at this stage that Barton's accusations of her intimacy with convicts surfaced.

Alexander Berry and John Coghill in a statement to the court claimed Charlotte Barton was not a 'fit and proper person to be the Guardian of the Infants the Plaintiffs in consequence of [her] imprudent conduct...since her intermarriage with George Bruce Barton and for various other reasons'. The other reasons included their opinion that the children would be better educated at a school than 'Charlotte Barton could possibly educate them'; that she was living separate from her husband for which 'there is as much blame to be attached to the said Charlotte Barton as to the said George Bruce Barton'; and that she 'had thrown many obstacles in the way of the Executors in settling matters for the benefit and advantage' of the children. They left the question of the appointment of a suitable guardian to the court. They suggested that the two children over ten, Charlotte and Emily Atkinson, be sent to a school run by Mrs Harvey at Liverpool and that when James J.O. Atkinson reached ten he should also be sent to a 'proper school'.[6]

The Master in Equity investigated many avenues in trying to find a guardian for the Atkinson children. In the absence of maternal or paternal grandparents, many people were suggested— Mr Fitzhardinge, a solicitor, was ruled out because he was involved in the case; their uncle John Atkinson of Mereworth when approached refused to act. When it became apparent that the Court would appoint a guardian other than herself, Charlotte Barton suggested Mr Burlingham, whom she described as 'formerly a very intimate friend of my late husband,[7] but this was not accepted. The children's solicitor found an Anglican clergyman, Rev. George Edward Turner of Hunters Hill parish, residing at Kissing Point, who was willing to be guardian of James J.O. Atkinson and to take him into his rectory and educate him at a cost of £100 a year plus £50 for clothes and books.[8]

In the light of subsequent events it is possible twelve-year-old Charlotte Elizabeth Atkinson attended the school at Liverpool run by Mrs Harvey, which had been suggested by the executors, for a very short time, but the suggestions regarding the schooling of

Emily and James were overtaken by events. There was no recommendation concerning the future of the six-year-old Louisa, but if the trend of these suggestions by the Court had been acted on, eventually she would have been educated at a boarding school.

Charlotte Barton, furious at this attack on her right to bring up her own children, replied with a blistering petition in which she refuted the statements made by Berry and Coghill. She stated that she had not been guilty of improper conduct since her marriage with George Barton, she lived apart from him because 'his habits of constant intoxication render him unfit to live with and comparatively if not altogether insane', his conduct 'being violent and dangerous' to herself and her children. His violence was such that she had applied to magistrates at the Police Office, Sydney, for protection. Barton had made no defence and had to find sureties for a good behaviour bond. She denied Berry and Coghill's statement that the breakup of the marriage had been as much her fault as Barton's. She had left him solely because of 'his intemperate habits and bad treatment' and because of her 'anxious desire to remove her children from his control and example and to devote herself to their moral and intellectual improvement'. She also gave evidence of her own extensive education and her experience and competence in teaching. Her children should not be sent to a school because she did 'not consider that Ladies can be educated properly at a school even in England and that consequently that it would be less possible to educate them properly at a school in this Colony'. They would be brought up with 'stricter attention to their morals if they be placed under her charge'.[9]

In an effort to decide the issue of schooling the Master had the children brought to his office, where he examined them individually on the progress and proficiency of their education. His finding was a vindication of Charlotte Barton's competence as a teacher. He found that the children had been instructed with care and attention 'and in some branches of education not generally taught at Public schools'.[10]

This was to no avail. George Barton's sworn statement concerning her cohabitation with convicts, even though a withdrawal had been offered by Barton's solicitors,[11] continued to have a veiled effect on her reputation. This, combined with Alexander Berry and John Coghill's opinions of her 'difficult' nature, and their general view that she was not a fit guardian for her children, must have outweighed her outraged reply.

In an interim report the Master in Equity found that she was not fit to be guardian of her children and appointed a young solicitor, Edward James Corry, as temporary guardian. Charlotte Barton regarded this decision as extremely insulting. Corry was 28, had been in the Colony only eight months and was involved in the case as Chancery Clerk for James Norton, the solicitor for Atkinson's estate. 'His youth...his connection with this suit, his local inexperience and his position in society render him an unfit person to be guardian of the said infants,' she claimed.[12]

She also denied other statements in the report of the Master, for example, that the 'children were in a state of want and were often left alone in their residence without any person to be in charge of them in consequence of Mrs Barton's frequent visits to town on business'. It must have been a bitter experience for Charlotte Barton to hear that she was blamed for leaving her children when her frequent visits to town were occasioned by the legal battles over them. She replied to this accusation saying that she had always left them in charge of a proper person whenever she was obliged 'to leave her residence at Double Bay to come to Sydney as she has been frequently obliged to do to consult legal advisers upon the subject of this suit'.[13]

The Master concluded his report by stating that because of Mrs Barton's 'peculiar circumstances', (this seems to be a reference to her separation from her violent husband) he could not approve of her being guardian of her children particularly as the eldest girl was 'approaching an age that would require peculiar care and attention'. The children should be taken from under the care of 'Mrs Barton, their mother' and placed at a proper boarding school.

During the course of the interim inquiry Charlotte Barton had tried to have the hearing delayed while some information she had that Barton was a bigamist was pursued, but nothing came of this. She also asked for the inquiry to be delayed because she was unable to leave her children because of an epidemic of fever in Sydney, but the children's solicitors countered this by claiming that the inquiry should proceed quickly because the children were 'in want'.

Fortunately for Charlotte Barton and her children, the Master's report was an interim order only and the case was listed to come before the Chief Justice. If carried into effect its result would have been devastating for Charlotte Barton, not only in being deprived of her children but in its financial consequences. Separated from her husband and with no support from him, her only prospect of income was as guardian of her children. Her financial position was very difficult; the £1000 which should have been paid to her from James Atkinson's estate on her remarriage had not been paid[14] and during the period from December 1839 she and her children had lived on credit. It was at about this time when she was desperately in need of money that Charlotte Barton wrote a fictional version of the stories she had been telling her children and arranged with publisher G.W. Evans for their publication as *A Mother's Offering to Her Children*. Her book was released in December 1841 in time for the Christmas trade. It was the first children's book to be published in Australia.

On 9 July 1841 *Atkinson Versus Barton and Others* was again before the Equity Court on the petition of Charlotte Barton who asked the Court not to confirm the interim report by the Master in Equity. The Court described her petition as 'unnecessarily long' and 'impertinent and scandalous' and the Master in Equity was ordered to consider whether the costs of the 'unnecessarily long' part should be disallowed.[15] Charlotte Barton was ordered to pay the costs of the reference because of her 'impertinence'.[16]

Apart from this the July 1841 hearing was a triumph for Charlotte Barton as the Chief Justice, Sir James Dowling, in an interim judgment, disregarded the conclusions of the Master in Equity and appointed her guardian of her children and ordered that she be paid £350 a year in quarterly instalments for their maintenance and education. Elated, she wrote to Sir James Dowling:

> Permit me to offer my most grateful thanks to your Lordship for your truly humane decision on behalf of myself and dear Children my utmost efforts shall be exerted to prove myself worthy of the confidence reposed in me. I would also express my grateful sense of your goodness in the sum awarded me as an Income: but would humbly implore that while the Bills to the amount forwarded are paid quarterly I may be permitted to receive £100 per annum (also to be paid quarterly) to defray the unavoidable expences [sic] in bringing up a family for which I cannot keep open accounts. Having been for sometime without money I have not only been put to great distress at times but have been obliged to pay extravagantly for everything which might be avoided by having ready money: as everything is now reasonable. No fears need be entertained respecting Mr Barton benefitting by it; as nothing should induce me to give him anything; or to have the slightest intercourse with him. My habits and those of my Children are frugal not a portion of it should be extravagantly expended...without a portion of ready money I do not know how I can manage. My sufferings for a long course of years have been extreme but I can humbly and conscientiously affirm that I have struggled hard to do my duty and to preserve our property; and could have done so but for the opposition met with.[17]

The request for ready money does not appear to have been granted as she submitted many accounts to the Court in subsequent years, as well as for the period prior to the judgment. They covered rent from February 1841 to February 1842 at £90 a year on a house at Rose Bay (Double Bay), and subsequently on a house in 1842 at Darlinghurst; for meat, bread, shoes and boots, educational books and stationery, servant's wages, clothing, medicines, washing, and the keep of a horse.[18] It does not seem that Charlotte Barton was ever recompensed for expenses she incurred from December 1839 to the beginning of 1841.[19]

Very soon, as the effects of the economic depression into which New South Wales was sliding became apparent, the £350 which Charlotte Barton was to be paid annually must have become an unrealistic sum to be expected from the Oldbury estate. The tenant Humphery may have paid rent for the first six months of 1841; if so, this was the only money ever received from him and soon he was to be declared bankrupt. The administration of Oldbury continued to be a problem for the executors. Early in 1842 Alexander Berry wrote to John Coghill asking him to call at Oldbury on his way from Braidwood to Sydney to investigate Humphery's non-payment of rent. 'I am very unwilling to send up a special Bailiff from Sydney on account of the expense—& else out of consideration for the family of the late James Atkinson—because if Humphries [sic] is sold off at this moment no one else will give so much for the farm', he wrote.[20]

As Sir James Dowling's order of July 1841 was an interim one only, *Atkinson Versus Barton and Others* was before the court again on 15 April 1842.[21] At a detailed hearing the Chief Justice declared the will of James Atkinson proven and ordered (eight years after his death!) that his debts, funeral expenses and legacies be paid. He also ordered a complete examination of the financial management of the estate since his death. All books, deeds, papers and writings regarding the administration of the estate were to be presented to the court on oath, and all rents and profits, all money paid out for the support and education of the children, and all money paid by the executors to the estate were to be declared. This investigation by the Master in Equity, which took a year, brought all financial dealings regarding Oldbury under scrutiny and there were some recriminations. One verdict went against Alexander Berry who was required to pay George Barton £95 on account of the Oldbury estate, the case having arisen because of arrangements made by Coghill. 'The whole is a fine specimen of legality,' Berry wrote to Coghill at Braidwood, 'and of course I must submit to repay the money out of my own pocket—as it is now impossible to alter the accounts'. He continued:

All the lawyers say that you acted quite wrong. . .by leaving the property in the hands of the woman Barton. . .you will most likely be

James Atkinson became friendly with Captain John Coghill when he travelled on Coghill's ship, the *Mangles* on a visit to England in 1826. By the time Coghill became an executor of Atkinson's estate, he had left the sea and had become a landowner and a magistrate at Braidwood. (National Library of Australia)

made liable to the children to the amount of £600... This is an affair of which I know nothing except from hearsay and therefore although I have been doing my best, I fear that I shall be unable to produce what will be considered sufficient proof that you left the property with the woman...

Had it not been from this difficulty the papers would ere now have been sent before the Master—and if you do not come down yourself & furnish proof, I will be compelled to send an affadavit stating that I know nothing of this part of the affair except from hearsay—This no doubt must be very annoying to you but is far more annoying to me because being originally totally averse to having any connection with such a notable she dragon I was only prevailed upon to act at the earnest remonstrance of Mr Norton & yourself—of course your own statements will be of no value but perhaps you may be able to get some evidence at Berrima.[22]

In another letter Berry wrote of a further claim by Barton against him, warning Coghill, 'It would not be safe to trust our case to a copy...in the hands of Barton, as both copies being in his hand writing his copy may have undergone some attention.' Again he expressed his bitterness at being required to pay Barton £95—'the verdict was almost as outrageous as knocking a man down in the street', he wrote.[23]

Following the detailed examination of the estate by the Master in Equity, the case came before the Court on 27 June 1843. The report exonerated Berry and Coghill from any suggestion of misappropriation of funds. The Chief Justice decided that £2171/13/4 was due to Alexander Berry and John Coghill and that they had not 'by their wilful neglect' or default omitted or neglected to receive any money. The Chief Justice found that James Atkinson had no debts at the time of his death, and the only legacy, that of £1000 to Charlotte Barton should she remarry, had been paid. The executors had received £7769/5/5 and had disbursed £7118/7/6, including £2228/9/5 for the education and support of the Atkinson children, leaving a balance of £650/17/11.

The judgment revealed that T.B. Humphery had not paid rent due on Oldbury, had been declared insolvent and no dividend had been declared. Consequently the amount allowed to Charlotte Barton for the maintenance and education of the children was reduced to £215 a year, which represented the whole of the permanent income of the estate, until 'the estates of Oldbury and Galgal be let'. The permanent income appears to be the yearly interest paid on money raised from the sale of livestock and other assets and money left by James Atkinson which the executors had lent on mortgage to the Auditor-General, William Lithgow. The executors were ordered to pay over the surplus of £650/17/11 they had received from the estate.[24]

Alexander Berry and John Coghill had found the administration of the Atkinson estate so onerous and difficult that they applied to the court to be relieved of their duties as executors. This was refused but Sir James Dowling decided to appoint a receiver to administer the personal and real estate and receive all rents and profits. The appointment of a receiver was not finalised until 25 October 1843 when on a petition from Charlotte Barton, Alfred Welby, a farmer at Sutton Forest, was appointed. Welby had to provide a surety of £2000 plus a surety of £250 from his father-in-law Rev. William Stone of Sutton Forest. His duties were to let the Atkinson properties and collect rents.[25]

Although the judgment by Sir James Dowling settled the major problems in the administration of James Atkinson's will, it did not end the court appearances in the case. In succeeding years, sometimes at intervals of only a few months, the case was before the court, and it was continually in the hands of solicitors. Welby's actions as receiver at Oldbury were scrutinised, as was Charlotte Barton's allowance for the children and her bills. On several occasions she petitioned for more money. Early in 1846 the amount was raised to £300 a year.[26]

It is obvious from the frequency of Charlotte Barton's appearances in court, and the amount of time she must have spent in lawyers' offices preparing material, that these legal battles dominated her life and that of her children for very lengthy periods during the six years they spent in Sydney. Apart from appearances in court there must have been visits to solicitors and endless family discussions as Charlotte Barton prepared her attacks on Alexander Berry and John Coghill for their alleged mishandling of the estate, and fought the entrenched prejudice of male executors and a court system which, until her case reached the level of the Chief Justice, was weighted against a woman fighting veiled attacks on her morals, character and stability.

Observing this as a child, Louisa absorbed her mother's views. In her novels she was to include several unflattering descriptions of lawyers and of visits to them, particularly in *Debatable Ground*. One of the characters in this novel, Le Bois, while trying to prove that he is Arnold Woods and the heir to Carlillawarra, makes many visits to Messrs Giles, Curten and Curten, his lawyers in Sydney:

Now, indeed, began days and nights of uneasiness and anxiety; journeys to Sydney upon matters trivial, in answer to hasty and imperative messages. Hardly would he have reached home, before some such note followed: 'Dear Sir,—We require your presence without delay.' Then, when he had obeyed it, his solicitors looked surprised, and said—
'Oh, you came down again.'
'Did you not send for me ?'
'By the bye, now you are here, what was the date of so and so—?'
Money melted away like dew drops before the summer's sun; patience, hope, happiness, all followed suit—the young man began to feel old.
'What must we do first?' had been answered, 'Prove your identity.' Then arose the serious difficulty of tracing Arnold Woods from his birth, twenty-eight years before, till he left Australia, thence to connect his history with Jean Baptiste le Bois, of Paris, and to fill in the links till le Bois of Paris became tenant of Woodacres.
'You must prove you were born, sir!' said one of the legal gentlemen rather testily, when his client had been talking for some half-hour.
'That requires no proof surely.'
'You must find registers and witnesses. There is a nurse or some one living, I suppose?'
'Yes, this Norah Coe I mentioned was my mother's female domestic, and her sister, Margaret Blair, was midwife; it was from these women that I discovered much which led to my discovering who I am.'
'Very good, sir; [these] women must be kept at hand till they are wanted at the trial.'
'When the identity is proved, what then?'
'You must prove that Animus Woods was seised of the land.'
'Was what, sir?'
'Seised of the land—taken possession—taken hold, sir.'
'That will be easily proved, I should think,' interrogatingly.
'Very probably.'

'After that?'

'You must prove your heirship.'

M. Le Bois thought that having established the other two points, that would be readily accomplished, for he was of a hopeful, elastic temperament.

The legal gentleman again said it was probable; and turned to his papers; and Le Bois went back to Woodacres to suffer a fever of excitement, and anxiety.[27]

Le Bois's action eventually came before the court, 'in certain legal circles' his case having become 'a standing joke'.

Messrs. Giles, Curten and Curten, the solicitors for the plaintiff, and his counsel, 'the cleverest man at this sort of case that could be got in Sydney for money,' bustled about with a sort of subdued enjoyment, evidently supremely happy, and trying to look perfectly indifferent. Their client made no such pretence; he was pale, haggard, and nervous, like one whose all depended on the moment—who was then to make a move, which should decide the game of life for or against him. The legal gentlemen had tried to calm him, and now and then urged him to leave the court, and take a glass of wine at a tavern over the way; but no persuasion could induce him to lose sight of the black gowns and white wigs of the learned judges and councillors—the case might come on in his absence.

'Not the slightest danger, my dear sir,' said they in chorus; indeed they had another difficulty, they were in constant dread of their client forgetting, or wilfully setting aside, the proper etiquette, for he was evidently disposed to rush over to his counsel, and give him instructions without a medium, viz., Messrs. Giles, Curten and Curten. Such shocking breaches of decorum scandallised that worthy fraternity, so as almost to ruffle their seraphic humours, ever though it was the trial of a pet little case, which was by no means likely to come to a speedy conclusion.

After the presentation of the plaintiff's very lengthy case and the defendant's evidence the jury considered their verdict and returned with a verdict for the defendant:

The words fell clear and sharp on Le Bois' ear—fell like burning shot, pitiless, deadly. Mr Giles took him by the arm and drew him behind the crowd, and his legal partners moved for a new trial, which was granted. Le Bois did not speak; he was stunned; not forgetful, as his companions supposed; nor could he communicate to them the fear of poverty which the failure of his suit had awakened. The costs, of course, he had to pay; and he now felt how much he had indulged hopes from the blank he had experienced.

'We must really moisten this dry affair,' said Mr E. Curten pleasantly, 'nor would a little lunch be unacceptable; come, my dear sir, let us step down to a restaurant, and talk the affair over.'

Le Bois yielded to the suggestion, and the four walked in the direction indicated.

'I had the promptitude to beg leave to move for a new trial without waiting for your instructions; in fact, the verdict is monstrous, and could *not* so happen again;...I consider the result certain.'

'Certain failure,' groaned Le Bois.

'Certain triumph, nothing less; it *must* be.'

'Must be,' repeated the other two gentlemen, filling their glasses, and passing the decanter to Le Bois.

The plaintiff was growing reckless; like a gamester, resolved to stake all on a throw, 'All, or nothing,' was now his motto. So preparations for the new trial were entered upon.[28]

Inevitably Le Bois's legal battles end with his insolvency and destitution.

A sheriff's sale, insolvency, nay, worse than all to Le Bois—the case—
the case on which hung everything—lapsed through want of means
to pay the costs. He was as destitute as the blind beggar on the
pavement—worse,—he had no Benevolent Asylum nocturnally to
shelter his head. He stood on the street, homeless, penniless,
friendless, and without hope.

Eventually Louisa's character, Le Bois, obtains employment as a shepherd, living a solitary life following his sheep 'far into the silent stringy bark forest'.[29]

Another of Louisa's novels, *Tom Hellicar's Children*, is a story about children who are deprived not only of their inheritance but of their mother. It has striking resemblances to the story of the Atkinson children, taken to a nightmarish conclusion. Although nothing so drastic happened to the Atkinson children—and their mother was diametrically opposed in character to Ruth Hellicar, who allowed her children to be taken from her with a submissiveness that Charlotte Barton would have been unable to contemplate—it is obvious the impression made on Louisa as her own mother faced having her children taken from her was long lasting.

In *Tom Hellicar's Children*, the executors, Tom's brother Richard and Max Ibotson, are portrayed as villains, as Berry and Coghill were to the Atkinson children. Richard Hellicar, married to a woman with great social and financial aspirations, resents his brother's property falling into the hands of his sister-in-law, whom he despises. He is depicted as rapacious while his friend, Max Ibotson, a Sydney wine merchant, is described thus:

...corpulent and bloated, with a red pimply face and dim little blue
eyes, you saw the man who would fawn upon wealth and power, and
bully and bluster the weak and lonely; who would be great in
reprimanding a beggar or a vagrant; he was a Justice of Peace, and
came out in all his glory in the affairs of the widow and orphan.[30]

47

Razorback Mountain on the route between Sydney and Sutton Forest was the scene of several murders committed by John Lynch, formerly a convict assigned to Oldbury. This illustration of 'Razor Back on the Goulburn Road' is believed to have been engraved from a drawing by Louisa Atkinson. (*Illustrated Sydney News* 18 February 1854)

In a chapter ironically entitled 'The Executors Look to the Children's Interests', Richard Hellicar, on the pretext of considering the children, arranges their separation from their mother. He divides them 'into two parties, antagonistic to each other', as Charlotte Barton and her children had been in the Atkinson versus Barton cases. In an echo of the sale of livestock at Oldbury, Ruth Hellicar says of the breakup of her former home, Biribang:

> This was the first time—but not the last; oh no, not the last—she was to hear it every day—to hear it when the sleek, fat cows *he* was so proud of were driven from the pastures at Biribang to be sold; to hear it when even his favourite riding horse was disposed of, and when she found in the papers an advertisement announcing the sale of his valuable library at an early day, then she interposed. 'I too' she said with decision, 'forbid the sale'.
>
> 'Madam,' returned Richard Hellicar coldly, 'our duty to my brother's children must be considered rather than an idle whim'...[31]

6

She does not appear to have received any instruction after her twelfth year

Once she had won custody of her children, Charlotte Barton was able to consider their education free from intrusion and advice from courts and executors. Her view that boarding schools did not provide a good education remained firm, but by now the older children had reached an age when they would gain from the wider opportunities of being taught by a variety of teachers and competing with other children. Charlotte chose for them a day school, College High School, run by the distinguished scholar James Rennie, formerly professor of natural history at King's College, University of London. Records exist which show that both Charlotte Elizabeth and James Atkinson attended this school in 1842 and James probably continued to be a pupil there for some years. It is probable that Emily also was a pupil at College High School. Louisa's attendance is uncertain but it is possible that she had some schooling there between 1842 and 1846. That year she turned twelve and according to William Woolls her education ceased at that age—'her education was so much neglected', he said, 'that she does not appear to have received any instruction after her twelfth year'. With her delicate health it is doubtful whether she attended school regularly. According to Woolls, she was 'constitutionally delicate' and had 'suffered much from a severe practitioner of the old school (from whose treatment, it would seem, she never altogether recovered)'.[1]

College High School was run on relatively advanced educational principles. Professor Rennie placed an emphasis on providing a basic education although 'ornamental' branches were not neglected. He also had an enlightened attitude to physical punishment and was proud to claim that there had been no floggings at his school. The aims of the school were:

1st. To make the useful branches of a sound English education (Reading with Grammar and Dictionary, Writing and Accounts) take the lead of the ornamental branches. But 2nd. Not to omit the ornamental branches, and to charge moderate fees, without the usual extras for masters, an expense so often preventitive of pupils learning Drawing, French, Music, &c.; yet to spare no expense in procuring the best instructors: and during the year *seven* efficient teachers have actually been in regular attendance. 3rd. To substitute the discipline of kindness and punctual diligence for the usual harsh system of flogging and beating, and so strictly has this been adhered to in this School, that no pupil has been flogged during the year [1842].[2]

Rennie believed parents appreciated his system, pointing to the fact that 160 pupils were enrolled in 1842, the first full year of the school's existence. James Rennie had begun his school for boys in a building which faced Elizabeth Street and backed onto Castlereagh Street just north of Market Street. He was assisted by his son Edward Alexander Rennie, later New South Wales auditor-general, and his daughter Christina who in 1842 started what was referred to as the 'Ladies' Department'.

Charlotte Barton may have responded to an advertisement for 'Miss Rennie's School' published in December 1841.[3] In it Miss Rennie offered to take a few 'Young Ladies' as 'Day Pupils' to be accommodated in a temporary apartment of her father's College High School until other premises were found. The fees were to be two guineas for pupils in the junior school and three guineas for seniors, payable quarterly in advance.

By great good fortune detailed academic results for College High School in 1842 were published in the *Sydney Morning Herald*. From these it is possible to discover that two of the Atkinson children were very successful students. In the results for the first half of 1842, Charlotte Atkinson, who turned fourteen that year, came first in drawing and geography, second in Italian and ornamental needlework, and third in 'Letter Writing and Keeping a Daily Journal of Lessons' and history. In the boys' section James Atkinson, aged ten, came first in the second class in Geography and second in Drawing.[4] Their results were even more remarkable in the second half of the year. At the prize-giving presentation by Colonel George Barney of the Royal Engineers on 14 December 1842, Charlotte Atkinson of Woolloomooloo achieved the great distinction of being dux of the girls' section receiving the '1st Medal' for general superiority. The award was made on the number of tickets received by the pupils for merit in their different classes; Charlotte Atkinson received 2988 tickets, the runner up receiving more than 1000 less. In the boys' section James Atkinson came fourth for general superiority. He came first in both the senior and junior sections in drawing, second in mathematics including algebra and third in 'Writing a Daily Journal and Letter Writing' and in grammar; in the junior section he came first in Geography, second in 'Reading with Dictionary and Mutual Questions', writing and arithmetic and fourth in 'Etymological Spelling and Dictionary'.[5]

The results of Charlotte and James Atkinson were a remarkable tribute to the education they had received from their mother. No published results have been found for succeeding years so it is not known with certainty whether Emily and Louisa attended the school or, if so, whether they shone in the prize lists in later years. It is interesting that both Charlotte and James shared the family talent for drawing, which was to be one of Louisa's great accomplishments.

Miss Rennie's school gained popularity rapidly. Ten months after it began, she was employing seven masters and two governesses.[6] An indication that Louisa Atkinson may have attended the Rennies' school with its emphasis on basic education can be drawn from the scathing criticism in her novels of the education inflicted on many girls at schools which concentrated on teaching ladylike accomplishments rather than more important subjects.

In *Gertrude* Mr and Mrs Settle, uneducated themselves, decide after they have become prosperous farmers, to do what they think is the best for their daughters by sending them to boarding school in Sydney: '...they all were down in Sydney for years; and the result was a little wool work, and bad music; and like many others in her position, old Mother Settle fell into the idea of keeping them ladies; so slaved herself, and let the girls be utterly idle'.[7]

In Louisa's novels the desire for 'refined' education is pervasive. Another character in *Gertrude*, Julia Lenny, who lives in Sydney, thinks her country cousin, Kitty Kenlow, should be allowed to 'have a year's schooling; she might go to the same lady I did, it would do her good...It's a sin she don't learn the piano.'[8] Another character, Mr Wedlake, remarks of his daughters, 'I always was for keeping up with the times; so my gals had a year at a boarding school, and learnt the pianny'.[9]

Louisa Atkinson observed life in Sydney for about six years, until the age of twelve. Her knowledge of city life was supplemented by another shorter stay some years later but she does not appear ever again to have lived for any length of time so close to the city as she did at Rose Bay, Darlinghurst and Woolloomooloo. Although the main settings of her novels were bush properties and small country settlements, she also wrote with great vitality about city life—the crowded streets, the markets, legal and mercantile offices, particularly shipping offices near the wharves, humble dwellings in the poorer streets and the beauty of the harbour and the bays around her home.

In *Cowanda* there are many scenes set in the warehouse of Ralph and Brent where one of the main characters, Gilbert Calder, works as a shipping clerk. Approaching the warehouse for his first day at work,

[Gilbert] entered a lane sloping down to the water; the dusty windows of warehouses looked down upon it; over or between these were visible the masts of shipping, and sailors' voices singing in chorus sounded and mingled with the rattling of dray wheels and the whistle of draymen. Then he paused before a door, above which was painted 'Ralph and Brent, Shipping Agents,' and, pushing it open, entered a large room, divided by desks, behind which were already assembling the numerous clerks employed there, pen in hand, or turning over the day's paper and chatting, for the principals were not there yet. . .

An hour later, and all pens were busy and the office had many visitors—stout, ruddy-faced men, who looked like sea captains and first mates; and others who appeared to be merchants, or clerks, from other commercial houses; and there were consignments, and sailing, and lading, and clearing talked of, and passing the customs, and many other significant terms in that locality.[10]

There is a similar setting in *Tressa's Resolve*:

It was a marine dealer's store; dusty, dull, and close. Gabriel Love's desk stood in a corner, with a high deal stool behind it, and a small window shedding a dingy light upon the dingy corner—the dust and cobwebs of years lurked there, and a scent of ropes and rusty iron, of salt fish, and tar, and slop clothing, hung around. Outside the door was the noise and bustle of Lower George-street, and between two roofs opposite the tops of a few masts were visible.[11]

In *Gertrude* the heroine, Gertrude Gonthier, stays briefly with Mrs Lenny who keeps a ramshackle cornstore near Brickfield Hill:

A shed with its dusty beams and posts knocking together, as if they had the palsy, rose before, the dwelling; and under this shelter of green decaying shingles, were displayed sundry tempting oranges, and apples; or peaches, and grapes, as the season might be, with cadaverous shrivelled pineapples, cruelly bruised bananas, with a jolly face melon, or trumpet pumpkin, backed up by trusses of hay, and bags of maize; among which, a steep flight of steps led 'the highest way' Mrs Lenny said to the house.[12]

In an effort to find a job in Sydney Gertrude goes to a registry office for the employment of females:

> The room was crowded with women, chiefly young, well, and even stylishly dressed: some were silent, and grave, others smiling, and whispering to some companion, or attending to those persons standing in the middle of the room. One was the Registry Agent evidently, and the girls looked up to her as if she were one of the three sisters, the Fates, commissioned by destiny to arbitrate between them and fortune; the two others were an elderly, and a young lady; the elder was scanning through an eyeglass, a little stout 'Maid of all work' before her, questioning her in a severe tone, whilst the younger played with her parasol, and appeared indifferent to the result.[13]

When Tyrell Love is wooing Tressa in *Tressa's Resolve* he takes her for a pull around to Woolloomooloo Bay in a boat:

> And what a day it proved. Dancing along on the sunny waves, or backing before a fresh breeze, always some exquisite view in sight. Now a rocky hill crowned with scrub, rusty and dense; white sand beaches, or villas clustering up the heights amidst their green shruberies. Then the shipping, and the numerous boats, the islands; why the very gulls were occasions of delight—were not their wings swift and their dives bold to charm the voyagers.[14]

She describes the harbour very differently as the scene of Gustavus Tinsley's suicide in the same book. Preparing to drown himself late one night,

> [Gustavus] creeps on—down to where the waves ripple against the steps—down to where there is a smell of tar and coal—where masts loom up against the dusky sky, and rats hurry past him, bold in the darkness, and dust, and solitude. There are black warehouse walls here, and black steamers and vessels lying in the tide, and there is a sickly smell of sea water which is not pure and free, and orange peel, and decaying onions in the stores near.[15]

In *Debatable Ground*, Amina Roskell visits Margaret Blair, a bedridden old nurse, who lives in a back street in a poor part of Sydney:

> A rather long and disagreeable walk had brought her to a door where she stood to knock, scarcely finding footing on the narrow landing, to which a flight of stairs had brought her. No fashionable parade ground this; no draper's window attractive with merchandise; no pavements, only narrow streets broken by open drains, uneven with primeval rocks, edged by cottages of every variety of form and size, with lines of clothing flapping in the wind, and dirty pale children playing on the door-steps, and wrangling over the reversions of kiss-papers and glass beads.[16]

When the Atkinson children attended College High School it would have been known that their mother was the author of *A Mother's Offering to Her Children*. It was a collection of instructional stories, no doubt similar to those she had been telling her own children, arranged in the form of a dialogue between the fictional Mrs Saville and her four children, Clara, Emma, Julian and Lucy, who approximate her own children in age. Her book was published by G.W. Evans and printed at the office of the *Sydney Gazette* in December 1841. Conforming to the standards of the time, when many authors, particularly female ones, wrote anonymously or under a pseudonym, it was stated to be by 'A lady long resident in New South Wales'. In a contemporary review, however, the author was named as Mrs Barton.

Subsequent to this, the identity of the author of the book became, and was to remain, a mystery for more than a century, until recent research by Marcie Muir again established that the author was Charlotte Barton. The clue to the authorship of the book appeared in a review in the *Sydney Gazette*, at whose office the book was printed.[17] The reviewer wrote:

The work which embraces a variety of useful and entertaining matter, is got up under the form of dialogues, between a mother and her children. It is to be hoped that others will follow the noble example set by Mrs Barton, and from time to time dedicate some such work to the public; for nothing sooner gives young persons a taste for refined literature than books of this description, which while they are interesting, are also instructive.

The Mother's Offering which teaches 'To look from Nature up to Nature's God,' should be in the hands of every young person. It is quite impossible for us to give an adequate idea of the work from the limited space we can afford, suffice it is to say, that we can confidently recommend it to the notice of parents, guardians, and teachers, who will all find it a powerful auxiliary in inculcating true morality and profitable information in the minds of those intrusted to their care and supervision, and for whose mental improvement they are responsible...

The style is easy and perspicuous, and evidently shows that the writer is a person of cultivated taste, and an enthusiastic admirer as well as a close observer of the wonders of nature. The portion of the work dedicated to Natural History, will be read with great advantage by our juvenile friends. The account of Port Essington and Timor contains some amusing information, which will throw considerable light upon these localities, that are but little known either to Europeans or their brethren of the 'far north.'

We trust that the 'Mother's Offering' will obtain a cordial welcome in the home of every colonist in New South Wales, as, independent of its intrinsic merits—the successful attempt by Mrs Barton to elevate the character of the rising generation of her adopted land, by her excellent work, gives her a claim upon the public that entitle her to their best wishes and patronage.[18]

The *Australian* on 18 and 30 December 1841 carried an advertisement for the book:

CHRISTMAS GIFT
THIS DAY is published by Evans, price six shillings, 'A Mother's offering to her Children,' by a lady, long resident in New South Wales.

It was also reviewed in the *Sydney Herald* under the heading, 'COLONIAL LITERATURE':

A very useful little publication, entitled 'A Mother's Offering to her Children,' issued from the Colonial Press last week. The work is written, in a very unpretending style, similar to Aiken's Evenings at Home, and some of Mrs Barbould's works, and, to use the words of the authoress, 'it may claim some trifling merit from being the first work written in the Colony expressly for children.' It is written in the form of a dialogue between a Mrs Savelle [sic] and her children, in which the former relates the particulars of the wreck of the *Charles Eaton*, the loss of the *Stirling Castle*, the history of Joseph Forbes, the formation of the settlement at Port Essington, together with chapters on various natural phenomena in the Colony. As a Christmas present, more especially for new-comers, the work is well adapted, and the community are under no small obligation to the authoress for having provided such a fund of amusement and instruction for the rising generation.[19]

Although it is unlikely that she had any direct connection with the Governor, Sir George, or with Lady Gipps, Charlotte Barton, rather enterprisingly, must have sought and obtained vice-regal approval of her project, as her book was dedicated to their young son, Reginald. In the dedication, Charlotte Barton said the principal merit of her work was:

...the *truth* of the subjects narrated; the accounts of the melancholy shipwrecks being drawn from printed sources, and perhaps it may claim some trifling merit also from being the first work written in the Colony expressly for Children.
The Author is fully aware how greatly the value of these little Books will be enhanced by the high and kind patronage of Master REGINALD GIPPS...

Charlotte Barton's stories included descriptions of thrilling, frightening and intriguing events that had occurred in Australia's short history since settlement by Europeans. There was the loss of the *Stirling Castle*, the wreck of the *Charles Eaton* and the rescue of

PREFACE.

TO MASTER REGINALD GIPPS,
SON OF HIS EXCELLENCY SIR GEORGE GIPPS,
Governor of New South Wales and its Dependencies,
AND OF LADY GIPPS,

THIS little work is dedicated by permission, and the author hopes the incidents it contains may afford him some little entertainment in the perusal: its principal merit is the *truth* of the subjects narrated; the accounts of the melancholy shipwrecks being drawn from printed sources; and perhaps it may claim some trifling merit also from being the first work written in the Colony expressly for Children.

The Author is fully aware how greatly the value of these little Books will be enhanced by the high and kind patronage of Master REGINALD GIPPS, to whom she begs to subscribe herself his

Truly obliged,

And most obedient humble servant,

And well-wisher,

THE AUTHOR.

Sydney, New South Wales,
29th October, 1841.

Charlotte Barton gained vice-regal patronage for her book, *A Mother's Offering to Her Children* by dedicating it to Reginald Gipps, the ten-year-old son of the Governor and Lady Gipps. It was the first children's book to be published in Australia. (*A Mother's Offering to Her Children*)

Joseph Forbes, shipwrecked as a young boy. There was also information on natural phenomena, plants and animals and some extraordinary tales about Aborigines. It was the first book Australian children could read about adventures set in Australia and descriptions of Australian life and natural features.

The wreck of the *Charles Eaton* was a particular favourite with children as it involved the survival against great odds of two young boys. The *Charles Eaton*, a barque sailing from Sydney to the East, was wrecked on the Great Barrier Reef near the Sir Charles Hardy Islands in August 1834. Five seamen escaped in a boat and the remaining twenty-seven people got away on rafts but all except a ship's boy and a two-year-old child were murdered by Aborigines. The boys were rescued in 1836.

The more original stories in Charlotte Barton's book were those containing information on natural formations, plants and animals. Most of these were set in the country around Oldbury or Budgong and the mountains and gorges of the Shoalhaven. One, 'Sea shells', was set in Sydney. It describes a visit to 'Bondi Bay' in search of sea shells and ends with 'Mrs Saville' telling her children she will buy them a book on conchology when she finds a suitable one. It is comforting to believe that Charlotte Barton, in the midst of her legal battles and uncertainty about the future, found the time and interest to take her children on a trip to Bondi beach.

It has been pointed out that there was nothing original in the style of presentation of Charlotte Barton's book. The technique of a mother telling stories to her children was a tried and tested formula which had been used by many writers of children's stories in England.[20] What was new about her book was her use of heroes and heroines from true stories that had happened in Australia, stories that were very familiar to colonial children. In their emphasis on the sea and shipwrecks they were very close to the experience of many who had weathered the hazards of the long voyage to New South Wales. Charlotte's descriptions of native trees, insects, birds and animals were also familiar to Australian children, but had never before been presented in stories for them to listen to or read.

The longest story in the book, 'Anecdotes of the Aborigines in New South Wales', a story of infanticide and cruelty presented as true events that took place among the Aborigines on or near the Oldbury property, is very shocking to present-day readers. Like her mother, Louisa was to write about Aborigines. As only remnants of the former tribes of hundreds were left when she was writing, it is obvious she gained much of her knowledge of Aborigines from her mother's stories and some of the episodes in

'Anecdotes' are repeated in Louisa's articles. By the standards of the time, when Aborigines were being massacred and poisoned, Charlotte Barton's accounts of them would have been considered sympathetic. Compared with perspectives today, there is missing from her narrative any effort to apply other than European standards to their actions or any understanding of the catastrophic effect of colonisation upon them.

Even the children in Charlotte Barton's story talk in a cold-blooded manner, apparently acceptable to those guiding young readers in the 1840s, about what are terrible tragedies:

> *Clara.*—You know Jenny has left three infants to perish in the bush; because, she said, it was too much trouble to rear them: and when our cook asked her if native dogs had eaten them, she replied, 'I believe.' And I am almost sure she killed that little black baby girl, she had sometime ago; for it suddenly disappeared; and when we questioned her about it, she hung down her head and looked very foolish; and at last said, 'Tumble down.' It was buried in one of our paddocks; and some stones laid over the grave: when we were taking a walk, with our nurse, we met one of our men, who opened the grave; and it was evident the body had been burned; for there were remains of burnt bones, ashes, and hair.
>
> *Emma.*—Billy the black man killed one of his little babies.
>
> *Mrs S.*—Yes, he took it by its feet and dashed its brains out against a tree. Some however, are very kind parents: but I do not think they are in general, to their infants. I remember a tall woman, quite a stranger, coming with a black infant, of less than a month old. It was so ugly and covered with long hair, as not to look like any thing human: but worse than all, the poor little creature had been terribly burned by the mother putting it too near the fire; and falling asleep. From the ankle to the lip, on one side, it was nearly burned to the bone. It had been done some days; and the fire seemed out. I therefore had it dressed with lard spread on rags: soon after, I heard the bandages were off. The negligent mother had left it; and one of their hungry dogs, attracted by the smell of the lard, had torn off the rags; and dragged them away; notwithstanding they had been tied on carefully. They were replaced; but the cruel mother appeared quite indifferent to the sufferings of her tender babe.
>
> About a week after, I understood it was dead: probably made away with.
>
> *Emma.*—What tribe did she belong to, Mamma?
>
> *Mrs S.*— I do not recollect: there were a great many tribes collecting; to the number of perhaps 200 blacks on our estate: they were assembling to fight; and we found it a great nuisance. Bullocks and horses are very much frightened at them; and the men found it almost impossible to continue their ploughing.

Emma.—It is very odd, that animals should know the difference between black and white people.

Mrs S.—I do not suppose that it is their color altogether. It may be the unpleasant smell which they have; from want of cleanliness; and constantly rubbing themselves with the fat of the animals which they kill.[21]

Charlotte Barton's success in having her book published and her children's successes at school were the bright side of life in Sydney for the Atkinson family. Despite the extreme disruption to their lives caused by constant legal battles and the uncertainty of their outcome, a picture emerges of Charlotte Barton maintaining a close-knit family life in which learning and scholarship, drawing, music and a love of nature were fostered.

Before the Atkinson family left Sydney, they may have witnessed early in 1846 the amazing and triumphant return to Sydney of explorer Ludwig Leichhardt and his party after they had succeeded in crossing from the east coast of Australia to Port Essington on the north coast. The party had left almost two years previously and for long had been regarded as lost in the unknown interior of Australia. Their appearance on a ship in Sydney Harbour was greeted with amazement by huge crowds. There were official welcomes and public acclaim.

With their interest sharpened by Charlotte Barton's stories of Port Essington, Louisa and her sisters and brother would have felt a personal interest in the arrival of these heroes. On the way one of the party, John Gilbert, had been killed in an attack by Aborigines and two others, John Roper and James Calvert, had been badly injured. The party had survived the greatest of privations, including near starvation.

At the time she first heard of James Calvert, and perhaps was one of the thousands who lined the streets of Sydney to greet the returning explorers as they went to a welcome at Sydney Town Hall, Louisa was eleven and James Calvert was twenty.

7

The glass was broken in many places, and the walls cracked and damp-stained

When Louisa Atkinson was about twelve, her family left Sydney to return to Oldbury and she was to live in the house where she had been born for the next seven or eight years. On their return they found the house in disrepair. Although the land had been rented out to a number of small farmers by Alfred Welby, the manager appointed by the Equity Court, the house probably had not been occupied since Thomas Humphery left in 1842 or 1843. In its disrepair it probably resembled Aloe Hill, a property Louisa described in *Cowanda*. An estate on the Parramatta River left to minors, Aloe Hill had fallen into neglect before being rented by Captain Dell:

> ...it was then empty , and so gone to decay as to let at a merely nominal rent...
> A few fields, the wreck of an orchard, and a large dilapidated cottage, once plastered and whitewashed, constituted the property; there were, or had been, wide verandas and French windows, but the glass was broken in many places, and the walls cracked and damp-stained; in fact, it was a picture of minors' property.[1]

Oldbury was in such a state that Charlotte Barton was obliged to pay for repairs to the house from her allowance for the support of her children, which had been reduced to £200 a year. In 1848 in a letter from Oldbury to Mr S.F. Milford, Master in Equity, in which she complained about deficiencies in her allowance, she wrote, 'I am having the house and buildings repaired so that I am under heavy expense just now having *daily* occasion to pay away money or I would not trouble you with this letter.' She detailed payments she had received in the year from 1 July 1847 to 30 June 1848, totalling £170/18/10, a shortfall of £29/1/2 on her yearly allowance, and continued:

> I this day recd. a paper from Mr Welby which he wished me to sign as a receipt to shew that I had received my Income up to 1st of Octr 1847 inclusive but as at that time there was £27/8 due to me I have deferred putting my signature particularly as I shall be in Sydney the 1st week in July.
> I have had to pay £1/8—for Quit Rents as Mr Welby could not be found and at the time Mr Norton *lent* me £31/16 towards my Income on 7th July 1846 Mr O'Reilly insisted on my *lending* him £5 for which he gave me a receipt acknowledging the loan and stating that the money was to be repaid to me from money owing him by the Court. I have never troubled you about it because I always found you had no funds in hand but as the half year's Interest became due on 3rd of May will you do me the favor to have the £29/1/2 paid in immediately and keep some money in hand for the sums I have mentioned and for my next quarter's Income.[2]

The move back to Oldbury may have been forced by economic circumstances. From Charlotte Barton's letter it appears the estate was not producing enough income, even when added to interest on investments, to provide more than a meagre allowance for the children's maintenance. It would have been much easier and more comfortable for a family of five to live on £200 a year rent free at Oldbury than in Sydney. Another consideration may have been that the heir to Oldbury, James John Oldbury Atkinson, turned fourteen in 1846. If there was insufficient money to pay for him to continue his education at a good school, this may have seemed a suitable age for him to begin learning to be a farmer.

The Atkinson family returned to a rather secluded social life. Gone was James Atkinson, a man of great respectability and standing, admired in the community. Had he lived, he would have attracted to Oldbury his farming and business associates, his friends from the landed families in the counties of Camden and Argyle and beyond, and those like him who were agricultural innovators. Instead his family returned to their estate associated with the scandals of George Barton, an incompetent farmer, a drunkard and a man held responsible for the crimes of the murderer Lynch. Charlotte may have been pitied for her misfortunes and misjudgments after Atkinson's death and might have attracted the sympathy of neighbours, but her striking independence of character and unusual if not abrasive manner probably earned her enemies rather than friends. Although the reasons were different, the family's social position at Oldbury was probably similar to that of the

James John Oldbury Atkinson was fourteen when the family returned to live at Oldbury. Only two when his father died, young James had no opportunity to learn farming from him. He inherited Oldbury when he came of age. (Janet Cosh)

widow, Mrs Doherty, Louisa Atkinson described in her first novel *Gertrude*:

'...in Dr Doherty's time we had many visitors, gentlemen principally, indeed entirely—travellers, and persons bringing out introductions from home—we had such persons here by the week together, sometimes for months—waiting till something offered suitable for them, or gaining experience, if they were going to settle...now many of these are influential men, and occasionally in Sydney we meet, and pass without recognizing; these sort of obligations are soon forgotten...and they don't like to remember that there was a time when they were glad to eat at our table; and perhaps borrow money of my husband, to start them in life in Australia.' She added fiercely 'I want no patronage from any one.'[3]

Louisa was probably less affected than the rest of the family by lack of social opportunities—she spent her time absorbing the scenes of country life and the beauties of nature around her and in drawing and writing. This period of her life from the age of about twelve to nineteen was very important in the development of her talents. Oldbury was to be the model for the property of Murrumbowrie, the setting for *Gertrude*, and her observations of plants, birds and animals at Oldbury were to feature in many of her nature articles. Her schooling ceased about the time the family moved back to Oldbury, presumably because her mother, by then 50 years old, felt unable to continue teaching her children in a

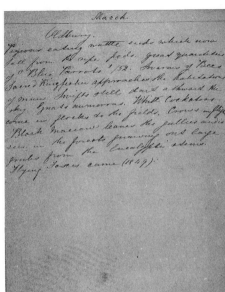

During her adolescence at Oldbury Louisa Atkinson began keeping notes on seasonal changes and the habits of birds and animals. When she began writing her nature columns for newspapers she referred to these notes and to the illustrations she had done to accompany them. (Mitchell Library, State Library of NSW)

formal way. Nevertheless it is clear that Louisa continued absorbing a wide ranging knowledge of plants and animals and birds, and she observed people closely, practising her skills at writing and drawing by keeping notebooks and sketchbooks.

Small vignettes of her life at Oldbury were to appear in her writing in later years. In one article she expressed her delight at finding the deserted nest of a wedge-tailed eagle while climbing Mt Gingenbullen. It was in the fork of a tall eucalypt in a very secluded spot, on a thickly wooded horizontal shelf between the base and the crown of the mountain.[4] In another article she related the adventures of a pair of curlews, given to her as a present, whom she named Peter and Petrea. When she released them she watched as Peter, using his wings and bill, drove Petrea to a pond surrounded by weeping willows and covered with white waterlillies. There he forced Petrea to eat the snails clustered around the waterlillies. 'Peter...was a lordly and arbitrary bird, but when Petrea was destroyed by the native cats, he long and mournfully bewailed her,' she wrote.[5] Though her fame as a naturalist is associated with the years she spent in the Blue Mountains, Louisa Atkinson found the district around Berrima 'a far richer field for the naturalist'.[6] By the time she left Oldbury she was accomplished in the study of plants and animals and in writing about them and drawing them.

While Louisa was absorbed in these pursuits, her sister, Charlotte Elizabeth, older and more restless, was searching for companionship and love. At the age of eighteen, not very long after the family's return to Oldbury, she eloped with a groom who worked on the estate. Charlotte Elizabeth appears to have been similar to her mother in force of character and independence. She was strongminded, perhaps domineering, and was described, in later life, as 'autocratic'.[7] Perhaps mother and daughter were too similar in character and disposition to live happily together.

At the age of fifteen, while they were still in Sydney, Charlotte Elizabeth had been the subject of a court case when she attempted to obtain the permission of the Equity Court to marry. In an application through the Atkinson children's solicitors on 5 March 1844, she applied as a ward of the Court to the Master in Equity to inquire and report on whether she would be permitted to marry William Cummings junior of Liverpool. The application stated that she was residing with her mother, Mrs Barton, and if granted permission to marry wanted arrangements made for her marriage settlement out of the funds and properties in which she was interested and which were under the control of the Court. In the application it was stated that Mrs Barton and several other interested parties had given their consent. The Court granted the request for an inquiry stating that it was very important for the Master to ascertain whether Cummings was a man of substance, 'as from the tender years of Miss Atkinson, the Court felt itself bound to be satisfied on that point before it could consent to a union, however much it might be desired by the young people themselves, or approved by their friends, relatives, and others interested'.[8]

Nothing is known about how Charlotte Elizabeth met William Cummings, a wine and spirit merchant, the son of William Cummings, a publican of Macquarie Street. His petition to the Court stated that he had proposed to Charlotte Elizabeth and she had accepted with the consent of her mother and her guardians.[9]

The result of this petition is not recorded in reports of Equity Court cases. As the marriage did not take place it may be assumed that either Charlotte Elizabeth or William Cummings had a change of mind or the Court did not give its permission. If the latter was the case, these remote judicial figures may not have realised how determined Charlotte Elizabeth was to marry—perhaps to assert her independence from her mother.

Returning to Oldbury at the age of eighteen, Charlotte Elizabeth, disappointed in her romance with William Cummings, may have found it difficult to meet men of a similar background to herself. She looked instead among the employees on Oldbury estate and fell in love with an attractive and charming Irishman employed as a coachman. He had dark hair and was described by a descendant as having 'winning ways.'[10] Her attraction to Thomas McNeilly, who could neither read nor write, was apparently physical rather than mental. Apart from the gulf in social position and education, there was also a religious gulf. He was a Catholic. No positive information on Thomas McNeilly's arrival in Australia has been discovered. It has been suggested that he was Thomas McNally, a former convict, but there is no firm evidence.

Whatever the truth of Thomas McNeilly's antecedents, his charm won the heart of Charlotte Elizabeth Atkinson. After their elopement, Charlotte Barton insisted they be brought back to Oldbury and formally marry.[11] She was present as a witness at the wedding at Oldbury on 22 July 1847, even though she disapproved of the marriage. The ceremony was performed by Father William McGinty, Catholic priest at Berrima, on Charlotte's nineteenth birthday. Thomas McNeilly was probably 30.[12]

Louisa was thirteen at the time. Although she claimed that none of the characters in the novels she wrote were based on actual people, the visit of Father McGinty for the marriage of her sister appears to form part of the background for the inclusion in *Gertrude* of the marriage of Mary O'Shannasy, an Irish maid on Murrumbowrie, to Dick McMaster, a sawyer, by Father Patrick O'Connor:

> Every thing being thus in readiness, the arrival of the Reverend Patrick O'Connor became a matter of unusual interest. Never was the worthy man met with such officious attentions, and such protestations of affection. He was a short, very stout man, so much so as to be a perfect caricature of corpulent humanity; and he came into the house panting and puffing alarmingly. Mrs Doherty welcomed him with a smile.
>
> 'We have some work for you,' she said in her own brisk manner.
>
> 'Indeed Madam,' he replied in a strong Irish accent, 'and what may it be?'
>
> 'Why Mary here is tired of freedom, and wants a Master, so you must tie their hands.'
>
> 'Indeed Madam my fatigue will prevent my attending to the matter at present, or I should feel great pleasure for your sake in so doing.' His Reverence had sunk into a chair, and was passing a large red hankerchief over his heated brow...
>
> 'In the meantime, if you could oblige me with a glass of milk, I should feel all the better,' he concluded.

THE WOOL-SHED.

Louisa's sister, Charlotte Elizabeth Atkinson, married Thomas McNeilly at Old-bury in 1847. In her novel *Gertrude*, Louisa Atkinson included a country wedding followed by a woolshed dance. This illustration from *Gertrude* was engraved on wood by Walter George Mason from a drawing by Louisa Atkinson. (*Gertrude, the Emigrant*)

> Gertrude ran for the desired beverage, and Mrs Doherty begged to add a little French brandy to take off the chill; and the good man tasted and relished, and spoke a few words, and tasted again, and so on, till no inconsiderable quantity of the mixture had vanished.[13]

In the fictional version, the wedding was followed by a dance in the woolshed:

> such a dance! no swimming in lazy ease through elegant saloons but real, active, violent exertion, such as a lot of spirited horses at play take: jumping, bounding, and stamping, while from time to time a visit to the two-gallon keg of rum, smuggled in by the slyest means, gave an additional impetus to their glee. Scarlet and yellow hankerchiefs fluttered on poles for flags, and old shawls were spread out as streamers. When evening came tallow candles, stuck in the necks of bottles, illuminated the scene, which presented a subject fit for the pencil of Cruickshank in his happiest moments.

Following the wedding, Mrs Doherty and Gertrude entertained Father O'Connor in the parlour:

The Rev. Patrick O'Connor is well versed in the genealogies of the old colonists: a subject always affording amusement to the long resident, and Mrs Doherty and his Reverence astonish Gertrude by their acquaintance with, not only the principal stems and branches, but also the twigs and endless saplings of the genealogical tree; each in his, or her turn, prompting the other by 'Was not she one of old Such-a-one's daughters?' 'Did not he marry one of the Smiths?' 'Was not her sister connected with the Browns by marriage?' 'Was she a "Red Rover"?' 'The man was a 'Veteran' I think.' On these little headings such a chapter opens out, as that most fertile brained writer of three volumned romances, J.P.R. James might envy.[14]

Louisa Atkinson's *Gertrude* was published ten years after her sister's wedding, long enough to distill the event into a part-fact/ part-fictional comedy. Charlotte's wedding was unlikely to have been such a carefree and happy event; it could hardly have been the marriage Charlotte Barton would have wished for her brilliant daughter.

Charlotte and Thomas McNeilly continued to live at Oldbury, probably on one of the small farms into which the estate had been divided. Their first child, a daughter, Flora Charlotte, was born there on 1 May 1848. When she was baptised by Father McGinty on 11 August 1848, Thomas McNeilly was described as a settler. Later children were baptised in the Anglican Church at Sutton Forest and one son who died was buried there. The family prospered for some time. On 13 May 1854 Thomas McNeilly is recorded as the purchaser of a 16 hectares block of Crown land at Cutaway Hill, north of Berrima, perhaps paying the £60 sum from money due to Charlotte from her father's estate. On 20 January 1857 he bought an adjacent block of 15 hectares for £37, also a grant by purchase, and the family farmed these blocks for some years.[15]

For the next twenty years Charlotte McNeilly's life, like that of so many other women in colonial times, was one of constant childbearing, with the heartbreak of the loss of several children. Of her living children Thomas James Lewin was born on 4 January 1852 at Berrima, Charles James E. on 27 December 1853 at Berrima, Ernest Adolphus at Cutaway Hill, Berrima on 25 January 1859, Louisa Emily on 3 May 1861 at Goulburn, Edwin Thomas on 5 October 1863 at Berrima and Henrietta on 20 April 1867 at Nattai. When her last child was born in 1867, Charlotte McNeilly had borne a total of eleven children, of whom six were living and five—three boys and two girls—were dead. Before the birth of her last child, her eldest child, Flora McNeilly was already married.

The birth certificates of the McNeilly children who survived document the rise and fall of Thomas McNeilly—from being a

On several occasions Louisa Atkinson kept pet possums. This oil painting of a ring-tailed possum is by her. A companion painting of a brush-tailed possum is at Old Government House, Parramatta. (Janet Cosh)

settler when his first child was born to being a farmer on his own land at Cutaway Hill, a labourer at Goulburn, a carrier at Berrima, and in 1867 a labourer at Nattai. His decline may have been like that of many other small settlers with insufficient land to make a living, particularly during times of economic depression.

For six years following her sister's marriage, Louisa acquired an extensive knowledge of plants, learning to classify them according to their genera. She studied birds and animals by observing and dissecting them, treating their skins and re-creating them employing the self-taught art of taxidermy.[16] As well as a scientific interest, she had a great love for animals and birds. Her pet koala

> ...was independent and rather capricious in temper, familiar, but resenting liberties and could, and would at times, bite severely. He was passionately fond of music, and, if performance was slow and marked, would beat time, nodding his head and [keeping] a low accompaniment. Its ordinary cry was gutteral, loud, and violent.

On one occasion she had three possums 'domesticated' in her home. One, a female, became a great pet having been fed milk from a spoon from babyhood. It spent the day rolled up in a cloak, asleep on a sofa, and the night in a cage:

> ...if not removed to the latter shortly after sundown she awoke and would run about the room, climbing to the top of the doors and casements, or, while young, romping with a kitten. She would sit on my knee holding a piece of bread and butter in her forepaws, and liked well a drink of sweet tea.[17]

On one occasion a 'beautifully spotted' koala skin was brought to her:

> In regard to this animal I could gain no positive information, many of the Blacks offering that they had never seen one like it before, others that such a species existed in the Great Shoalhaven gully, where it was killed by an aborigine who accompanied my brother as a guide when exploring. They were encamped for the night when he was startled by the shreiks and shouts of his guide, who had gone to the river, and presently he presented himself dragging the slain bear...It was a large one though not as large as they are said to grow—the size of a sheep.[18]

By the time she turned nineteen in 1853 Louisa had acquired sufficient knowledge and was practised enough in writing and sketching to seek publication of some of her work. This could be done more easily in Sydney and together with other events led Louisa and her mother to plan a move from Oldbury.

On 6 April 1853 the heir to Oldbury estate, Louisa's brother James J.O. Atkinson, turned twenty-one. It was not clear from his father's will whether he should on this date take possession of Oldbury or whether he had to wait until Louisa, the youngest child, turned 21 two years later. To clear up this point the case of *Atkinson Versus Barton* again came before the Equity Court. James J.O. Atkinson asked that he be allowed to take over Oldbury on his twenty-first birthday or, if it was decided that he had to wait until Louisa turned 21, that he be allowed to rent the Oldbury mill and premises associated with it. His request was supported by a

The large steam mill on Medway Rivulet at Oldbury, begun by James Atkinson and completed by George Barton, milled the wheat of a large number of small farmers. This watercolour of Oldbury mill is by Louisa Atkinson. (Mitchell Library, State Library of NSW. Calvert Sketchbook)

letter from his three sisters consenting to him being allowed to take possession immediately.[19]

These legal processes took some time and Louisa and her mother appear to have stayed at Oldbury until the latter part of 1854. During 1853 Louisa's sister, Emily, aged 23, married James John-

Louisa's favourite sister, Emily (Atkinson) Warren, died on 24 August 1854 after giving birth to a son, Henry, who also died eight months later. Both were buried in the Atkinson family vault at All Saints' Churchyard, Sutton Forest. (Janet Cosh)

son Warren, a farmer. Again Charlotte Barton was a witness to the marriage of a daughter, but she may have been happier to participate in this event than at her oldest daughter's wedding. James Warren, 33 at the time of his marriage, was the son of a Royal naval lieutenant, reputed later to have been promoted to admiral, although this has not been confirmed.[20] They were married on 12 October 1853 at All Saints, Sutton Forest in the presence of Charlotte Barton, and Emily's brother James.

Louisa was still at Oldbury when Emily, her favourite sister, died in childbirth less than a year after her marriage, on 24 August 1854. According to notes left by Louisa, Emily was a sweet-natured girl. A watercolour of her as a young girl shows her with a delicate profile, short straight nose, hazel eyes, brown hair and 'a sweet and modest expression'.[21] Louisa described her sister as 'pious, clever, amiable, her gentle face and graceful form rendered her at once an object of admiration and love'. Quoting the Bible, she wrote that Emily was 'An Israelite indeed, in whom there was no guile'. As she lay dying after the birth of her first child she said, according to Louisa, '"I rest entirely in Christ. Entirely." Her last words were addressed to me. Her eyes were large and prominent of a soft grey hazle [sic], her hair brown.'[22] In an article Louisa described their close relationship: 'Long years ago, when one who is now at rest, and I were cultivating our childish gardens and I would weary and wish to leave off work, she would say: "Let us sow the seeds first, L.; they will grow *while we are resting.*"'[23]

71

Emily was buried in the Atkinson family vault at All Saints churchyard, Sutton Forest. Her baby, Henry, was cared for at Mereworth, but he died at the age of eight months and was also buried in the family vault.

The year 1854 was a disturbing year not only because of the death of Emily, but because of the reappearance in the news of George Barton. Probably last heard of by Charlotte Barton at the time of his bankruptcy in 1843–44 and his appearances in the equity cases concerning James Atkinson's will, George Barton at some time after this left Sydney and moved to Bathurst. There he took up farming at the Yarrows (or Yarras) on Winburndale Rivulet.

George Barton had been living at the Yarrows for some time when in March 1854 he was indicted for murder at the Bathurst Circuit Court before Mr Justice Therry. Detailed accounts of the case appeared in the *Bathurst Free Press* and these were repeated in the *Sydney Morning Herald*, where they could hardly have failed to make disturbing reading for Charlotte Barton and her children, bringing back memories of his violent and erratic behaviour.

Barton was charged with the murder by shooting of William Rogers, known as 'Brandy hot', a reaper on his property. Barton claimed to have fired in self-defence after Rogers had entered his bedroom with an axe in his hand and threatened to 'cut him down'.[24] Rogers, shot in the lower part of the stomach, lingered in great agony in Bathurst Hospital for eight days. An inquest which began the day after his death lasted three days, the *Bathurst Free Press* commenting that all the witnesses except one had been drunk at the time of the shooting. The Coroner's jury returned a verdict of manslaughter and Barton was held in Bathurst gaol awaiting trial at the Circuit Court.[25] Despite this finding, the Attorney-General decided to put Barton on trial for wilful murder. Barton must have felt it unfortunate that his case should come before Mr Justice Therry, who had knowledge of him going back nearly twenty years when he had been assistant Crown Prosecutor at the first trial of Oldbury convict, John Lynch, for murder.

Evidence was given at the trial by John Waller, District Constable at Kelso, who said he had reached Barton's house at about 11.30 on the night of 11 January and found William Rogers, known as 'Brandy hot', shot. Barton told the constable he had gone to bed at about eight o'clock 'with the missus'. About half an hour later hearing a footstep in the bedroom he called out, 'Is that you Brandy hot?' and on receiving an affirmative reply said 'Go out of my room you old scoundrel.' He later heard Rogers say 'now I have got the axe I'll knock the old beggar's head off'. Upon this Barton said he jumped out of bed, took up his double-barrelled shotgun and the moment he saw Rogers inside the door, shot from the left barrel.

Catherine Byrnes (also known as Mrs Molloy) said she lived with Barton, with whom she was sleeping on the night of the shooting. She was not very sober 'having partaken of rum and water rather plentifully during the day'. During the night three or four drunk men had rushed into the bedroom and 'behaved indecorously, one of them raising her by the foot, which caused her to give the alarm'. Further evidence was given by several of Barton's employees including George Thomson, a horse-driver, and Henry Smith, a reaper, and by Dr Bushby, the Bathurst District Coroner.

Rogers's son, Edward Watson Rogers, testified that before he died his father had said 'Barton called me into his room to give me some grog, and when I went inside he refused to let me have any. Upon my saying I would have some, I perceived the woman Catherine Byrnes reaching something to the deceased, and the next moment I was shot.' He said his father and Barton had been on intimate terms for four years, and just before he died his father said he was as much to blame as Barton 'and that he could not make out how it was that Barton shot him'. Mr Justice Therry said the statement made by the deceased was supposed to have been made under the solemnity of death and went far to negate the supposition of malice. However, although 'the master and servants were all drunk together', drunkenness was not an excuse for the crime. He recalled the jury after they had retired to point out that Barton had not appeared to interest himself in the fate of Rogers after the shooting nor even to make any inquiries about him. The jury returned a verdict of manslaughter and Barton was finally sentenced to two years' hard labour in Parramatta gaol.[26] As no record of Barton's death has been discovered it appears that after serving his gaol sentence, he may have left New South Wales, perhaps returning to England.

When Louisa Atkinson turned 21 in 1855 she was entitled to her share of the assets of James Atkinson's estate, apart from Oldbury. As the estate had been keeping the family for 21 years through a period of drought, rural depression and bankruptcies, there would have been only a comparatively small amount left for the three daughters. However, it was sufficient to give Louisa some financial independence.

About this time she and her mother moved back to Sydney,

Louisa Atkinson was living at Burwood when she drew this scene of the eclipse of the sun on 26 March 1857. (Mitchell Library, State Library of NSW. Calvert Sketches)

living at Burwood, which, although on the rural outskirts of the city, was linked to it by train after the opening of the Sydney to Parramatta line on 26 September 1855.

Emily's death probably contributed to their decision to leave Oldbury. Following the loss of this daughter, a favourite with everyone, and some estrangement from her eldest daughter, still living in the district, Charlotte was probably glad to leave. Also, aware of the very unusual talent possessed by her youngest daughter, Louisa, she would have been determined to give her the opportunity to become known to publishers.

The walls cracked and damp-stained

This illustration of Louisa Atkinson is believed to have been painted by her eldest sister, Charlotte Elizabeth. (Janet Cosh)

Charlotte Barton and Louisa were reported living at Burwood in an article entitled 'Sydney to Homebush, 1855':

> Burwood, in 1856, and for some years later, contained but few houses; they were chiefly along the Parramatta-road. From my father's cottage, built in 1855, on Lucas-road, to the railway line and station, a distance of about half-a-mile, was all bush, and the road itself and land on its eastern side was bush to the Parramatta-road, except for Bottle's small dwelling, where an old brick-yard was situated, and one other house, occupied by MacKnight...
>
> Among the residents of the fifties, and later years, were Daniel Aldeton, storekeeper, a fine old Christian, one of the best; Mr Mosely Cohen, near the post-office already mentioned [opposite the Concord-road, on the main road, at a little shop kept by Paddy McGrath] and nearby Mr Daly and Mrs Charlotte Barton and her talented daughter, Miss Louisa Atkinson a great botanist. The last-named were friends of the writer's family.[27]

Louisa's writing career had begun before she left Oldbury; in the coming years it was to blossom, as was her fame as a naturalist.

8

The sketch for October will appear in our next number

Despite her stressful childhood, her chequered education and her delicate health, Louisa Atkinson at the age of nineteen emerged as a talented writer and illustrator and a disciplined observer of nature. In 1853 she was confident enough of her own ability to offer regular articles to the editor of the *Illustrated Sydney News*, which was just about to begin publication in Sydney. Apart from the desire to share her knowledge of nature and her illustrations with readers, there is every reason to believe that Louisa Atkinson needed to earn money and that this need remained a motivation for her writing throughout her life.

The *Illustrated Sydney News* was the second illustrated paper to be published in Australia, being preceded by the *Illustrated Australian Magazine*, which began publication in Melbourne in 1850 but ceased in 1852. The *Illustrated Sydney News* began as a weekly selling for sixpence. One of its proprietors was the engraver, Walter Mason, who had worked on the first illustrated paper in the world, the *Illustrated London News*.[1] At first the *Illustrated Sydney News* was extremely popular, 4000 copies of the first issue being sold.[2] It began at a time of economic prosperity, following the discovery of gold with an influx of gold diggers who were eager to buy illustrated papers, similar to those being printed overseas, to send home illustrations of Australia.

In the first issue on 8 October 1853, among the notes from the editor to contributors there was a reply to a letter from Louisa Atkinson: '"L.A." Notes on the Months. Have been received with their accompanying sketches. The sketch for October is in the hands of our engraver, and will appear, with the Notes for the month, in our next number. We shall take an early opportunity of acknowledging "L.A.'s" kindness in a private letter'.

76

The sketch for October

Louisa Atkinson's articles which appeared in subsequent issues of the *Illustrated Sydney News* set the pattern for the subjects and format of her later writing. Apart from her nature notes for the month—a formula she used with great success in the *Sydney Morning Herald* and *Sydney Mail*, beginning in 1860—she also had published in the early issues of the *Illustrated Sydney News* a story of bush life and articles on the Aborigines. These were to be topics that recurred in her writing for the press and in her novels. As promised by the editor her first article, almost certainly her first published article, appeared in the second issue of the *Illustrated Sydney News* on 15 October 1853.[3] Headed 'Notes on the Months. October', it began:

In these busy times, and in the universal pursuit of wealth which characterises the state of things among us, the beauties of nature are in danger of being overlooked. We believe that there are many old inhabitants—nay, even native Australians—who know little of the natural history of this great continent. Confined to the town, and engrossed by its pursuits, as they are, the thousand wonders of the creation vainly invite their attention. Perhaps a few remarks on our natural history, in a simple and popular style may be acceptable. So numerous are the writers who have illustrated the beauties of England that ignorance of them, on the part of any one who can read, must be voluntary. Australia, a land of many wonders, claims a similar attention.

Beginning, therefore, with the present month, October, we will notice some of her indigenous productions. In the high branches of the sombre Eucalyptus, we hear the *caw caw* of the clamorous young magpies, peeping out of their twig-built nests, and opening their large red mouths to receive the grub or butterfly presented by the parent bird. Most of the magpies have built in September, and even earlier, according to the warmth of the situation they inhabit. The magpie is a cheerful, noisy, familiar bird. They come flocking round our homesteads, quarrelling over a bone, or picking the crumbs cast out by the maid; or they may be seen trotting over the new turned garden-bed, dragging the earth worm, or cockchaffer grub, from beneath the sod. We have many annecdotes [sic] of the audacity of the English pie, and our native birds exhibit the characteristics of the family. The magpie constructs its nest in the forked branches of a high tree, and lays several eggs, of a deep blue-green, spotted and freckled with brown and purple. The parent bird displays much affection for its young, and defends them against intrusion with its beak and wings. The plumage is a glossy black and white. In the young birds the colours are dull and mingled; but as they advance in age the brilliancy of their appearance is increased.

That lovely little creature, the Diamond Bird, is still building. We see them on the roofs of our houses, stripping off the fibres of the stringy

77

bark to line their subterraneous nests with. They burrow in banks, or delve in masonry. For many years several of these little creatures built in the walls of the writer's house, by excavations in the mortar. Their cry of *na-nin, na-nin*, rapidly uttered, announces the approach of spring. The plumage varies according to the species; there are two varieties. . .

The article continued with descriptions of butterflies including the Admiral and Painted Lady, and the flowers in bloom in October— wild geranium, bird's eye, day-violets in the paddocks and, in the bush, the golden blossoms of the black wattle or mimosa, the English clematis, nightshade (with a note—'This species is not poisonous, and the writer has known children to eat of its berries without injury') and the love-everlasting or life-everlasting of which she wrote, 'The longevity of this flower has won it its names, and rendered it emblematical of the undying love of friends.'

The article was illustrated by her own drawing of two magpies, which had been engraved and signed G.F.A. by the engraver. It was the usual practice for the engraver's initials to appear on wood-cut engravings rather than the name of the artist. Walter Mason, the part-owner and chief engraver on the *Illustrated Sydney News* was, with Calvert in Melbourne, one of the best known engravers in Australia, although their work was said to be 'almost uniformly cold and mechanical'.[4]

In her article for December Louisa Atkinson wrote that the 'intense heat of summer heralds in our Christmas, and a brown tint settles on the meadows'. The article was mainly about birds—the bell-bird, the quail, their nests disturbed by the reaper, the skylark uttering its 'peculiar note', the house martin building under the eaves, the young 'essaying their first flights', and the sparrow-hawk 'hovering above the fields, or descending to seize a grass-hopper or a cricket'. She also wrote of attacks by black caterpillars on the oat crops and the ripening seeds of the native cherry, which were 'not *in*, but *out* side the fleshy portion'. She gave the botanical name for the native cherry, '*exocarpus expressiformis*' [*Exocarpos cupressiformis*],[5] a practice she was to follow in later aricles and which added to the educational value of her articles. Her drawing of 'The sparrow-hawk of the colonists' accompanied the article.[6]

In January her subject was possums and the article was accompanied by a delightful drawing of two possums, one on a tree branch, the other holding a decorative twig in its claw. She wrote:

The frolicsome little subjects of the accompanying illustration, are the liveliest, and perhaps the loveliest of the animals with which our

This engraving of 'The Sparrow-Hawk of the Colonists' was made from a drawing done by Louisa Atkinson to illustrate her article for the *Illustrated Sydney News* on the seasonal changes, published on 3 December 1853. The drawing was repeated in the issues of 2 June 1855 and 16 November 1865 (National Library of Australia. *Illustrated Sydney News* 16 November 1865)

This delightful drawing of possums by Louisa Atkinson illustrated her 'Notes on the Month. January' published in the *Illustrated Sydney News*. She was only nineteen when her first articles were accepted for publication. (*Illustrated Sydney News* 4 January 1854)

forests in time past abounded. Of the most playful disposition, and capable of much animal education, they essentially belong to the spring and summer times. In the warm nights in these seasons, they skip from branch to branch with a truly tropical celerity, now whisking their long and bushy tails, fan like, through the air, and now depending from an o'erhanging bough, musically swinging themselves in the atmosphere, and bathing in the falling dew-drops from the leaves. The opossum feeds principally upon herbage and foliage, and soon attains a most unfashionable obesity. The flesh forms a favourite article of food to the aborigines, and the invaluable qualities of the cloak made from the rich grey and buff fur of the animal, and, which is vulgarly called a 'possum skin,' has been attested by most travellers in the interior.

On moonlight nights, when the silence of the wood is only disturbed by the gambols of the opossum, the incipient and indeed the practised sportsmen of the interior employ themselves in shooting these little creatures, in some cases for the skins, but too frequently for mere pastime.

The flying squirrel is another of the beautiful little tenants of the forest trees, and if possible, is still more vivacious than the opossum. The wings of this singular and interesting little creature, consist of a membrane extending from the fore-arm to the hind-leg, and are attached to the body. The fur is long, and is in colour black on the upper part of the body, and white beneath. It also is one of the many lovers of the summer, and is alike perceptible at night.[7]

During the period when the notes for the month series was running, Louisa also had a short story published, entitled 'The Burning Forest. A Sketch of Australian bush life'. It was a topical story for the gold rush period, about a group travelling through a tract of wild bush on their way from the coast to the gold diggings, 'a fine group of men, chiefly new comers, with a few older inhabitants of the bush'. Despite being warned of the danger of starting a bushfire one of the group lights a fire to make a pot of tea. Again after being warned, he leaves a log alight as they continue on their way. When warned it may set the bush on fire, he replies, 'Bother the bush, it is better burned. There's plenty of it...' Inevitably a bushfire begins and races towards a bark-roofed hut, deep in the scrub, occupied by a family of settlers. They escape from their burning hut to a chain of ponds but the father leaves to attempt to save the eldest son who is watching their sheep on the hills.

> There was a silent grasping of hands—such as takes place in great extremities, when words fail—and they parted—the husband and wife—to meet no more. He lived to find his son struggling with the devouring element, and trying to drive the frightened flock to a place of safety. Father, son, and sheep, perished together.
>
> Down in the dell, the mother retreated farther and farther into the pond, shielding, with her dress, the children from the burning leaves showered upon them, and trying to pray, and move her parched lips to tell them 'all would yet be well.' And then she saw the flushed cheeks grow a dull white, and the tearful eyes glaze, and one precious babe after another, sink faint and dying into the watery grave. Then all incentive to exertion was over, and she laid her weary head beside theirs, and the wave rippled over them.

The only surviving members of the family, Minnie, the eldest daughter, and the baby, escape when Minnie, after covering the baby's face with a piece of material she tears from her dress, springs through the flames to safety. The story ends with the moral:

Taking place far from all civilisation, these circumstances did not reach the newspapers, and perhaps the travellers never knew the result of that burning log. 'Behold how great a matter a little fire kindleth.' The lighted match, or pipe ashes, in a dry country, are sufficient to fire a forest, sending desolation and death to peaceful homes. And once ignited where shall be the end?[8]

This technique of combining ordinary events and homely people with dramas of bush life, reinforced by a moral, which she first used at the age of nineteen, was to remain the pattern for much of Louisa Atkinson's novel writing.

Concurrently with her other contributions, she also submitted to the *Illustrated Sydney News* a series on Aborigines. This subject also was one that was to recur in her writing. The series, only two of which appeared, was called 'The Native Arts'. The first article described Aboriginal burying grounds, beginning with reports of graves found on the Bogan (by Sir Thomas Mitchell), the Lachlan, the Murrumbidgee, the Murray and the Darling Rivers. The main interest of the story, however, was in Louisa's description of a burial ground on Mt Gingenbullen at Oldbury:

We have inspected a grave, or perhaps we might call it a *tumulus*, which resembled a large hillock some 100 feet long, and 50 in height, and apparently formed the burying place of many persons. The last interred there was the body of an old man, and this was upwards of thirty years ago. The mound is oblong, and to all appearance, entirely formed of earth, probably on a low natural elevation. The large trees surrounding the mound, are carved with various devices, and others, at intervals, on the slope leading to the valley below. The *tumulus* is situated on the level of a mountain side, at an elevation of about 2700 feet above the sea, and 700 feet above the wooded table land. Below the *tumulus*, on the slope of the mountain, are extensive marks of excavations of the soil. The construction of this mound must have been a work of labour and time; and, in strong contrast, we may mention a few instances of interments within the last few years. A native black of the locality died, but was not buried in this tomb—a large nest of Termites being scooped out, and the body tied into a sitting posture, and enclosed within it. No trees were carved. It was a melancholy instance of the degraded state of the wretched aboriginal race, as a care of the body of the dead seems inherent in the human breast, in proportion to the advance of civilization. In the case of an infant who died, or was probably murdered some time since, the corpse was burned and interred in such a shallow grave, that portions of the half consumed bones were perceptible. The accompanying sketch will give a correct view of the locality. Even in connection with the idea of death and mortal decay, it is a pleasing spot, richly clothed with grass and flowers, and shadowed by fine trees, while between the forest boughs

This drawing by Louisa Atkinson was published in the *Illustrated Sydney News* to illustrate her article entitled 'The Native Arts' in which she described an Aboriginal burying ground on Mount Gingenbullen. (*Illustrated Sydney News* 26 November 1853)

we catch a rural scene of fields and dwellings. How great the change from the time when the native blacks toiled in the erection of that *Tumulus*? Now their foot rarely, if ever, treads there, and the sleepers are unknown and forgotten.[9]

The second article in the 'Native Arts' series began with a description of the use made of possum skins by Aborigines 'when independent of the Government blanket and the worn clothes of the charitable'. She described the making of a cloak:

...the skin is carefully removed and pegged by means of numerous wooden skewers to a small sheet of bark cut for the purpose. In some cases the raw surface is rubbed with fine wood ashes, and the fur always put next the bark. When dry, the skin is squared, and the process of carving commences; this is done by the females, and is a very tedious task. The operator seats herself on the ground, and folding the skin, still with the fur inside, places it within her knees, and with a sharp stone removes portions of the inner skin, or that part which formerly adhered to the animal, the process is very slow, and in cases where the carvings are in woves and circles, the operation is the work of patient labour, of some days' duration. So far prepared, the bark of the currijong is stripped and the fibres next the wood selected: two skins are placed together and pierced, and the currijong fibres passed through, securing and neatly sewing the skins together. The cloak is thus gradually enlarged, often to a great size, and is, when completed, a warm and durable robe. During the process of carving, the skin is softened by fat and ochre, and becomes, in consequence, of a red hue within.

When the skin was not required the animal was plucked of its fur before cooking, the fur being made into yarn by twisting it rapidly between the palms; it was then worn around the waist falling in numerous ends.

This, in the wild state of the aborigines, was there [sic] sole summer's dress. Of the more ornamental part of the costume we may mention the smooth white bone passed through the cartilage of the nose, and the Kangaroo teeth suspended from the ends of the hair. But perhaps the ladies of Sydney should like a complete description of a native belle—here, then, is her portrait. The naturally glossy black hair falls in many ringlets round her swarthy neck; but, with a copious lubricative of fat and red ochre, has assumed a sanguineous tint. A band, netted with currijong cord in round meshes is passed round the head; and the teeth before mentioned clatter gently when she moves; her necklace, many yards in length, is passed in increasing circles round the neck. It is of a golden yellow, and made of the jointed stalks of a parasitical rush found on decaying timber, which are cut into oblong beeds [sic] and strung. The opossum skin cloak is placed beneath one arm and secured on the opposite shoulder, falling with some taste round the slender form. The foot and ancle [sic] are always small and without ornament. An essential part of the dress is the netted wallet, suspended over the shoulders, and in which the extra raiment and food, and the carefully concealed and mystic charmed pebble are carried. The net is similarly made to the head-band—the latter, in cases of mourning, is whitened with pipeclay, and the face also. The arrangement of the cloak displays the tatooing on the arm and shoulders, which is effected with great agony. Such is an aboriginal girl in full costume; and with her large dark eyes and white teeth, her free movements and retiring manner, when as yet she is free from the evils gained about the settlements of the white men and public houses, she is an interesting object. Shall nothing be done for the *souls of such*? If the Prophet had bid us do some great thing, would we not have done it? We send our missions to the north and the south—the east and the west, while at home our black, aye and white populations are heathens.

In a future number we hope to describe the missions of the Blacks, and illustrate the articles here described.[10]

84

No further articles appeared in this series. In the same issue there was a drawing of the flying squirrel and the ring-tailed opossum together with a short description of each animal. Neither the drawing nor the note on the animals was signed but they are certainly by Louisa Atkinson as very similar drawings are among her paintings. Of the flying squirrel, the author wrote: 'The aborigines have a superstitious dread of destroying them, and it is only when severely pressed by hunger that they are induced to use them as food'.

After these few months of success in having her articles published, Louisa's two series ended suddenly, perhaps because of the uncertain future of the *Illustrated Sydney News*. In the 4 March 1854 issue a notice stated that William Edward Vernon and Ludolf Theodore Mellin had ceased to be part-proprietors and that the engraver, Walter George Mason, would pay all debts of the remaining proprietors.

Short unsigned articles that appear to be by Louisa continued to be published in a series on native animals and birds. One example is a note which appeared on 15 April 1854 on the koala accompanied by a drawing that is certainly by her. Some later articles and drawings in this series were supplied by the Curator of the Australian Museum or by William Woolls. A further change in ownership of the *Illustrated Sydney News* occurred on 15 July 1854 when the partnership between Henry March and Mason was dissolved and Mason became sole proprietor.

It is possible that Louisa Atkinson's burst of creative activity may have been affected, not by the upheavals at the *Illustrated Sydney News*, but by the tragic and disturbing family events which took place in 1854—the death of her sister and nephew and her stepfather's trial for murder. This may also have affected her health which since childhood had caused concern. She was said to have suffered from a weak heart, and it is clear from the explicit statement by her friend William Woolls[11] that she also suffered from pulmonary consumption, or tuberculosis. Tuberculosis was so prevalent in the nineteenth century that it was described as the 'white sourge'. There was no medical cure for the disease but victims sometimes recovered or had periods of remission under the influence of rest, healthy diets and fresh air. Louisa was certainly free of the disease for long periods of her life during which she was very active, but it may have recurred in times of stress. 1854 may have been one of these periods.

Perhaps as part of her treatment, Louisa, probably accompanied by her mother, went on a holiday visit by sea to the Illawarra and Shoalhaven areas on the south coast in February 1855. She referred

During a visit to Wollongong and the South Coast in 1855 Louisa Atkinson painted this watercolour of Five Islands. (Mitchell Library, State Library of NSW. Calvert Sketches)

to this trip in an article for the *Illustrated Sydney News* as 'the time I spent on the coast' and she also used this experience in her first novel, *Gertrude*. In the novel she describes a voyage by ship from Sydney to the Shoalhaven made by Gertrude Gonthier and her employer, the demanding Miss Markarld, who has been ordered a change of air because of her 'delicate health':

> The ludicrous confusion and bustle of a short steam trip promised to reach its utmost height, as the travellers exchanged a seat in the carriage for a place in the ladies saloon. Gertrude indeed, was not destined to remain there long, there were packages innumerable to see after, and to know the exact locality of.
>
> 'Gertrude,' said Miss Markarld, from among a pile of pillows and shawls.
>
> She approached.
>
> 'Where is my small bonnet box?'
>
> 'Quite safe miss, just there above that brass rod.'
>
> 'Bring it to me. I cannot see it.'
>
> The box was brought, and then returned to the same situation.
>
> 'Gertrude, where is my silk shade; I really think I dropped it on deck, go and see.'
>
> The waves of the wide Pacific were not acting in strict conformity

with their name, and the reeling movement of the vessel disposed the young girl to make sudden runs in a rather dangerous manner. The drawn shade was not on deck, and after a lengthened search, it was discovered beneath the pillows under Miss Markarld's head.

So often did the pretences arise for requiring her attention, that the notice of the other female passengers was aroused.

'I say young woman,' ejaculated a comfortable looking dame, clearly a farmer's wife, returning home after a marketing trip. 'You just let her be, if she wants them things, let her get up after them,' and she gave the shawl twisted about her shoulders an indignant jerk.

Gertrude replied that the lady was ill.

'And what are you I wonder,' demanded the zealous good wife.

The girl passed her hand over a white cheek, and smiled faintly.

The wind was getting up, and the waves in concert, there was rolling and tossing of the boat, and staggering up and down stairs, among the male passengers, and strong voices pronouncing opinions that 'a southerly buster' would overtake them. Miss Markarld's fears rose with the winds, and the stewardess and Gertrude were incessantly interrogated upon the subject. A certain concomitant to water excursions seized upon the inhabitants of the various berths, and the confusion increased apace.

Gertrude found she was in perfect ignorance of the coast scenery, or the appearance of any other objects than her young mistress, and the boxes and baskets legion by name, till they were seated in a dog-cart, which their future host had brought to convey them home.[12]

Louisa Atkinson also used her coastal holiday to write a factual story for the *Illustrated Sydney News* which appeared well over a year after the abrupt end of her series on nature and the Aborigines. The article, like those that had appeared previously, was signed 'L.A.' Entitled 'A Peep at a Coal Mine', it had many of the distinctive features of Louisa Atkinson's writing—it was written in clear, unadorned English, there were detailed descriptions of plants and the scenery and it included a few tantalising personal details. It was illustrated by one of her scenic drawings. She described visiting the Mount Keira coal mine near Wollongong:

It was about noon on a close sultry day in February last, that we paid a visit to the Mount Keira coal mine... As we ascended the mountain side the enclosures ceased, and the path was cut through forest. On either side of the road lay deep glens, thickly wooded. Vines bound together the cabbage, palm, myrtle and tea tree, and the large leaves of the tree nettle spread conspicuously among the branches of the red cedar, and the feathery plumes of the tree fern and Bangalee Palm, whilst the staghorn fern, and numerous other parasites clung to every branch. The clear notes of the Bell Bird rung from a hundred throats, and lesser feathered songsters twittered and chirped. Another cottage

'Mount Keira Coal Mine, near Wollongong', drawn by Louisa Atkinson, was published in the *Illustrated Sydney News* to illustrate her article on the mine. (*Illustrated Sydney News* 14 May 1855)

broke upon the almost solemn naturalness of the scene, and a decent young woman, with her chubby boy in her arms, offered us a rest in her neat dwelling. There is something affecting in the presence of these little homesteads in the wilderness; man must have toiled long before the dense wood has yielded to his hand, and that dwelling, albeit, rude and low, has arisen! A few geraniums and pumpkin vines added a grace to the scene, and from the door the good wife pointed out the noble view which offered a strong temptation to the pencil. . .

Still ascending, we reached the object of our visit. The face of a high pile of rocks had been cut away, and a small plateau or 'yard,' as the collier called it, built before the openings to the shaft. A spring dripping in cool drops from the rock was, during wet weather, swollen into a cataract, and swept away the yard repeatedly, he informed us, and a drain had been cut to carry off the water and prevent a like occurrence. The 'old shaft' is cut into the rock on a level with the plateau, but soon sinks as the seam dips, and being below the level of the outer yard, was damp, and a little drain was conducting a clear rill from the rocks when we visited it. Our guide, who might have been taken for the impersonation of a coal genii, lighted a little lamp and bade us follow him. Mounting a pile of coal, we stood before the 'new shaft,' also cut in the face of the rock, and here we entered. A coal waggon, capable of containing 1000 cwt., occupied the entrance, but a push from the collier's hand sent it lumbering away down its tramroad with a strange underground echo out of sight. Not far from the mouth a passage connects the two shafts, but it is filled with lumber, as the air entering it at the tunnel passed into the other without visiting the distant recesses of the mine.

The old shaft penetrates 100 yards, but the new one has not yet reached such a distance.

The height of the excavation did not permit of walking upright. We did not penentrate far, as our companions objected to a living entombment. The little flame of the lamp playing on the rock and coal wall and glittering on the pools of water, added not a little to the novelty of the scene, and the sooty form of the guide contributed to make a strange picture. Once again on the yard, we surveyed the beautiful picture before us, and turned an admiring eye upon the superb vegetation towering over the cliffs above the tunnels. The surface now presented was marked by seams and stripes, and was, we believe, traversed by belts of slate of different formations.[13]

The *Illustrated Sydney News*, which had begun so confidently, ceased production on 30 June 1855. The last editorial complained that the paper had been unfairly criticised for not being as good as English illustrated papers. It was also said that its 'engravings are neither so numerous nor so artistic'.

Towards the end, one of Louisa Atkinson's drawings—of a possum and a flying squirrel—was used again,[14] and after the paper was revived in 1864, some of her drawings were re-run, having apparently remained in stock. On one occasion both her koala illustration and the popular possum and flying squirrel drawing were published in the same issue.[15]

Although the *Illustrated Sydney News* after the first few months had not been a constant vehicle for her articles, its disappearance in 1855 must have been a blow. It is possible that Louisa found another outlet for newspaper and magazine articles in the years

This engraving from a drawing by Louisa Atkinson of 'The Great Flying Squirrel and The Ring-tailed Opossum' was first published in the *Illustrated Sydney News* on 4 February 1854. Her drawings were so popular they were reprinted on several occasions. (National Library of Australia. *Illustrated Sydney News* 16 September 1865)

from 1856 to 1860, when she began writing for the *Sydney Morning Herald* and the *Sydney Mail*, but, if so, these have not been discovered. It is more likely that she was occupied in writing novels and the lyrics for songs. Her first novel, the first by an Australian-born woman, was published in 1857, when she was 23. It was published under the pseudonym 'An Australian Lady'.[16] She also used this pseudonym for the lyrics she wrote for songs that were set to music and appeared as sheet music.

The first 'Cooey!', although it expresses trite and sentimental thoughts in conventional words, is authentically Australian. Although the word is more usually spelt 'Coo-ee', Louisa used the spelling 'Cooey' in her novels. 'Cooey!', published by John Davis,

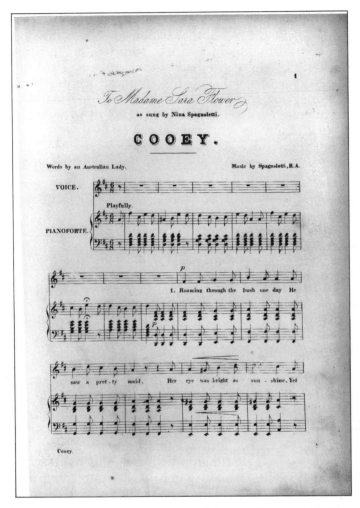

'Cooey', with words by Louisa Atkinson, may have had its first public perform-ance during a musical event to celebrate the opening of the Great Hall of Sydney University in 1859. Melbourne singer, Nina Spagnoletti, who sang 'Cooey', visited Sydney for that occasion.

draper of George Street, Sydney, probably in the late 1850s, was described on the cover as an Australian song. It was sung by Nina Spagnoletti, the wife or daughter of Ernesto Spagnoletti, tenor and graduate of the Royal Academy of Music, who wrote the music. During a residence of about eight years in Australia Spagnoletti wrote several songs including the 'Woolloomooloo Gallop'. 'Cooey' was dedicated to English-born contralto Madame Sara Flower, who had been famous since her arrival in 1850, the first singer of 'star' quality to sing in the Australian colonies. She subsequently appeared in several operas in Sydney, some with the prima donna Marie Carandini, whom she had taught. It is possible the writing of 'Cooey' was associated with the coming together of many singers in Sydney for the first musical festival in Australia, held to mark the opening in 1859 of the Great Hall of Sydney University. Among the 250 singers who sang at the festival were Sara Flower, Nina Spagnoletti and R.A. Spagnoletti.[17]

The music of 'Cooey!' was in 6/8 time. It consisted of three verses, the first being:

Roaming through the bush one day
He saw a pretty maid,
Her eye was bright as sunshine,
Yet soft as evening shade,
Her look was sad, her gaze was wild
And often did she sigh
And in a silv'ry timid voice
   she uttered the wild cry,
And in a silvr'y timid voice
   she uttered the wild cry.
Cooey Cooey Cooey Cooey Cooey
Echo caught the strain
Cooey Cooey Cooey Cooey
It echoed back again.

In the next two verses a romance develops and the man gains 'A trusting heart a loving wife'.

The second song by Louisa, 'The Light From the Mountain', which expressed sad sentiments with religious overtones, was described as a 'Favorite Ballad' when it was published in a second edition. The music in 3/8 time in D major was by composer and vaudeville performer Sydney Nelson, one of many entertainers who had arrived in Australia during the gold rush period. After making a fortune, Nelson appears to have left Australia by 1860—he died in London in 1862—so 'The Light From the Mountain' was also probably first published in the late 1850s.[18] The publisher was Edward Arnold of Elizabeth Street, Melbourne. 'The Light From the Mountain' was sung by Octavia Hamilton, a Melbourne contralto, another of the singers to visit Sydney during 1859, where she sang in a season of opera. The words of the song read:

Oh! the light from the mountain is fading away
and the shadows creep over it chilly and grey,
I see the dark rocks in their sternness and pride,
But the flowers are hidden that grow by their side.

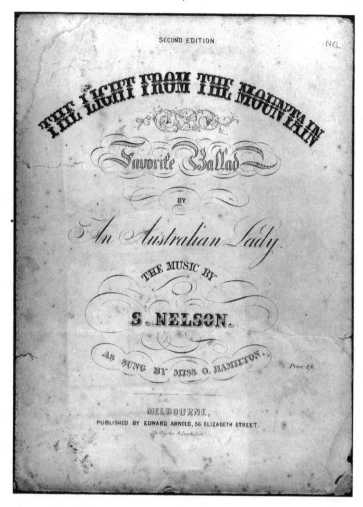

Louisa Atkinson wrote her first novels and lyrics for songs under the pseudonym 'An Australian Lady'. 'The Light From the Mountain' may have been first performed in 1859 when Melbourne contralto, Octavia Hamilton, visited Sydney to sing in a season of opera.

The tall trees are tossing their wild arms on high,
As the shreik of the curlew goes mournfully by,
The cold night is coming it will not delay,
for the light from the mountain is fading away.
The light from the mountain is fading away.

Oh! the light from Life's mountain is fading away
The shadows are closing o'er Earth's summer day!

The cold mists have gathered on heart and on brow,
The green leaves of friendship are lost to me now,
Up the steep rugged path I must wander alone.
For the blossoms of Love and of Beauty are gone;
Death's chill night is welcome why should it delay,
When the light from Life's mountain has faded away.

Louisa Atkinson's authorship of these lyrics has not been publicised previously. It is possible that other songs by 'An Australian Lady' may be discovered.

9

Her women were recognisably like Australian girls of today

In 1857, at the age of 23, Louisa Atkinson became the first Australian-born woman to have a novel published. Although written under the pseudonym of 'An Australian Lady', it was soon widely known that Louisa Atkinson was the author of *Gertrude, The Emigrant: A Tale of Colonial Life*. Early the following year, Blanche Mitchell, daughter of Surveyor-General Sir Thomas Mitchell, a young girl unacquainted with Louisa Atkinson, recorded in her diary (29 January 1858) that she and 'Miss Atkinson, authoress of *Gertrude*', were learning German in Sydney from the same teacher.[1]

Gertrude was a delight to readers at the time, providing a kindly and fresh look at ordinary colonial society, not previously described in this way in a novel, and written by an author who knew no other life. The gold rushes brought many newcomers to the Australian colonies, but they also increased the nationalism and pride in their own country of native-born Australians. It was an opportune time to publish a book about home-grown heroines and heroes. Well over a century later *Gertrude's* appeal is not in its plot or characters but in the authentic view it provides of aspects of Australian life in the mid-nineteenth century.

Gertrude opens with the arrival of a migrant ship in Sydney Harbour and in less than two pages conveys an enormous amount about the complex feelings aroused by migration. On one hand is the newly arrived Gertrude Gonthier, a friendless girl of sixteen, who while still on board ship is put up for hire. On the other hand is her employer, Mrs Doherty, a competent and commanding woman who expresses, with the directness that is cherished as an Australian trait, her disdain for emigrants who want to return home.

The deck was still crowded; some unhired, others waiting to depart; some lamenting, some rejoicing, a few stolid and indifferent, yet all desirous of quitting the confined area they had occupied for the last three or four months.

The land of promise lay before them in all its magnificent beauty, and yet many were wishing themselves back at 'home', that is in England again.

'Oh! why did I leave my own comfortable home,' lamented one. . .

'Let me never hear you say that,' said Mrs Doherty, flashing her keen eyes upon Gertrude, 'don't talk to me of what you have not been used to; of course you have not, did you expect to find England in New South Wales? If you were better off why not stay there.'[2]

Gertrude was first published in 'numbers'—a series of 24 sections released at intervals, each selling for sixpence—beginning in the first part of 1857. Reviews praised the recording of 'the ordinary incidents of every day occurrence in town and country'[3] and the recognisably Australian characters. It made for good reading 'particularly among the *native-born'*.[4] Nearly ten years later its 'Australianness' was still regarded as its chief attribute. Critic George Burnett Barton wrote in his *Literature in New South Wales*:

The scene is laid wholly in this Colony, principally in the bush; and nowhere are the peculiar features of bush life more accurately or more graphically pourtrayed [sic]. . .Her descriptions of Australian scenery are extremely good: anyone who has resided in the bush will recognize the faithfulness of her landscapes. The best character in the book is that of the 'new chum'—a supercilious coxcomb, who goes up-country with the idea of ridiculing the natives, and is signally discomfited. The contrast between this gentleman and the old residents in the bush, including the good old convict lady, the country doctor, and the young superintendent, is brought out remarkably well. Then there are several detached scenes which fix themselves in the memory; such as the child struck by a falling bough while playing at the foot of a 'woolly gum-tree'; the 'Dead Man's Run,' where the skeleton of a lost wanderer in the bush is discovered by a party of young stockmen; the narrow escape from a mob of wild cattle, careering down the side of a precipitous hill. . .[5]

The release in parts took six months. Successful in this form, it was published later in 1857 in book form by Jacob Richard Clarke of George Street. Clarke was primarily a publisher of music so it is possible Louisa had met him through her writing of lyrics. She may also have met him through engraver Walter Mason as Clarke also specialised in publishing illustrated books. In the same year that he published *Gertrude*, he also published *The Australian Picture Pleasure Book*, which contained about 200 engravings by

Mason, most of which had originally appeared in the *Illustrated Sydney News*. *Gertrude* also featured many illustrations. They appear with the initials WGM being engraved on wood by Walter Mason from 'sketches supplied by the fair authoress'.[6]

When she came to write *Gertrude*, Louisa's imagination, moulded by her family's experiences, must have embraced what was necessary for a novel of intense passions and hatreds and of single-minded and violent characters. Although she said in the preface to *Gertrude* that her characters were not based on real people, it was inevitable that she would draw on her childhood memories and the experiences of her youth. Apart from a few episodes, however, the life she portrays at Murrumbowrie is life at Oldbury idealised rather than the harsher reality. Some of her mother's attributes are present in Mrs Doherty and there is violence in Mrs Doherty's end, but it is a pale representation of the murders by Lynch and the violence of Barton. Louisa was very young when she wrote *Gertrude*, only 21 or 22 at most so it would be unrealistic to expect the maturity which would have been necessary to distill these events and characters into fictional form.

Gertrude is a story of thwarted but finally successful love against a background that moves from the Sydney wharves to a country property to outlying stations, back to Sydney, and finally to the Hunter, all in New South Wales. Gertrude Gonthier, the daughter of a German clockmaker and his English wife, following the deaths of her parents, is sent to Australia to make her own way as a friendless immigrant. When her ship docks in Sydney she is paraded to prospective employers 'like a slave put up at an auction mart'. She is fortunate to be hired as 'something more than a servant' by a widow, Mrs Doherty, the owner of a large property, Murrumbowrie. She had sought not a servant but 'a responsible person, a sort of housekeeper; one that will not be above putting her hand into the cheese vat, or the beef cask'.[7]

Mrs Doherty and Gertrude travel to Murrumbowrie in a tilted cart accompanied by two heavily-laden bullock drays carrying the supplies for the station property. At night they stay at an accommodation house where the main room, crowded with travellers, is lit by tallow candles, a huge boiler hangs over the log fire and rashers of bacon cool in a pan—a new world to Gertrude but a familiar scene to Australian readers in the 1850s.

Mrs Doherty's superintendent is Edward Tudor, an exemplary young man, 'about six feet high, rather thin, but well built; with serious, handsome features, and a healthy glow upon his brown cheek', a forerunner in physique to many of the tall, bronzed heroes who were to appear in Australian fiction. He is immediately

The illustrations in *Gertrude* were engraved by Walter Mason from drawings done by Louisa Atkinson. This illustration opposite the title page depicts the scene at a country inn where the newly-arrived immigrant, Gertrude Gonthier, stays during her journey to her new home at Murrumbowrie station.

attracted to Gertrude, but she prefers the unworthy Charley Inkersole, who is involved in stocking the Inkersole station by 'moonlighting' cattle.

The arrival of Mr Battaly, the nephew of Dr Doherty, Mrs Doherty's late husband, introduces a 'new chum', the first of many who were to appear in Australian novels. They were very popular with Australian readers as they presented an opportunity for the native-born to laugh at the assumed superiority and the inevitable downfall of these newly-arrived 'know-alls'. Through Mr Battaly, who has obvious designs on Mrs Doherty's property, Gertrude learns of Mrs Doherty's convict background. Soon after, the novel reaches a climax when Mrs Doherty is found lying dead in her sitting room, apparently murdered by a blow to the head.

After Mrs Doherty's death Gertrude has to leave Murrumbowrie and make a living as a needlewoman in Sydney. With Mrs Doherty 'Gertrude had been respected, and had respected herself; but now she was like John Bunyan's pilgrim, descending the valley of humiliation'. Tudor also leaves Murrumbowrie and he and Gertrude are brought together again only after Gertrude rescues a lost child and her action is reported in the press. Reading this, Tudor is able to trace her whereabouts and the story ends with the two preparing to marry and live on Tudor's newly-acquired farm on the Hunter River. By a contrived coincidence Tudor hears that Inkersole had died following a fall from his horse and on his deathbed had confessed that he had struck Mrs Doherty the blow from which she died because she had told him she believed Gertrude would marry Tudor.

The story finishes just before Tudor arrives in Sydney to marry Gertrude. While strolling in the Botanic Gardens she sees a ship arriving with 300 emigrants, in a similar situation to hers at the beginning of the story. She 'had too recently left her native land...not to enter keenly into the emotions which must have stirred those many bosums'.

Gertrude is more interesting than its plot. Everyday life in the bush, from the slang to the odd characters, the itinerant shearers, the station employees, magnificent descriptions of the bush, trees, shrubs, the birds and animals and scenes of city life are recorded with great vitality and remain in the memory long after the details of the rather contrived plot are forgotten.

Life at Murrumbowrie is drawn from the life Louisa knew at Oldbury. The homestead is a larger version of the simple home her father had advised settlers to build, with a wide verandah at the front on to which the main rooms open and which is used as a place to sit in the summer evenings. The activities at Murrumbowrie—wheat growing, sheep washing and shearing and visiting the cattle on outstations—all are similar to life at Oldbury as is its physical situation. Oldbury was dominated by Mount Gingenbullen and crossed by White's Creek and Medway Rivulet; at Murrumbowrie:

The ground fell gradually from the cone on which they stood down to the chain of ponds now alternately black with shade thrown by huge round topped Woollygums, or gilded with the rapidly spreading sun rays. On each side of the clover field and at the back of the cone was a heavy stringybark forest, while a high distant range of mountains bounded the horizon; the clear meadows lay on each side of the house, and the huts of the labourers with their log walls and bark roofs looked as quiet and solitary as the bush: only the gay grateful hearted magpies raised their heads to heaven and poured forth a noisy cheerful song; and on the wheat just rising in delicate green blades through the black mould a flock of cockatoos, white as the driven snow, excepting their golden crests and sulphur tinted quills, had spread themselves to feed.[8]

At the back of Murrumbowrie in the gullies were the sawyers' huts, as they were in the Shoalhaven gorges beyond Oldbury.

Gertrude is set in the post-convict era but, whether convict or free, the handing out of rations to domestics, farm labourers, shepherds and stockmen on Saturdays was a feature of station life.

Such of the men as were not at work were there, the 'sheep watchman' waiting to take the rations of himself and three shepherds, whose flocks he guarded of a night; the bullock drivers and ploughmen whose work was over for the day; a sawyer just up from the 'gullies;' Owen the stockman; John the dairyman; and several women, whose husbands were yet absent in their various employments, fencing, splitting timber, threshing, or what not; with a troop of children who had followed their parents.[9]

Cattle duffing was prevalent and accepted as a normal part of life to an extent which astonished Gertrude:

The broken nature of the country, the wide forests, and indolence of many persons in charge, enable the herds to stray; thus there have sprung up thousands of cattle for generations unclaimed, and unbranded. Gertrude did not know that many holding the rank of magistrates and even members of council, made, in days gone by, no scruple of appropriating these cattle, and if in driving them from their strong holds some were gleaned from neighbouring runs, that they also were made part of the spoil, and marked with the burning iron brand. Neither did she know that many moving in respectable circles made no hesitation in killing their neighbours fat cattle...[10]

There are many examples of distinctive Australian language, from 'mate' and 'cooey' to the 'moonlighting' or 'gullie raking' of cattle; a discussion on Mrs Doherty's wealth brings the comment 'What a long stocking Mrs Doherty must have?'.

On the surface *Gertrude* is a story of colonial life featuring episodes and characters that were to become staples of Australian fiction. The frightening approach of the bushfire from which Murrumbowrie and its inhabitants are saved only at the last minute is

THE BUSH FIRE.

Louisa Atkinson includes in her novels many dramas of bush life such as the bushfires and floods that were to become commonplace in Australian fiction. (Illustration from *Gertrude, the Emigrant*)

an example, as is the description of Tudor's horsemanship as he musters cattle in the wild Abercrombie Ranges. When he comes to a steep hill:

> ...scaling it was impossible; no steps, or path, gave promise of assistance: only the cracks and fissures in the sandstone offered a resting place for the foot...None but the accustomed eye dare loom without dizziness down those deep gorges, or up to those towering heights.[11]

Threatened by the approach of a mob of 300 wild cattle their 'tongues lolling from foaming jaws, eyes flashing, tails erect', Tudor escapes by clinging to the branch of a tree as his horse leaps over the precipice in front of the stampeding herd. These and many other similar incidents were to recur in Australian fiction for the rest of the century and beyond. It was for these episodes that Louisa Atkinson received the greatest praise at the time.

What was not noted then but is apparent now is the striking feminism of the book. Most of the main characters in *Gertrude* are women and it is interesting just how capable they are. The Australian-born 'currency lasses' as seen through the eyes of the immigrant Gertrude are women of marked independence overcoming difficulties with courage and initiative. Mrs Doherty, (not

101

native-born but a long-time resident of Australia) although she depends on her superintendent Edward Tudor to some extent in the overseeing of her property and outstations, is a strong leader and a capable manager, with 'an aversion to feminine pursuits':

> In a plain dress and sun bonnet, marching round her fields, or counting in a flock of sheep, she was at home. She might have changed places with half the hardier sex, and filled their stations in a thoroughly manly spirited manner. Gertrude quailed when she heard that stern commanding tone rating the indolent. . . [12]

But she is a practical woman uninterested in theory. When Mr Battaly, newly arrived from England, where the women's rights movement was much in the news, initiates a discussion on this subject, Mrs Doherty, oblivious of her own atypical role, comments, 'I do not see why women should try to be like men'. Gertrude's view is similar.

> I think women have much to reform, Sir, but not quite in the way they are doing. . .
> They do not seem fit to battle with the world, as men do; but there is much yet to learn, and unlearn in their homes, and pursuits; the mind might be elevated, the heart guided, and the taste refined; the home have an influence of higher and sublimer things; and woman become a companion spirit for man—not contend with him. A Bloomer dress leaves as much as ever to do. [The wearing of bloomers, a movement begun by American women's rights activist, Amelia Bloomer, in 1851, became a symbol of freedom for women.][13]

While she puts these measured words into Gertrude's mouth, Louisa portrayed a very capable girl in charge of her own life. When she arrived at Murrumbowrie, she had had no experience as a housekeeper, yet she immediately took over running the domestic establishment of a large sheep and cattle station. Under her charge 'the former disorder that had reigned supreme throughout the house gave way'. She organised and controlled staff, ordered stores and planned for the future. By day she supervised the kitchen, replenished stocks, cooked and cleaned, preserved fruit and made jam, by night she sewed for the household and mended and made new clothes for Mrs Doherty. When the sheep washing and shearing began and eight extra hands were taken on Gertrude was in charge of preparations:

> Gertrude had risen early to see two huge plum puddings in the pot; and the great copper was full of joints of beef; while a basket of potatoes stood ready to be put down, and two loaves of unusual dimensions were placed in the pantry, among tin mugs and plates, and

other requisites for carving, and eating and drinking: the can of tea had been sent down already, and a thin blue column of smoke rose by the water's edge, where the kettle was set to boil.[14]

She quickly learns how to handle the servants, her only failure being with Sarah, 'a hardened wicked-looking old woman' with an insatiable craving for rum. With Sarah she has problems with fires being neglected 'and puddings turned out raw; and joints of meat only warmed'.

When the story moves to Sydney and its vicinity, there are other capable women who have defined tasks and responsibilities. Mrs Kenlow's widowed sister, Mrs Lenny runs a corn store near Brickfield Hill, her sister-in-law, Miss Lenny has a dressmaking business with many clients.

Women who do nothing or bring their daughters up to be idle are condemned. 'Genteel' idleness is often associated with an education that emphasises acquiring accomplishments, not practical knowledge. The daughters in the Settle family at Wattle-tree Flat, a property some distance from Murrumbowrie, were allowed to run wild until they were about twelve, then 'committed to an inferior school in Sydney "to be accomplished," as Mrs Settle said, but what the next four years had accomplished, was debatable'. Their mother thought that 'gentility' consisted of exemption from occupation. In Louisa's view 'their misguided education had robbed them of all a woman's true happiness; that which springs from duties fulfilled, and competency for her station in life'.[15]

Apart from her physical tasks, Gertrude has another role in the novel—spreading knowledge of Christianity. To a present-day reader, the perception of religion in *Gertrude* and in other Louisa Atkinson novels is sanctimonious and stifling, but it is interesting to analyse her views in relation to her own time. The religion she portrays is not influenced by ordained churchmen, the heroines are usually its purveyors and they direct their efforts to moral and social reform rather than to dogma. The absence of clergymen is remarkable. In *Gertrude*, apart from one visit by a Catholic priest for a wedding, there is only a passing reference to a dissenting minister's occasional visits to the district. Even if they are superficial adherents of a branch of Christianity, most of the characters in Louisa Atkinson's novels are depicted as pagan, unaffected by the practices or the tenets of religion. In most of the novels one of the roles of the heroine is to spread a deeper understanding of religion and to lead others through her example. In this role, Gertrude finds a pervasive ignorance of Christianity among the native-born:

Comely, tall, and vigorous, and often wonderfully moral, when the tainted stock from which they spring, be accounted: but quite ignorant of religion; out of the way of churches, and sunday schools; taught to read, and write, and so on, by some ruined tradesman, or educated scamp, who settles down as 'the schoolmaster,' in those isolated farmhouses; educated the boys, and girls, and perhaps drops (how can it be otherwise?) some deadly poison into the young mind.[16]

At Murrumbowrie Gertrude seeks 'Wisdom from Above' and then goes out among the families on the property lending them her books, teaching their children, visiting the sick and condoling the afflicted. She found that many of the children 'had never heard of Christ' and knew 'the name of the Almighty only as a curse'. Her missionary efforts have an effect. Tudor gives up shooting cockatoos and reading newspapers on Sundays. Mrs Doherty allows Gertrude to read to her on Sunday afternoons and discourses on theological subjects, although mainly the 'mysteries and knotty points' of church doctrine and differences between the sects rather than 'mightier matters'. Mrs Kenlow remarks that her daughter Kitty, who has come under Gertrude's influence, 'is like a ray of sunshine on a cloudy day'.

Another message partly hidden beneath the scenes of station activity is the social fluidity of the society Louisa Atkinson depicts. Kitty Kenlow, the daughter of the sheep overseer, assumes the role of a 'lady' without great trouble, 'except for a little excess of gentility you might have supposed it her wonted place'. Apart from her aspirations to gentility, Kitty is a very capable girl, native-born, about the same age as Gertrude. She is much bigger built and she 'experienced a good natured pleasure in a sense of superior strength and bush knowledge'. Gertrude found 'so many good qualities and useful attainments in the Australian girl'.

Social fluidity applies also to ex-convicts. The prime example is Mrs Doherty, who after being transported from England, marries Dr Doherty, a landowner, and on his death becomes the capable and efficient proprietor of Murrumbowrie. When Gertrude hears that Mrs Doherty had been a convict she asks herself 'shall not the penitent be restored to a place in society? Surely so.' Another ex-convict, Hugh Dugdale, a 'short sentence' man, becomes a respected storekeeper. His step-daughters are 'so genteel' and one, Betsy, marries Dick Inkersole, from the property adjoining Murrumbowrie.

As at Oldbury, at Murrumbowrie there are remnants of the Aboriginal tribes that had inhabited the land before the coming of the Europeans. Louisa Atkinson had a comparatively sensitive if rather patronising attitude to Aborigines, but like almost all

Europeans of the time she had little understanding of the devastating effect that the occupation of their land had had on their social fabric and physical and mental health, even though she acknowledges their ownership of land. She has Tudor explain that among the Aboriginal owners land 'descends by regular birth right, like landed estates among ourselves.'[17]

The Aboriginal race was of great interest, even fascination, to Louisa Atkinson and to her readers. She had already written about some of the aspects of Aboriginal life she described in *Gertrude*— the drying of possum skins, for instance, in the *Illustrated Sydney News*—and she was to write about other aspects in future articles. Aborigines have no role in the development of the story of *Gertrude*, they are introduced because Louisa was extremely interested in them herself and because she believed readers were equally interested. Some of the scenes are nothing more than an account of events she had witnessed or had heard described by her mother or father, for example, the 'dance of death' corroboree described in the novel by Tudor. Louisa saw a similar dance to this on her visit to the Shoalhaven in 1855 and she was to describe it in later articles:

> There were probably a hundred or more Natives engaged in it. . . The Blacks had selected a well grassed level about a mile from the River, thinly scattered over with high and heavy timber. When we arrived only a few women were visible, squatting in a group on the ground, near a small fire of light wood; they had lying on their knees a 'possum skin clock, folded into a small compass, with the fur turned in. . . Suddenly there had started from behind the trunks of the trees various figures painted with pipeclay and ochre, chiefly to represent skeletons. In their hands they held a flaming bunch of twigs, or dry fern, which sufficiently lighted up their figures to enable the painting to show, leaving the sable skins in obscurity. Never shall I forget the scene! it was indeed a 'dance of death;' and the monotonous beating of the women on the skins, and their low chanting increased the solemnity: as it might be construed into a dirge for the dead.[18]

Apart from these set piece scenes, some of the references to Aborigines in *Gertrude* reveal little-known attitudes, for instance, the Aborigines' feeling of affinity with native-born Australians, presumably because of their longer association with the land. One says to Tudor, 'Me old friend Miss'er Ned, me native, all a same as you'. Tudor explains to Gertrude, 'the tie of nationality is very strong; they think much of a native'.[19]

The headings to the chapters in *Gertrude* are quotes from poetic or prose works. They are interesting in that they indicate the books Louisa had read and which were probably owned by the family.

THE EMIGRANT GIRL.

THE ABORIGINALS.

Aborigines do not play a major role in *Gertrude* but there are several descriptions of their camps and corroborees. This illustration depicts the 'do good' attitude of Europeans towards the Aborigines. (Illustration from *Gertrude, the Emigrant*)

Many of the authors were minor poets, now forgotten, a considerable number writers of religious or philosophical works. They included the English poet, Henry Kirke White (1785–1806), a clerical student; George Crabbe, a clergyman poet (1754–1832); Samuel Rogers (1763–1853), a poet who was a friend of Byron and Wordsworth; Mrs Caudle, the central figure in *Mrs Caudle's Curtain Lectures* by Douglas Jerrold; David Macbeth Moir, Scottish humorist (1798–1851); Mrs Mary Howitt, British author and translator

(1799–1888); Ebenezer Elliott, British poet known as the 'Corn Law Rhymer' (1781–1849); Richard Cumberland, British dramatist (1732–1811); Philip James Bailey, British poet (1816–1902); Martin Farquhar Tupper (1810–89), author of *Proverbial Philosophy*; and James Montgomery, Scottish religious poet (1771–1854).

There were also quotations from more famous writers, including the American poet Henry Wadsworth Longfellow; Samuel Taylor Coleridge, and from *Sartor Resartus*, a philosophical prose work by Thomas Carlyle; the ancient border ballad 'Chevy-Chase'; and there were references to the Italian painter, Salvator Rosa (1615–73), one of the founders of romantic landscape painting.

These links with the literature of the old world added scholarship to *Gertrude*, but it was its depiction of ordinary Australian life and attitudes that made it popular. Miles Franklin wrote a century later:

> The people were no longer merely sojourning here. The author had a kindly opinion of the aborigines. Her women, the currency lasses, were recognizably like Australian girls of today. The life of the country was gaining a sure outline, in which it was to continue till recently, Australianism is defined, the idiom is gathering. We read of a brick-fielder and burning-off, of wool-washing in the creek; strychnine is used to kill dingoes, there are flying-foxes and happenings still familiar, such as boating picnics and the children ready to take refuge in the creek at the approach of fire. The language is simple and direct, the characters homely—the nation's strength type, not the poor sweepings of vice and their jailers who hammered out the first roads and towns.[20]

Louisa Atkinson's next novel, *Cowanda, the Veteran's Grant. An Australian Story*, published by J.R. Clarke in 1859, was set in a different part of New South Wales, coinciding with a change in residence by Louisa and her mother. In 1857 or 1858 they moved to Kurrajong Heights in the northern part of the Blue Mountains, and they were to live there for about eight years. Louisa's delicate health may have led them to believe it would be better for her to live an outdoors life in the mountain air rather than on the flat terrain of Burwood. Also, although there was still bush around sparsely-settled Burwood, Louisa must have longed for the stimulation of the bush so that she could continue her study of plants and animals. Why they chose to buy a house at Kurrajong Heights rather than another mountain settlement is unknown. It may have been because they knew people associated with the area, perhaps George Bowen, who had served as Police Magistrate at Berrima. He had received an original grant of land at Berambing near Kurrajong Heights and his mother, Susannah Bowen, a grant covering the summit of Mount Tomah, further west.

Louisa was living at Fernhurst, a house on the north side of Bell's Line of Road at Kurrajong Heights, when she wrote *Cowanda*. The setting for the first part of the story, 'Cowanda', the property of the elderly veteran, Captain Dell, appears to be the orchard and farming country west of Kurrajong. Louisa may have been influenced in giving the sub-title 'The Veteran's Grant' to her story by the fact that veterans of the British Army had been given grants at Bilpin, beyond Kurrajong. Captain Dell, however, was not typical of the real-life veterans from the ranks, many of whom failed as farmers and abandoned their land. A similar settlement of veterans near Berrima was also a failure. James Backhouse, when he visited the district in 1836, found them living in poverty caused by 'drunkenness and profligacy'.[21]

The attraction of *Cowanda* was, like *Gertrude*, in the immediately identifiable Australian characters, situations and settings. There is the same emphasis on a young woman of strong character, strikingly competent and independent, in the role of heroine. There are also portrayals of situations and settings familar to readers— descriptions of station and farm life, of city offices and the streets and markets of Sydney, and of adventures on the goldfields.

Cowanda is set in the gold-rush period, later than the post-convict era of *Gertrude*, giving the book a particularly topical appeal. Most of the readers or their families would have witnessed, and many would have had a closer experience of the feverish rush to the goldfields that gripped Victoria and New South Wales after the early 1850s.

Like *Gertrude*, *Cowanda* had faults of structure, a lack of development in the characters, and intrusive homilies on religion and morals. A contemporay review pointed out these faults but believed that the author's work would improve with greater maturity.

> The tale is a succession of sketches, rather than a connected story, and some of the characters are indicated, rather than described, or developed...
> ...we cannot help expressing a hope that in her subsequent works she will seek to introduce the religious element, not less thoroughly in spirit, but less prominently in *words*...It is exceedingly difficult either to talk well or to write well on religious subjects...It is this which makes so many religious novels and religious biographies so intolerable to the cultivated taste of even the most pious Christians.

This is the only illustration in Louisa Atkinson's second novel *Cowanda*. It depicts a planned attack by an overseer and stockmen on an encampment of Aborigines in revenge for the spearing of a shepherd. Their attack is foiled by the hero of *Cowanda*, Gilbert Calder. (*Cowanda, the Veteran's Grant*)

But the reviewer praised the genuineness of Louisa Atkinson's writing:

> Altogether, we have been very much pleased with 'Cowanda.' It strikes us as having the great and unusual merit of being a *sincere* book—the production of the writer's own mind and heart. . .the vision may be limited—the knowledge of the human heart may not in all cases be searching or profound. Still, there is hope of better things, when wider and more accurate observation and deeper experience shall have furnished more abundant materials, and given greater mastery over language and thought.[22]

The main character in *Cowanda* is Rachel Calder, nearly fifteen at the start of the story, one of three grandchildren being cared for by Captain Dell. The Captain, believing he has been defrauded by his grandson, Rachel's brother, Gilbert, has to sell his property and rent Aloe Hill, a small rundown estate on the Parramatta River. He becomes ill and despondent, and the work of the farm falls to Rachel. Rachel soon has the orchard under culture, and the fences repaired. She bargains with a neighbouring orchardist for the sale of the fruit crop 'and she might be seen often in the bleak wind, with a shawl wrapped round her, counting and superintending the packing of baskets of fruit'.

Competent as a manager, Rachel is also shown as a girl of great independence. Defying her grandfather's command that her brother should be considered dead, she makes several adventurous trips by herself to the city in an effort to trace him and redeem his name. These take her to the offices of shipping agents where her brother worked, and involve her in getting lifts to and from Sydney with orchardists and market gardeners taking their produce to the markets. On one occasion she stays overnight and walks through the city streets in the early dawn to find the dray on which she will get a lift back to Aloe Hill.

> The sun was just rising; the golden ball of St. James's Church glistened in the first rays, and then the roofs of the higher buildings caught the amber tint, and so it travelled from gable to gable, and shot in at the upper windows to awaken the sleepers; but the streets were still in shade, cool, fresh, and quiet. A group of labourers passed her now and then, with flat baskets, from which protruded saws and squares, or a paint-pot or trowel in hand: then, near the tardy rising walls of the Cathedral, an old woman, with a temporary table, raised on benches, circulating large cups of coffee and thick slices of bread-and-butter among her customers, the workmen, and a few tall boys, masons, labourers, or 'bus boys, perhaps. Not much was said; they eat and drank quietly, and then filed away, and collected in groups, sitting along the curb-stones, and waiting for six o'clock.[23]

This episode and other similar ones show Rachel as a girl of independence and courage. As they are almost certainly written from direct observation, they also indicate the extent of Louisa Atkinson's experiences of life in Sydney.

Simultaneously with Rachel's search, Gilbert's adventures on the goldfields are recorded. Although the height of the treks to the diggings was over when *Cowanda* was published, Louisa would have observed some of the traffic to the diggings out west and it is possible that she had visited the goldfield at Sofala on the Turon River near Bathurst and the Ophir field nearer to Orange. Gilbert Calder, unhappy in his work as a shipping clerk and unaware that he has been accused of forging cheques, sets out for the Turon. He meets other prospective diggers and goes with them to the Ophir field instead. There they eke out an existence and discuss moving to Summer Hill on the Turon.

Louisa Atkinson's message about goldigging is clear both in *Cowanda* and in a later story *Myra*—it was an uncomfortable, unpredictable, lawless life with very little chance of making a fortune. In *Cowanda* Gilbert and his friends, struggling to get a return from goldigging, are washed out of their tent and lose their possessions when a sudden flood comes down the river. Later as they prepare to move south to the Victorian goldfields they are attacked by bushrangers, who kill one of the group. The impact of this murder is minimal as the victim, Frank Maclean, has only a fleeting role in the story but, in view of Louisa Atkinson's developing interests in collecting and the interest overseas in Australia's unique animals and plants, the role she gives him is interesting. In England he had been 'admitted to museums and collections' and had 'learnt to cure and set up skins' and was then employed by several amateur collectors 'to visit Australia and the Islands' to collect specimens. His greatest find is 'a *new* beetle' as yet unnamed.

When Gilbert moves to the Victorian goldfields there is an opportunity for Louisa Atkinson to state obliquely her view on the Eureka rebellion. In a scene reminiscent of the real-life conflicts at Ballarat and Bendigo, she has Gilbert Calder save the Gold Commissioner from being shot while collecting licence fees.

As the story moves from the goldfields to Aloe Hill and Sydney, Captain Dell's three grandchildren become involved in romances which come to contrasting ends, providing interesting insights into Louisa's very cautious views on marriage. Rachel's cousin, Elice Gilbert, finds after she marries a farmer, Frederick Fenwick, that her ideas are incompatible with his mother and sisters, who live with them. They were 'coarse robust women, who gloried in dairies and kitchens, who scorned books and 'bookish' people, and cordially agreed that Poor Fred was very unfortunate in having a sickly, useless girl for his wife. . .' This marriage providentially ends with the death of Frederick Fenwick from fever. The author has Captain Dell remark, 'Elly's marriage was a mistake—strange how often such mistakes are made'.

Gilbert Calder marries Clare Welton, a delicate English girl who had migrated to Australia in an effort to cure the consumption from which she suffered, but she was seemingly equally unsuited to bush life. Without interfering in-laws to worry her, however, she adapts to life on the Gwydir in a small bush cottage, its walls lined with newspapers and the slab floor covered with tea chest matting. She learns to ride, collects books to form a library for reading on winter evenings, plants a garden and in idle moments reads the newspapers on the walls 'gathering a heterogeneous mass of information'.

Befitting the two characters in the book most aware of religion and with the highest spiritual aspirations, the heroine Rachel Calder and Leigh Osman face the greatest obstacles in the pursuit of happiness. At the end of the book Leigh Osman sails off to 'Java or Sumatra' hoping to make money to free his property from debt. As she waits for him, Rachel remains 'the main-spring of the establishment' at Aloe Hill.

Some of the subjects in *Gertrude*, for example Aborigines, recur in *Cowanda*. The episode involving Aborigines depicts the race war that occurred on farms and stations as Europeans took over Aboriginal land, with conflicts settled by violence. While Louisa Atkinson's account does not show a deep understanding of the conflict, she is on the side of compassion. She has Gilbert Calder, working briefly on Captain Dell's outback station, save a group of Aborigines from being ambushed and slaughtered by the overseer in retaliation for the spearing of a shepherd.

Another recurring theme is her view on the worthlessness of much contemporary education for girls. She wrote of the daughters of a rich squatter, 'The Misses Rylston did not agree with the received opinions of young ladies, as modelled in boarding-schools: excelling rather in the dairy, or equestrian pursuits, than at the piano and embroidery frame.' The Rylston girls do not play any further part in the novel, but this remark makes them unusual characters. They are members of the newly-rich class that Louisa Atkinson usually depicts as aspirants to a false gentility—their mother, for instance, was always 'trying to be very genteel'. She 'could not be contented to appear the homely, good-natured woman she was, but, in conformity with the modern spirit, was desirous of passing for what she was not, and so laid herself open to many jokes and satirical remarks'.[24]

Cowanda was not as good a novel as *Gertrude*—G.B. Barton thought it was a disappointment[25]—and was probably not as successful in sales. It was the last of Louisa Atkinson's novels to be published in book form. Four more were published as serials. By the time the first of these, *Debatable Ground*, was published in the *Sydney Mail*, under the author's initials of 'L.A. Fernhurst', these initials were well known for another series of a very different type. These were Louisa Atkinson's nature articles, beginning in 1860, in which she conveyed to readers her own sense of wonder and delight at the finds she made in the bush at Kurrajong.

10

Every step reveals some new treasure to the lover of nature

Living at Kurrajong Heights Louisa discovered a new world of nature. In her travels she discovered plants never before known to naturalists and to honour her discoveries her name was given to several of these plants.

Fernhurst, the house where she lived with her mother, was in the small settlement then known as Kurrajong, now called Kurrajong Heights, at the top of a hill so steep that a zig-zag track had to be cut into rock down its western side. From her home the bush was only a short walk down a narrow path. Leaving Fernhurst she could descend quickly out of sight of gardens, orchards and corn fields into 'the depths of wooded seclusion'. In the gullies the vivid green of magnificent tree ferns with their feathered fronds contrasted with the glassy green of the myrtle and sassafras, all profusely entwined with creepers. A mosaic of flickering light dappled the undergrowth and here and there a ray of light scattered 'flecks of gold among the branches', or illuminated a vista through which 'mossy foliage piled in luxuriant prodigality up the sides of the gully'.[1]

Louisa flourished in the climate of Kurrajong Heights. Not nearly so elevated as the more southern parts of the Blue Mountains, it was not so cold in winter and there was neither snow nor ice. It was also more moderate than the extremes of cold in winter and heat in summer at Oldbury.[2] Absorbed and excited by the different vegetation and terrain, her health was restored and she became fit enough to spend arduous days in the saddle, climbing up steep and rocky mountains or down into deep gorges. By herself in the gullies near her home, and accompanied by friends on longer journeys, she gathered material for her readers.

The series of articles she wrote from Fernhurst, entitled 'A Voice

114

Louisa Atkinson did this ink and wash illustration of a house at Kurrajong Heights believed to be Fernhurst after she and her mother moved to the district in the late 1850s. (Mitchell Library, State Library of NSW. Calvert Sketches)

From the Country', began in the *Sydney Morning Herald* on 1 March 1860 and appeared at roughly monthly intervals. After the weekly *Sydney Mail* began publication on 7 July 1860, they were usually republished in that as well. 'A Voice From the Country' was the first series of articles written by a woman to be published in a major Australian newspaper, and predated by well over a century the recent concerns about the environment. That her articles were still being published eleven years later—although the locale had changed and there had been a break for about four years in the latter half of the 1860s—is evidence of their great popularity.

Louisa Atkinson's first articles in the series were similar in format to those she had published in the *Illustrated Sydney News* seven years previously. In them she described in an engaging, easily-read style the changes in nature month by month. In the first article covering January and February 1860, she wrote of January:

A warm drowsy month, without the opening promise of Spring or maturing riches of Autumn. In dry seasons the grass is scorched and white, the dust flies along the road before the least puff of wind, much to the annoyance of the traveller. The observer of nature finds his field of observation limited, yet not altogether barren.[3]

115

She continued with descriptions of birds—the water wagtail or dishwasher, the laughing jackasses nesting near her home, the flocks of lowries devouring the crops, and a story about the pair of curlews presented to her while living at Oldbury.

From the regularity of their appearance it seems that Louisa had made an arrangement to write a regular series of articles with the editor of the *Sydney Morning Herald*, John Fairfax, who was to become her friend. Originally the series seems to have been planned to be on the changes in nature month by month, but Louisa had more general articles in mind and it was not long before an article entitled 'Flying Fox Hunting in the Blue Mountains' appeared. This was followed by many more, describing journeys, botanical finds and the birds, insects and animals around Kurrajong. In them she recorded a remarkable series of journeys by horseback and on foot through precipitous gorges and dense undergrowth and over the sublime heights of the Blue Mountains.

In the gorges she discovered ferns then unknown to science, from the heights she described and sketched the breathtaking views. With her riding habit looped up[4] to form trousers, she collected plant specimens she stowed in a plant wallet, slung securely over her shoulders,[5] which she had designed herself. Sometimes the journeys spread over two days of hard riding and walking, at other times the party returned home in the dusk after travelling all day. That night Louisa would sort and mount her plant specimens. 'The treasures of the collecting bag furnished employment for the evening in laying them in press, and not a little work in the morning in planting rooted specimens,' she wrote.[6]

She found Mount Tomah, further west, even more profuse with varieties of ferns than Kurrajong and at the Grose River she made one of the finds that was named after her. 'Descending to the Grose by an almost precipitous path down the sides of the mountains, I gathered Deodea [Doodia] Caudata, and in another tributary to that stream found Asplenium attenuatum, a curious plant, the points of the fronds of which strike root'.[7] A form of *Doodia caudata*, a small rasp fern, was named *Doodia atkinsoniana*.

Frequently her companion on these expeditions was Emma Selkirk, the English-born second wife of Dr John Selkirk of Richmond. Emma Selkirk, an enthusiastic plant collector, had two young children and the care of at least four step-children, making her journeys in some respects more remarkable than Louisa's. William Woolls, then conducting his own school at Parramatta and a renowned botantist, sometimes joined the expeditions. Other local residents in the groups probably sometimes included Mr J. Doug-

Louisa Atkinson travelled many kilometres on horseback and on foot over mountain tracks and through dense fern gullies searching for plants and for subjects for her nature articles. This sketch appears to be of the party which Louisa Atkinson describes in her article 'Flying Fox Hunting in the Blue Mountains', published in 1860. The female figure at the left looks a little demure to be a self-portrait of Louisa Atkinson on a plant collecting expedition. Perhaps it depicts another member of the party. (Mitchell Library, State Library of NSW. Calvert Sketchbook)

lass and James Comrie and his wife, but the identities of others are now unknown. Douglass was a son of Joseph Douglass, who had received a grant of land at Kurrajong Heights, known at first as Douglass Hill, where he was the first settler. James Comrie, a former member of the Tasmanian Parliament, had moved in 1857 with his family to Northfield, a property near Tabarag Ridge renowned for its gardens. Louisa's dog, Aime, sometimes accompanied the group. On these journeys she ranged from Burralow to Mount Tomah in the west, to the Kurrajong waterfalls, the valley of the Grose River and Springwood Creek and north as far as Colo and Wiseman's Ferry.

Louisa Atkinson's articles describing these trips educated her readers not only in the scenic delights of these mountainous regions few had visited but brought them to an appreciation of the native plants, birds and animals she observed.

In the first—'Flying Fox Hunting in the Blue Mountains'—there is a vivid description of the difficulties she and her party experienced on this trip and which were common on future trips. Setting out on horses the party rode towards Colo, where they came to a steep descent. Here they dismounted and led their horses 'down a narrow, rocky bridle-way, which might more properly be called a flight of rude stairs'. At the foot they crossed a stream and ascended a mountain by a steep path which wound along the edge of a ravine. During the ascent the horse carrying one of the women riders (possibly Emma Selkirk) lost its footing and rolled down a steep decline towards the creek, the rider being able to spring from the horse's back as it fell and being saved from crashing further down the ravine by a tree. 'The tortuosity of the path had carried all the party out of sight; but the repeated "cooeys"', Louisa wrote, brought them back to rescue the fallen rider.

After struggling along a cattle track through scrub which reached the riders' shoulders, they stopped enraptured by the view of a wild gap in the range. It ended in an almost perpendicular cliff, through which flowed Big Wheeny Creek. Beyond they glimpsed the cone of Mount Tomah. Tying up their horses they made the steep descent into the gorge, led by a man who had been there often shooting ducks and collecting cabbage tree palms for hats. At the bottom they met, by prearrangement, a group of 'Colo chaps' who knew where flying foxes were to be found. Louisa's description of the camp of the men from Colo is an example of her ability to convey to readers a pride in the improvisations of people used to life in the bush:

> Intending to encamp there all night, some had rolled blankets swung over their shoulders, other displayed the gaudy linings of their

reversed and folded coats, one had thrown his saddle bags across his shoulders, and another a large canvas bag of provisions; indeed, had they dressed as brigands in some stage effect they could not have chosen the colours and 'trappings' better.[8]

Failing to find the flying foxes, the party retraced their steps 'through vines, over rocks, leaping streams, creeping beneath fallen trees, and otherwise pursuing our difficult march'. After stopping for lunch they located the flying foxes, but delayed shooting them until Louisa had sketched the scene:

> . . . literally thousands of these great bats on the wing, gyrating round high tree tops, ever and anon settling and suspending themselves by their hind feet, then fired among, and rising into the air in the utmost state of consternation, yet not forsaking the accustomed roosts, the chirping, clucking and buffetting of the whole; the cries of the wounded; the report of firearms, and shouts of the men in that dense copsewood combined to make a scene rarely equalled for wildness and interest.

Nowhere in this article does Louisa Atkinson state why the flying foxes had to be eliminated but in a previous article she had described their depredations as being 'as much to be dreaded by the gardener as the wandering Arabs of the deserts by the merchantmen of the richly laden caravans'.[9] In other articles she deplored destruction of animal and bird life.

At the summit, after a walk that had covered eight kilometres over extraordinarily difficult terrain, the party found that two of the horses they had left behind had escaped. They were discovered a couple of kilometres away; on the way Louisa noted a wonga wonga pigeon, a black snake and tracks of the lyrebird and kangaroo.

In an article published in August 1860 she described three separate visits to the Kurrajong waterfalls. While others in the party observed the scenic splendours, she had another task—the search for a 'choice and beautiful fern'. On their first visit the party followed a sawyer's road along the ridge of a hill then plunged into the green shades of a dell where crystal-clear waters encouraged a luxuriant growth of moss and fungus, which clothed each rock with a green velvet pile, or in the form of ferns, clustered in every crevice and patch of sand:

> The shade was deep, for high hills rose abruptly from the stream, often broken by masses of rock towering far over head, and affording shelter for that wonderfully fleet-footed and agile creature, the rock wallaby. . . The silence was almost oppressive; the very birds were silent. But on that first visit the merry voices of childhood and the

119

barking of dogs put silence to flight;—it was on our second visit that the full solemnity of these voiceless solitudes struck us.[10]

They were more adventurous on the second visit. Reaching the top of a gully above the long fall, they left the track and walked through a scrub of dwarf mimosa, eucalypts, woody pear and waratah, to the point of the spur. From this vantage 'The view was extensive and solemnising in its utter solitude, its extent and beauty—this feeling of the littleness of man, and supremacy of the Creator, is a sensation which we always experience in such scenes...' The descent from the spur was slow and difficult 'now a huge rock to pass round, now a fleeting sand to mistrust'. On the way Louisa heard a cry of pain and imagined her dog had lost its footing and fallen into 'the abyss of leaves and waters spread in such profound shadow beneath us'. The cry came not from the dog, however, but from a lyre bird, which she later saw flying swiftly to the stream below, the first lyre bird she had seen though she had often heard them.

On a third visit the party crossed the stream and, ascending above the rocks on the edge of the water, made their way with great difficulty to a rock from which they had a fine view of successive falls. On this visit they could not follow the bed of the stream because the water level had risen and 'in trying to keep equidistant from the top and bottom' they 'reached a dizzy height, where progression was nervous work'. While struggling along the ledge they discovered a lyrebird's nest, to Louisa a great find, and she could not resist taking the egg the bird had laid. It was 'too great a treasure to be left, though nest-robbing is our aversion', she wrote. At home she put it in the nest of a setting hen hoping it would hatch, but its sad fate, being crushed by its foster mother when nearing maturity, was described in a later article.[11]

On the first visit alone, she collected 26 distinct varieties of ferns, which she planted in her fernery. They varied from the 'almost microscopic' to the *Dicksonia antarctica*, which she expected would reach up to nine metres in height.

Louisa's articles describing the changes in nature month by month ceased after August 1860.[12] Her more general articles had proved more interesting and they were to continue for several years. In October she described a visit to the sunken plain at Burralow.[13] The route was not as testing as some other rides, nevertheless, the party had to lead their horses for about eight kilometres over broken stones, 'ready to slip from under the feet on that steep incline'. When they reached the grassy plain their first impression was of the desolation: 'the bleached dead trees, the encircling rugged hills, bristling with sandstone and sombre forest

Louisa Atkinson often crossed Wheeny Creek on her plant collecting expeditions. This ink sketch is entitled 'Big Wheeny'. (Mitchell Library, State Library of NSW. Calvert Sketches)

trees'. No outlet was visible, the narrow path through which they had entered the valley being lost to sight. 'Is it the "Happy Valley" shut out from all the world?' Louisa asked.

In December she described a visit to Tabarag Ridge, the topmost point of Kurrajong Heights, known as the Cut Rock.[14] As they rode on the upper pass the party turned to look down at the zig-zag path, with its hairpin bends cut in the rock by convicts, its edge marked by a rough wall which supported the embankment. On the journey she reported discovering the tree fern *Alsophilia australis* growing freely, a forest of stringybark interspersed with *Persoonia* (geebungs) and *Epacris* (heath) and the beautiful white blooms of the *Quintinia sieberi* (possum wood).

Another visit was to Cabbage-tree Hollow, a favourite spot for collecting palms for making hats. This had been a considerable industry occupying a large number of men, women and children. When the Duke of Edinburgh visited Sydney in 1868 he was presented with a cabbage-tree hat by the President of the Horticultural Society, but by then the hats were going out of fashion in closer-settled districts.[15] Louisa's party set off through South Kurrajong to Wheeny Creek then on to a property known as 'Cabbage-Tree Hollow'. A small stream ran through here, later joining the Grose River. Here Louisa left her companions at the farm to follow the course of the stream. She found *Alsophilia australis* and many other ferns. Rejoining the party she travelled with them along the top of a range until they reached a place where they could see below the magnificent valley of the Grose:

A sketch by Louisa Atkinson showing in the distance from left Grose Vale, Mt Hay, Mt George, Mt Tomah, Sugarloaf. Louisa Atkinson made some of her greatest botanical finds at Mt Tomah, now the site of the Mount Tomah Botanic Garden. (Mitchell Library, State Library of NSW. Calvert Sketchbook)

We stood on a rock looking down into the deep gorge, through which flowed a turbulent stream, yellow and froth-laden from recent inundations, while tributaries, which in their course clove asunder the mountains, dashed down the steeps. The heights are wooded to their summits with grand masses of yellow sandstone varying them, and the rich greens of *Backhousia myrtifolia* [grey myrtle], *Pittosporum*, and *Tasmannia aromatica* indicating the course of the various rills.[16]

After she had sketched the scene the party rode on to another spur. From the ranges on the right fell the waters of Burralow and to the left those of Springwood Creek. When they returned to the settled farms of South Kurrajong they had been in the saddle almost uninterruptedly for six hours. It was then 3 pm but after having lunch at the home of a woman who was one of the party, they again rode up the mountain—another difficult ride along a road used to haul timber—their aim being to trace one of the tributaries they had seen rushing headlong into the Grose. The track was through dense forest overarched with luxuriant vegetation, the 'trees being so festooned by creepers as at times to threaten to put a stop to further progress'. By the time they started for home up the hill along a narrow stony path, the valley was 'already grey with evening hues', ending another exceedingly long and strenuous trip.

In February 1861 she undertook another major journey, beyond Tabarag Ridge to Mount Tomah, following Bell's Line of Road, 'the great thoroughfare of the cattle and sheep' which supplied the Sydney market from the western plains. Beyond Tabarag the party came to what had been a settlement of small farms on land granted to British military veterans at Bilpin. Louisa noted, 'not one of them or their descendants live here now, and there is only one homestead, inhabited by a family of more recent possessors'. At Berambing, a few kilometres from the summit of Mount Tomah they stopped for lunch and then began the walk to the top of the mount. In the rest of this long article she describes the profusion of plants she found on Mount Tomah, now the site of the Mount Tomah Botanic Garden:

> It is impossible to convey a correct description of vegetation so profuse as obtains on the summit of this mountain to those who have not witnessed similar scenes. The barren heights of the coast, the tea tree or ironbark forests of parts of Cumberland, and the scrubs of Bargo leave an impression on the mind of more or less sterility; to the botanist they may be interesting—to the woolman valuable, but we rarely speak of them without the addition 'barren'. Here, however, the words, luxuriant, fresh, green—all epithets which can be piled together to express a superabundance of beauty in tint and form—are in constant use...
>
> To enumerate all the treasures gathered or observed, would require too great a space...[17]

This journey yielded a treasure trove of plants, two of which were later named after her.

Louisa returned several times to Mount Tomah and also made many trips to the Grose River. On one occasion travelling with a small group she described riding from Kurrajong towards the Grose through stands of *Microgamia spiralis*, some plants being higher than a man on horseback, and coming to the Grose Vale lookout above the junction of the Burralow and Cabbage-tree Hollow Creeks. Riding further they reached an overhanging pulpit-like rock from which they could view the river. They then rode on a short distance but the horses could be taken no further and they left them before beginning a descent of about two kilometres to a sandy beach, a favourite fishing spot.

The ascent from the river took a fatiguing three-quarters of an hour. One of the party had remained with the horses and had 'kindly occupied himself' in collecting plants for Louisa's inspection. One of the most interesting was a coniferous shrub she had previously found at Bundanoon Creek, between Sutton Forest and the Shoalhaven gorge. After resting for a while and making selections to add to her 'herbal treasures', the party mounted their horses and started for home 'making a detour to a part of the river where the hills, though rough and rocky, were sufficiently inclined to permit of our riding down'.[18]

The following year she made another journey to the Grose undertaken because', having seen it from above, she was anxious to explore the valley further. Descending to the river they forded the stirrup-high water and followed a barely passable track, hacked out of the bush by surveyors assessing the route for a railway. Every step added 'to the wildness of the scenery'. Rugged mountains, bristling with rocks and trees, towered above them.

At the junction of Springwood Creek with the Grose River Louisa decided to explore this stream further as it had been the scene of some of the discoveries of the explorer and botanist, Allan Cunningham who, while collecting plants for Sir Joseph Banks in 1823, had travelled through the area as far as Mount Tomah. To Louisa this made the area 'classic ground'; she had already described the Mount Tomah area as 'doubly interesting from having been the scene of some of Allan Cunningham's botanical wanderings'.[19] On the first expedition she did not succeed in reaching North Springwood. Rugged boulders strewed the rocky and uneven path. Floods had washed away the smaller stones, leaving sharp pieces which quickly removed two shoes from her horse. Later she returned on another journey to this spot and was able to find a path up the range, eventually reaching a lookout from which she could see in the far distance 'the most prominent buildings in Sydney, the Heads, a steamer's smoke'.

Then the party continued towards Springwood, hoping to find a way down the cliffs, forcing their way through dense undergrowth so thick 'that at a horse's length we lost sight of each other'. All their attention was centred on 'preserving dress and skin from jagged twigs and thorny smilax creepers [sarsaparilla vines]'. When they had not reached their destination after struggling for about three kilometres, they decided to return 'leaving Springwood still a terra incognita, to be explored at some future period'.[20]

She returned to Springwood Creek on another expedition in an endeavour to follow Allan Cunningham's tracks, hoping to find some plants he had described, but after much investigation found she had come to the wrong location. She followed a track beside a swiftly flowing stream, broken by waterfalls, but found little animal life, and in the plant line, 'no novelty greeted the eye'.

The heat was excessive, which, added to the great labour of progression made it desirable to retrace my steps, though the results were so unsatisfactory. It was evidently not here that Cunningham gathered his treasures, but nearer its source in the western mountains, many miles distant.[21]

The longest trip Louisa Atkinson wrote about in her articles was to Wiseman's Ferry, on the Hawkesbury River north-east of Richmond. She made the journey in a party of four during two cloudy days in December 1862. She had apparently stayed overnight with her friend, Emma Selkirk, at Richmond, as they started from there in the morning, cantering along on their horses 'to the music of one of the party's tin mugs or pannikins which, slung from his saddle, proclaimed at once the experienced bushman'. They travelled to Windsor then to McGraths Hill and along the Maroota Road, crossing Big Cattai Creek then Little Cattai Creek. Then they came to Maroota Forest, settled in a similar way to Bilpin by British Army veterans on small farms. Like Bilpin the settlement had been a failure:

... one only appears to have made any improvements, and he must have been a man of taste, as the beautiful trees left dotting his clearing bear witness; in fact, the green meadow and park-like wood were the beau ideal of a picnic ground. The ruins of a stone cottage uttered their own sad lesson of man's decaying hopes. On either side of the way flows, at a short distance from the road, a delightfully clear, cool stream. What could have induced the desertion of such a charming and desirable spot by all the grantees is not a little surprising.[22]

These ruins set the atmosphere of desolation which pervaded the rest of the article, although Louisa still found new plants to collect:

The trees, chiefly eucalypti, were low and stunted, but the scrub, even at this season, was decked with flowers, many of them new to me, and which, owing to the assiduity and observation of one of my friends, on the homeward way yielded specimens, and quickly filled the wallet suspended round my shoulders.

The Hawkesbury River came into view below them, bordered with cultivated land, mountains towering above, 'like stone sentinels guarding the entrance to fairy-land'. As they passed a cave they discovered it had been used as a courtroom where convicts in the road gangs had been tried for offences, a bench and chairs having been cut in the rock. At a church which had been allowed to fall into ruin, its floor dirty, communion rail broken and the velvet cloth covering the table soaked by the rain and faded from crimson to dingy brown, the Bible and prayer books bursting out of their swollen covers, Louisa reflected:

> Oh, shame upon a so-called Christian community that could so slight a place dedicated to the worship of the Most Highest, that could suffer his written Word to decay in the sun and rain. What a frightful tale that ruined church tells of lukewarmness and unfaithfulness;

Crossing the river in a boat belonging to the innkeeper, they found Wiseman's Inn also greatly 'out of repair', but they were received kindly. They had completed a 70-kilometre ride by 3 pm; Louisa thought this was fair travelling as two of the party of four were women. By 8 am the following day they had started for home, completing a journey of 140 kilometres in two days. Louisa arrived home with specimens of several new plants.

Interspersed with articles on collecting expeditions Louisa Atkinson contributed many specific articles on natural science. They included 'A Winter's Garland', 'Antechinus. Bees', 'Orchidaceae', 'Epacrideae', 'Ferns and Their Haunts', 'Insects and Insect Feeders', 'Balonne Lizard' and 'Spiders'. In writing these articles she constantly referred to her 'collection of drawings',[23] to which she kept adding. By referring to her collection she refreshed her memory of finds she had observed in the Oldbury district and described them in addition to those at the Kurrajong.

In these articles, as in her descriptions of journeys she drew her readers into an intimate world in which she shared her delight in her new discoveries. Never dwelling on one subject at great length, she developed a facility for letting one topic lead on to others. Many times she reminisced over experiences at Oldbury, at other times she explained her methods of collecting, or made observations on human behaviour and the influence of religion.

In 'A Winter's Garland' she pleaded for the bestowing and use of popular names for native plants known only by their Latin botanical names. 'Hardly would the English child hail the delicate blossoms of the snowdrop so warmly as the harbinger of spring, did he recognise it by no other name but *Galanthus nivalis*', she wrote.

> It is a pity that so few of our native flowers have popular names: unless we study botany and recognise them by a Latin cognomen, they remain strangers. How can we make a friend or a pet of a thing which even to our inmost minds we have labouriously to describe as *that* plant with the quinate leaf, or lance leaf, or so on...
>
> In occasionally writing on the flora of the Kurrajong, I purpose, therefore, giving the vulgar or familiar title—where one has been

Louisa Atkinson's sketchbooks contain many illustrations of flowers. These are *Acianthus caudatus* (native orchids). (Mitchell Library, State Library of NSW. Calvert Sketchbook)

bestowed—and occasionally may suggest one where it has not to my knowledge. It may be that many of our favourites have names differing in different places, but to establish an universal appellation is very desirable for the end contemplated; and if the simple 'Voice' may help to that end it will be a source of satisfaction to one who loves nature with a deep devotion as an outward manifestation of Him—the source of all perfection and beauty.[24]

She cited many plants with popular names including the *Lambertia formosa*, called by some the 'Honey-flower' which she had found at Jervis Bay and at Kurrajong; the *Correa virens* or native fuchsia; *Prunella vulgaris*, the meadow mint (also known as 'self heal', its leaves being applied by early settlers to cuts and wounds); the *Solanum Laciniatum*, the kangaroo apple; *Acacia floribunda*, the native wattle; *Pittosporum revolutum* or wild lemon; *Rubus hillii*, the native raspberry and the *Cissus heterophylla*, a creeper which she had found on Razorback Mountain, for which she gave no popular name.

She was later also to decry the use of names from 'old-world places' for localities in Australia. Writing of the incongruously named New Sheffield near Mittagong, she said the name 'over-stepped the narrow line between the sublime and the ridiculous'.[25]

In 'A Peep Into the Herb Doctor's Basket' she again deplored the use of Latin botanical names rather than familiar names because it detracted from the use of the plants. The main purpose of this article was to publicise the medicinal and culinary uses of bush plants, information she had culled from 'those who were guiltless of science'.[26] The plants she mentioned included the *Smilax glyciphylla* (native sarsaparilla) or 'sweet tea', found on the shores of Port Jackson, the Shoalhaven and Jervis Bay districts and at Kurrajong. It was used as a beverage and a tonic by early settlers. A plant of the gentian family she described as 'in good repute as a stomachic' and also used as a 'decoction'; the 'Vervain' of the Verbenaceae family, was favoured for its emetic properties; the leaves of the green and black wattles and the smooth-barked gums were valuable astringent medicines and the green bark of the apple tree *Angophora* when burnt into ash could be used as a lye to treat irritation caused by mosquito bites and other stings.

In other articles she made suggestions for new uses for plants. On one expedition she stopped at a homestead at South Kurrajong where she was shown large tubers from an asclepiadaceae creeper, which she thought to be *Marsdenia flavescens*. She recommended eating these tubers, which were like a Swede turnip in flavour. With potatoes subject to disease, 'this root deserves attention', she wrote, adding that a similar species called the 'gibben' was a favourite food of the Aborigines of the Balonne River area in Queensland.[27] She made a similar observation about the *Brachychiton* (Kurrajong), whose turnip like roots were eaten by Aborigines and who gathered to feast on the ripe seeds.[28] In 'Orchidaceae' she described the rock lily, the dried stems of which had been used by Shoalhaven Aborigines to make necklaces.[29] Another observation was on the intoxicating property of *Duboisia myoporoides* with its cork-like bark and lilac-white blossoms growing at the foot of Kurrajong Hill:

It grows also on the Shoalhaven and at Illawarra, and has an intoxicating property. The Aborigines make holes in the trunk and put some fluid in them, which when drunk on the following morning produces stupor. Branches of this shrub are thrown into pools for the purpose of intoxicating eels and bringing them to the surface. I have known an instance in which giddiness and nausea have arisen from remaining in a close room where branches of it have been placed.[30]

In an article on 'Insects and Insect Feeders' she expressed her concern at the recent increase in insects which attacked plants— the aphis devouring cabbages and other vegetables, scale on oranges, American blight on apples and other species of aphis on roses and honeysuckle. She observed the 'provision nature makes to keep the balance of creation perfect, that each part of the vast machinery may adjust to the other, and the whole display the hand of the God of order'. But sadly, 'It would seem as if the insects had increased in a greater ration than their consumers'.[31] She praised the fern owl which ate slugs, the sacred kingfisher which removed spiders and beetles, the robin removing worms, and crows which ate larvae of beetles and caterpillars, but she found nothing that attacked the aphid.

An indication of the great success of Louisa Atkinson's articles was the number of readers who wrote letters to the editor concerning them. (There were also a few imitators—one correspondent headed his letter to the editor of the *Sydney Morning Herald* 'A Voice from the Lower Darling'.[32]) When appropriate Louisa Atkinson replied to correspondents in following articles. At the end of her article 'Orchidaceae' she welcomed readers' letters:

> As one of my chief reasons for writing is to call the attention of scientific and amateur collectors to the numerous objects of interest in the Kurrajong, and to share with them the enjoyment I derive in these researches, the courtesy of better informed persons in imparting either through the columns of the *Herald* or privately, further information on these subjects is particularly esteemed. One of these correspondents suggests that the Asplenium [fern] referred to is *proliferum*, that we have abundantly here, but it has a bi-pinnate leaf, while the frond of the other, *A. attenuatum*, is simple. He suspects my *A. nidens* [bird's nest fern] to be 'Neoporteria madens,' as the learned delight in changing the names of plants, it may be so designated now. If 'H.' has never visited Tomah, he has the pleasure yet in store of renewing the delights he has experienced in exploring the lovely glens and mountains of Illawarra.[33]

The article on 'Orchidaceae' brought a letter from a correspondent, 'E.M.B.' in Rockhampton, Queensland. He claimed there were several very interesting species of orchids to be found in the valley of the Nepean and in other places near Kurrajong not mentioned in her article.[34] When she noted 'E.M.B.'s' letter in her column Louisa wrote, '. . . very probably some more are to be found which have hitherto escaped me.'[35] Another correspondent, 'Accri' wrote

Louisa Atkinson's interest in nature was well known throughout the Kurrajong district. When a native cat was shot near Mt Tomah the skin was sent to her to study and she wrote about it in her nature column published in the *Sydney Morning Herald*. She was an expert taxidermist and kept many stuffed birds and animals to aid her research. (Janet Cosh)

under the heading 'Autumn in the Kurrajong', 'A gifted lady contributor of yours has left nothing to describe but two plants...'[36]

At the end of her article on 'Botanical Ramblings'[37] she acknowledged a letter from 'G.K.' of Woolloomooloo, who believed he had identified a native cat she had written about as *Dasyurus maculatus*. Louisa Atkinson ended her note on this letter 'I hope one day to get a perfect animal, and be enabled to enrich my folio with a sketch of it'. A few years later she gained her wish. In 'Stray Notes' she described in detail a *Dasyurus maculatus* (native cat) which had been shot at Mount Tomah by James Sherwood and its skin brought to her for examination. She sent an urgent request for the skull but did not receive it.[38]

Although plant collecting was the main purpose of her journeys from Kurrajong, she was equally interested in birds and animals and her columns were rarely without some notes on them. Her interest was well known and local residents alerted her to rare animals, birds, reptiles and insects, as well as plants. When some sawyers working in the bush found two apparently dead lizards they brought them to Louisa, who kept them by her dining room fire. Eight days later they revived and when after two weeks one escaped she liberated the other.[39]

When she heard that some settlers had captured a white squirrel in the hollow of a tree they were felling, she rode over to Bilpin to sketch it. She found it had the run of the settler's hut and when awakened:

> ...suffered itself to be lifted from some old shawl or coat that had been given it as a bed, and crawled about the young woman who obligingly engaged its attention while the sketch was in progress. It rubbed its soft fur against her, ran up on to her shoulders, and by its manner testified thorough enjoyment of her caresses. Yet this animal was full grown, but a week in captivity, and in the centre of its native woods, and within sound of the calls of its former companions. It was a victory of kindness.[40]

Despite her wide-ranging interests in all forms of animal life, it was her plant collecting that brought her the greatest satisfaction and she excelled in conveying her enjoyment when she made some new find. In 'Botanical Ramblings' she described a return trip to Cabbage-tree Hollow in search of more specimens of *Piper*. After eating lunch in the bush with the accompaniment of 'quart-pot tea', Louisa and her party went in search of this plant.

> Scrambling over rocks, fallen trees, leaping the creek, and so on, a mile or two was passed, when a tuft of pendous green fronds caught my eye. Fern-gatherers will understand the eager nervous fingers which grasped them, as if they were a living thing which would presently elude the extended hand; not so, however. The prize, an asplenium, was one not found by me before, with long attentuated fronds, of a dark green, not divided...

131

Although the ranges surrounding the watershed were almost dry because of drought, she also found on this trip an 'immense' plant of *Asplenium nidens* (bird's nest fern). She wrote that she had never, at Illawarra, the Shoalhaven mountains, or the Kurrajong, seen anything to equal it in magnificence: 'the fronds were like fresh expanded banana leaves, only far more solid, and several feet in length. There were many of these plants, all luxuriant, although this particular one exceeded all the rest'.[41]

11

Atkinsonia ligustrina *will ever remain a living monument to her exertions*

Already known as a novelist, Louisa Atkinson, while still a young woman and quite untrained in science in a formal sense, gained considerable fame as a naturalist through her series of nature articles and her activities in collecting botanical specimens. Her friendships spread through the scientific world. This was a period when the strange world of Australian flora and fauna with its novel and endless variety was a source of wonder both in Australia and overseas. Famous naturalists, botanists, zoologists, entomologists and geologists wrote learned works about its peculiarities and diversities. In addition to their own expeditions they depended on gifted amateurs in the field.

One of the roles of most exploring parties penetrating new country was to gather plants and seeds, but even in country already known to botanists there were still many new species to be discovered as well as new localities for plants already known. This was so of the Kurrajong district, although as early as 1804, nearly a decade before the first crossing of the Blue Mountains by Blaxland, Lawson and Wentworth, the naturalist George Caley had penetrated as far as a mountain he named Mount Banks overlooking the Grose Valley. A later explorer, Allan Cunningham, 'the king's botanist' during his 1823 Blue Mountains' journey, had discovered many new plants. But as Louisa Atkinson and William Woolls demonstrated, there were new plants still to be found in the mountains in the 1860s. Louisa was one of a very small number of talented women in the Australian colonies who, despite the fact that formal scientific training was unavailable to them, became expert botanists and plant collectors. In Western Australia Georgiana Molloy, for about seven years before her untimely death in 1843, had brought the unique plants of the southwest of the colony

133

William Woolls, a schoolmaster at Parramatta, was a friend of Louisa Atkinson's and fellow botanical collector. He introduced her to famous botanists and scientists and accompanied her on some of her plant collecting expeditions. (*Sydney Mail* 10 August 1872)

to the notice of international botanists. Louisa Meredith in Tasmania, Ellis Rowan in north Queensland and Helena and Harriet Scott in New South Wales, also skilled in botany, gained recognition as botanical illustrators and flower painters. Although she too was a gifted illustrator, Louisa's strength lay in her disciplined scientific interest in searching for, collecting and describing new plants in the localities where she lived.

One of her first contacts in the botanical field was William Woolls, a teacher with an interest in and extraordinary knowledge of botany. Born in 1814 in England, he was in his forties when he met Louisa. The friendship began when he decided he wanted to meet her after reading her articles on natural history and seeing her drawings.[1] These must have been her articles in the *Illustrated Sydney News*, as they were acquainted before her articles began in the *Sydney Morning Herald*. The friendship developed through their mutual interest in botany and flourished after Louisa's move to Fernhurst in the latter 1850s, which placed them within riding distance of each other. Sir James Fairfax, a pupil of William Woolls, believed that Woolls was 'led to study botany in the first instance through interest in Louisa Atkinson—a lady devoted to the flora of her own part of the country',[2] but Woolls's interest in botany was well developed before he met her.

Woolls had emigrated to Australia in 1832 at the age of eighteen, joining the King's School soon after it began, in charge of a cottage of boarders. After he left King's he became a classics master at Sydney College. In 1841 at 'Harrisfield', the first site of the King's College at Parramatta, he began his own school, which was to be remarkably successful. For 30 years he remained associated with the school, which was moved to 'Newlands' (renamed Broughton House after it was acquired by King's in 1909) in 1865. He became renowned as an able and sympathetic school master, encouraging his pupils in a love of the countryside. Regular walks he conducted through the grounds of old Government House to Baulkham Hills and Toongabbie and in the country around Parramatta were features of his school. On the walks he encouraged pupils to study plants and other natural phenomena. He himself studied botany intensively and attracted the attention of the famous botanist Baron Ferdinand von Mueller, Victorian Government Botanist, following publication of a series of articles beginning in 1856 in the *Sydney Morning Herald*.

Woolls was afflicted by several personal tragedies in the early 1860s. His second wife died on 7 March 1861 and his younger daughter from his first marriage a few days later. A few years later, his remaining daughter was to die. In 1862 at the age of 48 he married Sarah Elizabeth Lowe, who became a close friend of Louisa's. William Woolls and Louisa, apart from a deep interest in botany, shared a similar outlook on the importance of the influence of Christian belief and practice. Woolls was a staunch Anglican, a trustee of All Saints' Church, Parramatta. For the period of his friendship with Louisa he was a lay member of the Church of England.

Woolls accompanied Louisa on some of her plant gathering journeys into the bush and through him she met some of the famous scientific figures of the day, including the world-famous Baron Ferdinand von Mueller, the naturalist William Sharp Macleay, and the geologist/clergyman Rev. William Branwhite Clarke. All were to correspond with her and enjoy her friendship.

From the start Woolls recognised her unusual talent. As early as 1861, he acknowledged her great contribution to the study of the plants of the Kurrajong. She had already sent through him to Ferdinand von Mueller no less than 300 specimens of plants she had found in the Kurrajong district, many of them, according to Woolls, 'exceedingly interesting'. In a long letter to the *Sydney Morning Herald* in 1861 he expressed 'on behalf of Dr F. Mueller' and himself admiration for the 'untiring zeal of your correspondent of the Kurrajong'. He concluded by hoping that her life would be 'long preserved, and may a generous public afford every encouragement for the development of native genius'.

In another part of the letter he commented on Louisa Atkinson's 'Mount Tomah', article referring to her as 'my accomplished friend'.[3] One of the plants Louisa Atkinson discovered on this trip, a new species of *Xanthosia*, was named *X. atkinsonia* by von Mueller in honour of her discovery. Another find was a species of *Nuytsia* (*N. ligustrina*) of the *Loranthus* (mistletoe) family. It differed from previous known specimens as it was the size of a small shrub, with yellow and crimson blossoms and exuded a rather sickly odour, not a parasitical plant as was usual with the *Loranthus* or Australian mistletoe. It was originally regarded as a species of *Nuytsia*, but Baron von Mueller decided that it was a separate genus and named it *Atkinsonia ligustrina*.[4] It was, Woolls wrote, 'a plant ever to be connected with...Louisa Atkinson...a living memorial of a lady who, by her various collections and artistic skill, contributed materially to the natural history of the Blue Mountains'.[5] It would 'ever remain on the Alpine heights as a living monument of her exertions', he wrote.[6]

When von Mueller published his twelve-volume listing of Australian plants, *Fragmenta Phytographiae Australiae*, in addition to *Atkinsonia ligustrina*, he named after Louisa *Erechites atkinsoniae*,[7] an erect herb growing several feet high, which she had found in the Blue Mountains, and *Epacris calvertiana*, a heath, which she discovered on the Medway Rivulet near Berrima.[8] A small rasp fern, *Doodia caudata*, which she discovered in rock crevices at Kurrajong, had already been named *D. atkinsoniana* by Woolls. After checking with his friend William Sharp Macleay, he decided it was a new form of *Doodia* which 'seems to have escaped the notice of collectors, and as far as can be ascertained at present, the species appears a new one'.[9] When the first volume of von Mueller's work appeared in 1858 he sent Louisa a copy inscribed 'Miss Atkinson very respectfully Ferdinand Mueller'.[10] He also sent her the first volume of his book *The Plants Indigenous to the Colony of Victoria* with the inscription, 'Presented on behalf of the Victorian Government to Miss Louisa Atkinson, very respectfully by the author 8/4/62.'[11]

Apart from plants previously unknown, Louisa Atkinson also discovered specimens of plants previously noted only on one or two occasions. In *A Contribution to the Flora of Australia*, Woolls noted her discovery of a moss—'...lately my friend Miss Atkinson has been so fortunate as to find *Polytrichum aloides*, which I regard as an interesting fact in the cryptogamous botany of the Blue

(3) *Doodia aspera*
L. atkinsoniana (2) *media*
caudata

Louisa Atkinson prepared about 40 watercolour illustrations of ferns, apparently intending to publish a book on the subject. This watercolour, numbered Plate No. 20, includes *Doodia atkinsoniana*, a fern Louisa Atkinson discovered in rock crevices at Kurrajong, and *D. aspera*, *D. media* and *D. caudata*. (Mitchell Library, State Library of NSW. Calvert. Ferns)

Mountains'.[12] When George Bentham, the British botanist, with the assistance of von Mueller, published his classic seven-volume *Flora Australiensis* in the years between 1863 to 1878, he acknowledged Louisa's specimens 116 times.[13]

Louisa's trip to Mount Tomah, with its magnificent stands of the tree fern *Dicksonia antarctica*, during which she had been so successful in discovering plants, was also important in another field. She reported on this trip to William Sharp Macleay (1792–1865), a trustee of the Australian Museum in Sydney. His home at Sydney's famous Elizabeth Bay House, set in acres of beautiful gardens and planted with exotic and indigenous trees and shrubs, contained a treasure trove of specimens collected from many parts of the world. His library contained 4000 books. A man of 'broad culture and worldly experience, a fine classical scholar and an accomplished conversationalist',[14] Macleay had a wide circle of

137

This watercolour of *Dicksonia antarctica, Alsophila cooperi, A. leichhardtiana* and *A. australis* is numbered Plate No. 2 in Louisa Atkinson's book of ferns. (Mitchell Library, State Library of NSW. Calvert. Ferns)

intellectual friends, both in Australia and overseas. Louisa Atkinson, despite her inadequate schooling and her lack of friends and sponsors in society, corresponded with Macleay on equal terms and was welcomed as a visitor to his home.

Many of Macleay's records were lost in 1882 in a fire at the

Garden Palace, the building in the Sydney Domain which had housed the International Exhibition of 1879. The library and herbarium of the Linnean Society of New South Wales were also destroyed, but a remnant of what appears to have been part of a continuing exchange of letters with Louisa Atkinson is preserved in the Macleay Museum at the University of Sydney. It is headed 'Notes on the Sphaeria [fungus] and Grub' and although unsigned and not complete, it is displayed with Louisa Atkinson's visiting card. Like William Woolls's letter to the *Sydney Morning Herald*, it relates to Louisa's trip to Mount Tomah early in 1861. The letter demonstrates the great time and care she took in reporting scientific finds, the reason why her collections, writings and drawings were so valuable to the scientific world.

22nd April. Went to Mt Tomah and visited the hill where the Sphaeria is found. None evidently had grown since my last researches and all that were found were of a dark hue almost black while many had become hollow in the centre of the top and that portion of the stem above the frond. We dug up about 18, two of which were laying [sic] nearly laterally with the surface, the others perpendicular. One very small grub was found infected by fungi which had not risen above the ground. None had passed into the chrysalis state. In one instance three heads branched from the same stem which had apparently arisen from another that had died away, embryo fungi were found rising beside those fully grown in several instances. But the shells of escaped perfected insects were found. The lad who I employed to dig them up stated that he had yearly seen the Sphaeria for 4 years but had not been aware of its springing from a grub. The fungi he states are nearly white when young and become yellow deepening to black. He chopped out of *Acacia decurrens* two living grubs they were of a small size but one immediately began to spin white silk. The head and shoulder was cased in a hard shell the other parts being white masked by red spots and only covered with skin. Having wrapped them up in a hankerchief when I reached home and took them out, one had sown up a fold into a case with silk. [B]eing then placed in a vessel of damp mould they endeavoured to cover themselves. On the following day some pieces of green bark and wood of *A. decurrens* was furnished them, of which one eat eagerly the other crawled beneath a concave piece of bark, on the 24th it had woven it to the mould with white silk and remained quietly within. The earth was excavated slightly. The size of the Sphaeria differed considerably one was 6 inches above the ground another 2. While the stem from the earths surface to the head of the grub was from 1 to 14 inches.

Within a few hours after being dug up white mould appears over them and a clammy exudation from the upper part of the fringe.
26. [April] The second grub has spun a nest beneath a piece of *bark* similar to the others.

I am informed by a very intelegent [sic] man that he has seen the Sphaeria springing from the grubs while still *in the tree*. The fungi growing out of the holes, [?parted] by the grubs.[15]

Only this remnant of what appears to have been a number of communications to William Macleay remains, and the few surviving letters between Louisa Atkinson and William Woolls, Ferdinand von Mueller and Rev. W.B. Clarke are only a minute part of a voluminous correspondence that extended over a period of more than ten years. In one of these few extant letters, dated 26 September 1864 from Parramatta, William Woolls thanked Louisa for 'hunting after specimens'.

My dear Miss Atkinson
I feel somewhat puzzled about your little specimen. As far as I can judge, it is the fruit of *Celastrus australis*, for the seed vessel is generally two-celled & the pedicels are articulated. I found a similar shrub in the Cabramatta bush.
   In my last letter I forgot to mention amongst the introduced grasses, the *Holcus lanatus* which you were so kind as to send me from the Kurrajong, I do not think it is indigenous. With regard to the Poppy I did not mention it, because I saw the plant growing on Ash Island & I think Mr Krefft[16] told me it had escaped from some garden. I am aware that it is now regarded as a weed, but I cannot say for certain that it was introduced by *accident*. It seems to me to be *Papaven nudicaule* or *Arjemone Mexicana*, but without seeing the leaf and capsule I cannot determine. I am very much indebted to you for your kindness in hunting after specimens. Mrs Woolls is pretty well. She has her sister & two children here just now but we are proposing to start for Berrima on Friday next for a short visit to the Revd. J. Hassall. I am anxious to see the 'Sassafras'. Did you see Mr Walker's lecture. I am sorry he omitted Mr Macdonald from the list of Australian Poets. Will Mr Halloran[17] be pleased with the term 'fugitive' poet? Mrs Woolls sends her kind love to you, and with my best wishes,
I remain, My dear Miss Atkinson
Your sincere friend
W. Woolls[18]

Apart from contributing to the *Sydney Morning Herald* and *Sydney Mail*, Louisa Atkinson found a new outlet for her articles when the monthly *Horticultural Magazine* began publication in Sydney in January 1864. In the second issue an editorial on the front page drew attention to a letter she had written to the editor on the possible use of native plants as a source of food. Her letter appeared over the initials 'L.A.', by then well known in naturalist circles. Her identity was obviously known to the editor, as he referred to her as 'our fair correspondent'. In her letter she re-

Louisa Atkinson spent hours exploring fern gullies in the Kurrajong district. The fern gully at the back of her home, Fernhurst, was known as 'Miss Atkinson's gully'. (Mitchell Library, State Library of NSW. Calvert Sketchbook)

peated views she had expressed in 'A Voice From the Country' articles on the edibility of tubers she had found in the Blue Mountains. The editor asked her to send seeds or roots so that an attempt could be made to cultivate them. The tubers she named were '*Sarcopetalum Harveyanum*', which, she said, could be developed in size and might prove to be a hardy yam, and '*Marsdenia flavescens*', which could produce three distinct and valuable products—gum, hemp and flax, and esculent roots.[19]

She continued this theme in another letter that appeared in the April issue, in which she added the '*Brachychiton populneum*' (kurrajong bean tree, known as rattle-trap) to her list of possible edible tubers. It had a root which was 'extremely pleasant in flavour' and could be eaten uncooked or roasted. The bark, she said, was used by Aborigines for cordage, hence it was known as kurrajong and its seed eaten by them after roasting. The Aborigines, she wrote, 'used to assemble at a cattle-station of ours on the Wollondilly to gather them, which being accomplished they left the place till the following harvest'.[20] Urging the cultivation of this plant, she wrote, 'the cauliflower and red cabbage, with all the wide varieties of "white hearts", sprang from no more promising a source'.

The first of her series of three articles on ferns appeared in the form of a letter in the July 1864 issue. Other papers followed in the August and October issues.[21] The issue for the following February reported that Miss Atkinson of the Kurrajong had sent a jar of jam made from *Lissanthe sapida* (native cranberry). In an accompanying letter she described how to make the jelly which, she wrote, made a pleasant tart filling. When the jam had been handed around for tasting at the January meeting of the Horticultural Society, members decided that if available it would be a favoured jam, because of its pleasant acid taste. The meeting moved a vote of thanks to Miss Atkinson, not only for sending the jam 'but for the general interest manifested by her in bringing to practical use our colonial fruits and plants'.[22]

Louisa appears to have joined the Horticultural Society when it began in 1864, but she must have let her membership lapse, as when lists were published in 1867 and 1868 she was not a member. It is possible that the fee would have been more than she was able to pay out of her small income.

Louisa's interest in plants led her to search for magazines in this field, both to read herself and as possible outlets for her writing. In 1859 through her mother or someone writing on her behalf, she communicated with the editor of *Farm and Garden*, published in Adelaide. When the editor, E.W. Andrews, replied on 10 November 1859 enclosing copies of the magazine he said, 'You may well imagine how much it pleases me to hear of its being useful in other places besides South Australia'. The *Farm and Garden* magazine had ceased when the first issue of the *Horticultural Magazine* was published in Sydney in 1864. In February Louisa sent a copy to Mr E.W. Andrews, who in his reply on 6 April 1864 said it was a work 'which promises to be very useful to those who are engaged in garden culture. One of the gentlemen on our literary staff looked through the magazine as soon as it arrived, and inserted a very favourable notice of it in both our papers.'[23]

William Woolls admired Louisa's largely self-acquired ability in botany and drawing, but he also admired 'the moral worth' of her character. He is the only commentator on this aspect of her life during her years at Kurrajong Heights. During this time, Woolls said, she imitated 'the beneficient example of her great Master in going about doing good'.

> She visited the sick, gave counsel to the perplexed, and was kind and gentle to all; whilst her affection for the children of the district was manifested in her anxiety to secure for them the advantages of education. She not only felt a deep interest in the daily life of the neighbourhood but in a period when ministerial visits were few and far between, and the district did not possess so many religious blessings as it now does, she established a Sunday school in her mother's house and taught a large number of children herself.[24]
>
> Great was the anxiety which she displayed in the cause of education, and equally great was her desire that the children should be kindly and gently treated. Well do I recollect the concern which she manifested, when a former teacher at the Kurrajong had been too severe with some of those which she termed 'her children,' and well do I recollect the little conspiracy which she entered into with me to render him more merciful for the future.[25]

This picture of a woman so involved in the community in which she lived, so active in scientific research, in writing and in drawing, probably already caring for her mother, depicts a far from retiring life. Her health restored, it would be interesting to know whether Louisa at this time thought of marrying. She was not deprived of social encounters that could lead to marriage. She had friends all over the Kurrajong district, she was well known in Richmond where her friend Emma Selkirk lived and where she was a regular communicant at St Peter's Church of England. On visits to Sydney she called on William Macleay, she knew John Fairfax and through her activities, in science, writing, music and horticulture had friends and acquaintances in many fields. Implacably against any idea of marriage was her mother who had always been concerned about her youngest daughter's delicate health. Although Louisa's health had improved in the clear air and under the influence of an active life at Kurrajong, her mother feared that she was not strong enough to withstand childbirth. Charlotte Barton had lost one daughter soon after she had given birth to a child and had no wish to lose another.[26]

Events were developing, however, which were to lead Louisa to the man she would marry. During the early part of 1863 she and her mother spent some time at Oldbury visiting James Atkinson. Oldbury was never far from Louisa's thoughts when living at Kurrajong, as the number of reminiscences she interspersed in her articles indicated. Her return to Oldbury provided her with new experiences in the Berrima district and reactivated her memories of life at Sutton Forest and at the Shoalhaven. The results of this visit appeared in several articles in 'A Voice From the Country', first 'A Ride to the Fitzroy Mines' and later a major three-part series on Aborigines.

Louisa's brother was an investor in the company which developed the Fitzroy iron mine and smelter, the first iron works in Australia, around which the settlements of Nattai, New Sheffield, Fitzroy and Mittagong had developed. Smelting had begun in 1848 but following a financial crisis was suspended in the 1850s. The iron works reopened in 1863 when the company received an order for rails to be used on the southern railway. To Louisa, the journalist, this was an opportunity too good to miss. She visited the mine and described the trip for readers. Leaving the iron works she and her party rode through heavily timbered country up a steep pass. On one side were overhanging rocks and on the other a deep ravine where she glimpsed tree ferns and heard the murmur of a stream. As they rode they passed drays drawn by bullocks laden with coal from the mine or fireclay taken from the ceiling of the narrow mine shaft. Once in the mine, the group found breathing increasingly difficult and Louisa was glad to escape—'Oh, the relief of a breath of free pure air of the blue sky for a roof, and shady trees for walls'.

After leaving the coal mine she commented, as she often did, on the wealth of material for the naturalist in the Berrima district. Studying plants had developed her interest in the geology of different regions. The interrelation between vegetation and geological structures was a subject she was to comment on more frequently in her later articles.

There are several places around Berrima which would be mines of wealth to the naturalist. Here are, comparatively bleak whinstone

In 1863 Louisa Atkinson and her mother returned to Oldbury for some months. During the time she spent there she wrote some articles on local subjects including a series entitled 'Recollections of the Aborigines'. This is an unfinished sketch of Oldbury. (Mitchell Library, State Library of NSW. Calvert Sketchbook)

ranges, with their peculiar vegetation and geological formation; sandstone elevations, very rugged, very desolate, but embroidered with exquisite flowers; cedar gullies, groves of tree fern and sassafras; vast woods, silent and monotonous; and streams—where zircon, cornelian, crystals (apparently from iron formation), flints, gypsum, titaniferous iron sand, iron ore, topaz and coal, may all be gathered in one day's walk. Salt springs and salt earths occur in places.[27]

Memories of long past events came flooding back to her while visiting Oldbury. One she included in an article entitled 'A

145

Summer Picture', dated back to her father's time as magistrate and was obviously something she had heard from her mother. The story concerned two sawyers living in the cedar country beyond the Fitzroy Falls, their only connection with the settled districts being a monthly trip to get provisions and the occasional arrival of a dray driver to pick up their sawn timber. They were visited one day by Aborigines, who lured them away from their hut with stories of cedar trees of great size, one leading the way along a ridge of rocks, the other walking between the two sawyers. At a given signal 'each turned on his victim, and with one blow of his club felled him to the ground, and hurled him over the pass.'

At the bottom of the pass the Aborigines found the body of one of the sawyers and '... in their dread of discovery, they cut out his tongue, that he might not speak if the body were ever found'. Thinking the other man also dead they returned to the camp and took the food and clothes of their victims. However, the second sawyer's fall had been broken by some tangled brushwood and eventually he was able to struggle to a settler's hut and the police were informed. Unable to find the alleged murderers the police arrested a relative and brought him before Louisa's father, the chief magistrate.

> The man professed his ignorance of the whole affair, yet there was reason to suspect that he knew where his relative was, and a metal crescent which had been given him for former good services it was decreed should be removed till he redeemed his character. Meekly, with tearful eyes, he bowed his head while the much-cherished ornament was taken from his neck; his gun, too, was forfeited. In course of time both were, however, restored to him.[28]

Eventually one of the murderers was found and sentenced 'returning years afterwards to his native tribe, a wiser, if not a better, man'.

What appears now as the insensitivity of this article, the reporting of facts without any explanation about the motives that would have led Aborigines dispossessed of their tribal land to attack the interlopers, appears also in parts of 'Recollections of the Aborigines'. This three-part series was published in *Sydney Mail* in September 1863. Indicating the great interest they aroused, the articles were republished in the *Sydney Morning Herald* a few days after their appearance in the *Mail*.[29] As her opening sentence indicated—'these unhappy races have become rather a tradition, than reality, already in many districts'—the strength of the articles was in the factual reporting. Like almost all Europeans at the time, Louisa did not dwell on the causes of Aboriginal discontent. Given

Atkinsonia ligustrina

this limitation, and another—her pervasive belief that Christianity could uplift the Aborigines—Louisa's articles are valuable for her reporting of attitudes of both Aborigine and white.

The first two articles contained many stories, similar to the one in 'A Summer Picture', obviously told to Louisa by her mother, some of which had appeared years before in *A Mother's Offering to Her Children*. These included the story of the visit to Oldbury by Aborigines of the district after her father's death, during which they expressed horror at being shown a lock of James Atkinson's hair. In *A Mother's Offering to Her Children* this incident is described as taking place when Louisa was about four, but in 'Recollections of the Aborigines', it appears to take place soon after her birth. There are also stories about Yarrawambie, known as Jim Vaugh (sometimes printed as Jem or Jemmy, Vaughan or Waugh), the chief of the local tribe. He had guided her father on his explorations of the Shoalhaven. Other stories were of events Louisa had witnessed herself, for instance, the pathetic gathering of the 'remnants' of three tribes for a corroboree.

In the first article she described the appearance of Aborigines, their life as hunters/wanderers, their dwellings, methods of food gathering, their occasional practice of infanticide contrasted with the loving care of their remaining children, and their family relationships. She followed her usual style in interspersing these objective descriptions with personal anecdotes, for example, a description of a gathering of Aborigines:

> On one occasion, when the remnants of three different friendly tribes had assembled for a grand *corroboree* or dance, I made a plan of the encampment; each tribe was slightly apart from the other, divided by a sort of street. Thus the inviters were clustered in the centre, having, I think, seventeen camps; the Picton tribe on the right hand, five camps; and the Shoalhaven on the left, comprising ten or eleven gunyahs; consecutively forming a village.

Elsewhere in the article, among rather patronising commendation of Aborigines who act as guides and show kindnesses to Europeans, there are illuminating comments, for instance:

> The aborigines appear to pity the Europeans, as persons under self-imposed slavery to toil, holding themselves as quite their superiors. The difference of employer and employee they appreciate, and distinctions of Australian born, or otherwise: 'You brudder of mine; all same as me, native,' is a high mark of esteem.

Developing this theme she told the story of 'Neddy', who expressed his standing in a gauche but genuine way. One day when

147

acting as a guide he was given a horse to ride but complained that the stirrup irons would hurt his bare feet, so he was given an old pair of boots:

> ...a servant standing by began to laugh at the poor creature, saying, 'You are no gentleman—you are no better than a beggar.' Instantly irate, the black turned from one to another, demanding if he was not a gentleman. The scene was excessively ludicrous; the tattered clothes of the claimant of honours was like a burlesque upon his assumption. It required repeated assurance that he was quite a gentleman, and his tormentor an ignorant fellow who did not know a gentleman when he saw one, to appease his feelings.
> Some time after this he said to a member of the family he was then about to act as guide for, 'If you want me write to me, Missis,—' he returned, with the air of a sovereign, 'Mr Edward Rex, care of Mrs—' 'Edward Rex! Are you a king, then?' 'Yes Missis—; yes, ma'am, you write me Edward Rex, when you want me, an' I come.' Of course some person had called him this title.

Like so many others Neddy fell a victim to the alcohol provided by Europeans and Louisa commented:

> How frequent is the paragraph in the country paper of an aborigine's death from this cause; how many have sunk unrecorded! A great sin lies on us as a people, for much has been done to injure, and little to benefit the poor original possessors of our farms and runs.
> 'Only a black fellow,' is carelessly uttered. The soul is unheeded and untaught, or it is said, that they are incapable of instruction.[30]

The article ended with speculation about the possible religious beliefs of Aborigines. They liked 'to draw a veil of mystery round their beliefs and actions', she wrote.

She continued this subject in the next article with an account of Aboriginal burial practices. After describing a huge conical burial mound on Mount Gingenbullen, 30 metres long and 12 metres high, surrounded at its base by trees on which were carved forms suggesting an Aboriginal shield and boomerang, she wrote that she had not been able to get further information from the Aborigines. Without comment about the reasons why they might have abandoned their former practices, she wrote,

> Of late years they have excavated the large ant hill, and buried their dead in them, neglecting the carving of the trees. It was the custom of the women to asemble around the grave, probably those related to the departed only, wailing and lamenting, striking and lacerating themselves with sharp instruments, and drawing strings across the lips till they bled.

In the second article she included a description of 'the dance of death' which she had witnessed during her stay at the Shoalhaven. It is very similar to the event described in *Gertrude*. In neither case does Louisa comment on the significance of Aborigines portraying the deaths of their own people.

> I witnessed two dances on the Shoalhaven. A Bathurst black had been some months located in the tribe—the dancing master, in fact, teaching them new dances; the result was what I saw...the partial illumination revealed the white or yellow lines painted on them in the form of skeletons...It was a dance of Death. A circle was formed, each performer leaning at an angle impossible to a civilised being, unless after great practice, then with a pave-driver's breath they simultaneously fell at an opposite angle. After several such changes of attitude, a more stirring movement took place; the heels were brought with great violence to the ground, and a tremulous agitation given to the muscles. A vibratory motion was communicated to the ground for some distance...
>
> I was told by a medical gentleman that many years ago he witnessed a dance in which two figures were introduced, daubed over with spots of paint, and that the performance was a representation of the sufferings of the blacks under the small-pox.

With the understanding we have today of the devastating effect on the Aborigines when they were deprived of their land, Louisa's articles appear insensitive, condescending and racist. For their time, however, when in some parts of the country Aborigines were being hunted like dingoes, as she herself had portrayed in *Cowanda*, her articles conveyed humanity and understanding. Referring to unsuccessful attempts to educate Aborigines at Blacktown —the children simply walked out of school and returned to their tribes—she reported the experience of a lubra:

> 'Liberty's sweet,' said a gin, as she mended an old dress which had been given to her. 'I can work and I can read too; but it's confined living with white people, and I get tired of it—these are inconveniences; but then I'm free—'

The incident continued with Louisa's comment, one of the few direct comments she made in these articles:

> A gunyah and a scorched possum before a house and white bread, and the bowing to another's will—
> 'For Britons never will be slaves,' might have been the benighted creature's catechism. 'I was at black school, and can read,' was a decided boast; but there the scholar's satisfaction ended.

149

Towards the end of this article she returned again to the spirituality of the Aborigines. She thought in all their customs:

> ...there is a reference to spirits, a recognising of Deity, in some crude, uncertain, mystic way—a mystery which shall be carefully kept a mystery from the curious white invader. It is a matter of course to pronounce them the lowest scale in the human ladder; the last link between man and monkey; a degraded people incapable of improvement; beyond the scale of civilisation, and destitute of religion, and, recognising only an evil spirit. An idolator accustomed to worship the ostensible would look on the Christian religion as a mystery—bowing the knee to the Invisible our stand point is not such as to enable us to clearly limit the beliefs of the Australian aboriginal. For my own part I would be loth to come to any conclusion, and state it as a fact.[31]

The final article in the three-part series was quite different in subject. In it she told the story of Jackey Jackey, the Aborigine from Patrick's Plains in the Upper Hunter district who accompanied the explorer, Edmund Kennedy, to Cape York in 1848. To Louisa this was a story about an ideal Aborigine, a 'faithful black', because he was devoted to his white master. It was an epic story of courage and to European eyes it portrayed an Aborigine in a positive way. She concluded:

> A mournful interest is attached to the name of Jackey Jackey, not only on account of his unwavering fidelity and courage, but in connection with this brave and intelligent commander, Mr Kennedy, and his unhappy party. This interest heightens our regret that his end should have been an untimely one, and that while Government settled on him the sum of £20 per annum, he appears to have fallen into the vice which the poor aborigines so generally become prey to, when brought into connection with the white people, intoxication. In this unhappy state he was burned to death...[32]

Explorers were the heroes of the age and the fact that she devoted a whole article to this exploring trip indicates the fascination exploration and explorers held for her.

In another article that year, entitled 'Incidents of Australian Travel', she included further stories of Aborigines and their relationship with explorers:

> Several of these explorers have perished by the spear of the black, but others have met with not only a peaceable reception but even kindness. It will be fresh in the minds of all how kindly Burke's party were treated by the tribe who inhabited the district where their wanderings ended.

Atkinsonia ligustrina

While many accuse the Australian blacks of every mean and evil propensity, and represent them as destitute of all generosity or noblesse, how strikingly does the conduct of these poor creatures controvert such sweeping censures. Could the white, educated Christian have done more? Of their need they gave to these strangers, not angered at their intrusion upon their territories, but weeping over their deaths, and hastening to the survivor with the joyful intelligence that the whitefellows were coming when succour arrived. There is something in this which should not readily be forgotten, while a murder by blacks is so loudly proclaimed. In the latter case, while we view with rightful horror such murders as those committed recently upon Mr Wills and his servants, we should bear in mind the aboriginal law, which requires expiatory blood for blood—not the blood of the injurer, but of any of his tribe. There are a lawless class among the whites who are incesssantly aggressing upon the blacks, heedless of the result. They may escape, and the innocent fall victims to their crimes, while the blame rests less with the savage than the Christian and educated men, so called.

The few efforts which have been made to Christianise the aborigines have been almost failures, and the idea has been taken up that they are past redemption.[33]

She ended this article with a nostalgic evocation of the quiet happiness of bush travel—the camp at night with the quart pot bubbling on the fire, the cross sticks laid on the top giving the tea its peculiar bush aroma, the cooking of fresh 'leather jackets' (circular cakes formed from a damper mix), and a sound sleep on the ground with a saddle for a pillow, while flying foxes and opossums cry in the distance.

There is a charm in this nomadic life, which they who have not tried can form no idea of, and they who have tried grow so attached to as to be quite averse to a settled mode of existence. There are now many of our old colonists who delight in nothing more than seeing the equipments strapped upon the staunch horses, and starting upon their five or ten hundred miles' journey.

It is not certain when Louisa Atkinson met the explorer, James Snowden Calvert. Having survived as a member of Ludwig Leichhardt's exploratory journey to Port Essington in 1844–45, he settled in Sydney for some time where he became a friend of Lieutenant Robert Lynd, Barracks Master, who had been Leichhardt's friend and executor. Lynd was Secretary of the Committee which began the establishment of the Botanic Gardens and Museum, later the Australian Museum, in Sydney. Through this friendship and through his own great interest in botany Calvert knew many of the people who were Louisa Atkinson's friends and colleagues. He was acquainted with Ferdinand von Mueller, William Woolls, William Sharp Macleay and others. If Louisa had met James Calvert by the early 1860s, her interest in explorers may have been heightened by this acquaintance.

After their stay at Oldbury mother and daughter returned to Kurrajong Heights to resume their life as it had been prior to the holiday. There Louisa had an extraordinary diversity of activities to absorb her. Not only was she devoting an immense amount of time to searching for flora and fauna, collecting and preserving, writing and sketching, she was also continuing her other career as a novelist. During the period of her greatest activity as a collector and writer in the Kurrajong she also wrote two novels, which appeared during the first half of the 1860s.

12

Meanness is not one of my sins

Louisa Atkinson's work as a naturalist and plant collector and her journalistic writing popularising the study of native flora and fauna are usually regarded as more important achievements than her creative writing. Nevertheless, her novels, including those published only in serial form in newspapers, have their own importance in presenting in an unselfconscious way many aspects of ordinary life in colonial Australia. Her characters and the situations they encounter were easily recognised by readers, whether they lived in Sydney or the bush, and her stories have the added significance of casting women in major roles.

The four novels she wrote after *Gertrude* and *Cowanda* were published as serials in newspapers, not in book form. Serialisation fostered rather than cured the flaws in her writing. It encouraged the use of coincidence in place of a more deeply thought-out plot, the introduction of cameo characters who played little or no further part in the story and, most of all, a loosely woven structure with separate strands of the story developing almost independently in different episodes. She was never to master the welding together of disparate stories.

The first of her serial stories, *Debatable Ground: or, the Carlillawarra Claimants*, ran for a little over five months[1] in weekly episodes in the *Sydney Mail* in 1861. Within this very long story, set mainly at a country estate in the settled districts around Sydney, she included several sub-plots set in different locales. They included Will Shenstone's battle to establish his cattle station in wild bush country, his encounter with back country cattle rustlers and his thrilling escape from them and from a bushfire; the squalid, drunken life of the Fairwater family at a delicensed inn, the 'Hut-i'-the-Bush'; the heroine's visits to Sydney legal offices and to slums in the city's

Louisa Atkinson (Mitchell Library, State Library of NSW)

narrow back streets; and a governessing episode on the Monaro. Some of the episodes are only loosely linked to the main story. Although difficult to follow, this structure had some advantages for serial publication, allowing readers to enjoy discrete episodes without troubling too much about the main story. Nevertheless it must have been difficult for readers to follow the complicated plot and to remember characters who reappeared after an absence. They were not helped by the misprints of the names of some characters, a fault which occurred not infrequently in this and in her other novels.[2]

One of the main achievements of *Debatable Ground* is the portrayal of a more complex female character than Gertrude Gonthier in *Gertrude* or Rachel Calder in *Cowanda*. Amina Roskell, the heroine, appears at first as a jaded and bored young lady accompanying her aunt, Mrs Adler, to society events, where they are regarded as 'leaders of *ton* in their own especial circle'.

> Coldly, proudly walked the tall handsome Miss Roskell by her side; looking on a scene in which her heart and interests did not mingle, with an air of perpetual polite weariness... Amina's was a false life, at variance with her sense of right; wearisome in its aimlessness, its want of sympathy—it froze her geniality. She hated life as she saw it; she hated humanity as her own restless distempered heart rejected it.[3]

Often, Amina slips away from her shallow life in society to aid an impoverished family living in a back street of Sydney, but she remains unfulfilled. Half way through the novel her life is still discordant.

> Amina... had seen enough of the world to distrust it; she had been saluted as 'dear' by those who covertly envied and traduced her; and that, too, among the young of her own sex, where innocence and truth might be expected to dwell. She had met with flattering attentions from those who, indifferent to herself, where [were] yet proud to display an acquaintance with a handsome and stylish young woman. Miss Roskell had learnt to look through the outward gloss, and beneath the varnish... She had been early taught the way of truth, and she had turned aside to a life of worldliness; she knew that her mother was a Christian; and, with a vivid sense of what that name implies, she knew that she was not a Christian; and dissatisfied with herself, she viewed life with bilious eyes, and saw all its evil, and caviled at the existence of good in it.[4]

Although only partly realised, the main story of *Debatable Ground* is the development of Amina's character and her attainment of a higher form of Christianity, manifested in actions rather than religious forms.

Having created a female character with ability and personality who is frittering away most of her life in trivial pursuits, it is amazing that Louisa did not allow Amina to develop some overriding interest, as she herself had done, and which could have led, as it did with Louisa, to personal development and achievement. Instead Amina's role is domestic. She is typical of Louisa's heroines in being very capable in running a large establishment and the author is lyrical in praise of this domesticity.

> ...little as the fine lady of *ton* may believe it, there is much enjoyment in the little toils of domestic life... Oh, believe it, wife and mother, who seek your joys in the ball-room and promenade, or you who are declaiming on 'women's rights,' that your real happiness springs from duties fulfilled—your real exaltation on that Christian holy spirit in which those duties are performed; and she may be a far greater and

more useful woman who sits in her neat little parlour, sewing buttons on her husband's shirts, and rocking her baby's cradle with her foot, than that clever sister lecturing in a large hall to a numerous audience, on what women ought to be.[5]

Louisa makes a similar point in most of her novels. She seems unaware that she herself was not a typical domestic female. Although she did not lecture on 'women's rights', her life was that of a liberated woman. All her activities—writing novels and articles for the press, wearing male-style clothes to ride over mountains and through scrub, studying animals, birds and insects, drawing and painting them and mounting their skins, not for amusement but to delineate their characteristics in the cause of science, were atypical of the domestic scene she idealised.

Debatable Ground is a complicated story about a large property comprising Carlillawarra and Woodacres, owned by Mr Roskell, a magistrate who had gained the property in the absence of an heir to the former owner, his cousin, Aminus Woods. A Frenchman, John Bapist Le Bois, arrives in the neighbourhood and rents Woodacres. Eventually through the help of an old ex-convict, Norah Coe, he discovers that he is Arnold, the son of Aminus Woods, who after being shipwrecked had entrusted his son to French monks. Le Bois makes many visits to the Sydney legal firm of Giles, Curten and Curten and gathers witnesses for a legal challenge to Roskell's ownership. Amina, convinced of the justice of Le Bois's claim, also makes many visits to the lawyers. These scenes are written with great fidelity and feeling—Louisa had only to call on her memory of her own family's unending legal battles for the raw material for these scenes.

There are many sub-plots in the story. One involves a relative of the Roskells, Clemence (or Clemency) Fairwater, who at the beginning is living an unhappy, deprived life with her father and step-mother in a rundown former inn, the 'Hut-i'-the-Bush', a similar setting to the derelict buildings Louisa had seen on her horse ride to Wiseman's Ferry.

Later Clemence, aged sixteen, answers an advertisement for a governess to instruct three young ladies and two small boys 'in a plain education and dancing'[6] for £25 pounds a year in the Monaro district, 250 kilometres south of Sydney. Her employers, Mr and Mrs Munn, are storekeepers with a branch post office and she soon finds that she is expected to run the post office too. Like many other characters in Louisa's novels, Mrs Munn aspires to gentility, a subject for gentle satire. Mrs Munn had named one of her daughters Victoria Adelaide because she had a cousin who was a skullion maid in the Dowager Queen's kitchen, and she has another claim to connections in being related through a great aunt to a 'first fleeter'.

Clemence's pupils bear out Louisa's views, often depicted in her novels, concerning the lack or poor quality of education.

Her pupils were ignorant even of the rudiments of education; overgrown, red faced, utterly untutored beings, whom Clemence found very difficult to control. Like natives generally, they were strong minded, and shrewd, and had quite business dispositions. The little boys 'swapped' sticks to ride on, and Victoria Adelaide lent her sisters her thimble for an hire in sugar-plums; and already dealt in stock, and paraded the good points of her pony.[7]

Clemence, to the amazement of her employers, rejects the advances of their wealthy neighbour Tasker Knox, although he offered 'a good position in society, and so much wealth to support it' but Clemence felt 'no holy love, no sympathy of soul, no kindred minds'. Instead she returns to her squalid life at the 'Hut-i'-the Bush' to look after her alcoholic step-mother. She is grieved to see in each room the accumulation of empty bottles, 'ranged in the fire-places, beneath the side tables, in every accessable [sic] spot, labelled hollands, cognac, stout and trebble X'. Later Clemence trains to become a teacher. 'To earn an independent and respectable livelihood, and to be useful, was the acme of her ambition'[8]—another example of the contradiction between Louisa's idealisation of domesticity and the fact that many of her female characters—and she herself—have roles outside the domestic realm.

Another strand of the story involves William Shenstone, who is developing a cattle run at The Gibbers, in a gully so isolated and rocky that supplies have to be taken down by sledge on a narrow tortuous path, a locale reminiscent of the Shoalhaven gorges. With Shenstone is Paul Baron, a young Englishman trying to rebuild his fortunes after losing his small inheritance in a farming venture soon after arrival in Australia. This situation allows Louisa to introduce some exciting bush adventures and descriptions of nature. Shenstone, while trailing lost cattle in wild and inaccessible country of 'high mountains, dense scrubs, steep ravines, and precipitous watercourses', comes across a band of cattle rustlers and is injured while trying to escape. When he recovers he tries to escape again but becomes lost in attempting to cross 'ridge after ridge of high scrubby sandstone'. Before him 'rose a high, rugged mountain, a sandstone ridge, clothed in scrub; waratahs, banksia, and various flowering shrubs, now gaudy with bloom, splendid moths hovered above them; and the fern owl and flying fox winged their way over head'.[9] Ahead of the lurid light and tongues of flame of an approaching bushfire, he rides his horse to the top of the mountain, where the horse collapses and Shenstone continues on foot.

In the midst of these sub-plots the story of the heroine, Amina, surfaces at intervals. After her father's death she inherits Carlillawarra and is courted by the local clergyman, referred to as 'Monsieur le Cure', a man of 'much self-conceit' and narrow mind. In much of Louisa's writing, clergymen are either absent or ineffectual but her condemnation of 'Monsieur le Cure' goes further. He was

> a man who, had he lived a few centuries back, would have lighted a stake fire, with a pious hatred of heresy—but it is well in these days when that fire is extinguished, not to say what latent hate, power might have aroused in men. There are a class of narrow minds which view all deviation from their opinions, as *the* sin; and who hate the bold thinker, as good men, alas! will often hate.[10]

Amina, after giving Carlillawarra to its rightful owner Le Bois, moves to an overseer's cottage and achieves happiness in a relatively humble life. As her husband she chooses Paul Baron, who in contrast to the clergyman came to an independent view of religion through a study of the Bible. Thereafter 'M. Le Cure' saw her

> tinctured with the heresies of Mr Baron's creed; perverted to his untrammelled courses of thought, riding roughshod over established customs, and orthodox faiths; without due reverence for the Fathers and Church authorities; nay, not even confessing it as *the* Church, but recognising every believer in Christ as part of the Church, though he were a Methodist or a Puritan.[11]

The heroine of Louisa Atkinson's next novel, *Myra*, is similar to her earlier heroines, Gertrude Gonthier and Rachel Calder. Unlike Amina, Myra Kershaw is not on a voyage of self-discovery, her role is the simple one of uplifting the spiritual lives of the people around her. The interest of *Myra*, a much shorter novel than *Debatable Ground*—it was serialised in the *Sydney Mail* over only two months of weekly episodes[12]—is not so much in the plot or the heroine than in some of the unusual characters. There are also descriptions of farm and domestic life in the closely-settled district on the Nepean River south-west of Sydney, particularly a very true to life depiction of the ravages of a flood.

The novel opens with the arrival in Sydney of a steamer from the Hunter. Passengers alight with their carpet-bags, leaving on board a child who is still unclaimed when the steamer is due to sail. No-one knows anything about the small girl except the negro steward, Jann,[13] who had taken her on board when approached by a lady who told him the child would be collected in Sydney by her mother.

The descriptions aboard ship and at the wharf are based on a real life experience of Louisa's. She had made a trip to the Hunter district by steamer, which she described in an article, apparently never published, called 'Recollections of the Hunter District', which began

> Flat, dusty, unsightly—so had Maitland been described to me, and the expectation of scenic beauty therefore did not prompt a trip to the Hunter. Early in the evening a cab deposited me at the wharf and by dint of enquiries the night steamer was found and her cabin reached. It was long before the time of starting and no other passengers were on board. The steward obligingly brought a number of a magazine with the remark that 'It was dull alone'. . .Then came ladies and children to claim the empty berths, then the bells rung [sic] and we started.[14]

The story of *Myra* continues with a passenger, Miss Janet Bean, returning to collect a shawl she had forgotten. A tall, strong woman with a square-cut face who 'crashed her great foot on the floor with emphatic *manliness'*, she decides to look after the child until her mother is found. When it becomes apparent that the mother will not appear, she takes the child, whose name she discovers to be Myra Kershaw, to her farm homestead on the Nepean River. There she braces herself for a confrontation with her companion, Miss Roberts. 'If ever Miss Janet approached to six feet in her stockings it was then. No quarter asked or given, was the banner flying over the ranks of her artillery.' Janet Bean offers that 'the expenses of the bairn can go to my side of the account'.

> 'It's sad for such a wee lassie to be alone in the world.' remarked Miss Bean, after a pause, 'there's the Orphan School —' she did not finish the sentence, for Miss Roberts broke in indignantly.
> 'For shame on you—could you have the heart to send that little lonely thing to be ground down to a mere automaton? I know what orphan schools are, with ever such good masters and mistresses; if children are herded, they will have no more brains than a sheep. I do hate such selfishness. Our old clothes run up would do her to play about in, and the bit a child eats is nothing. You never see such a spirit in me; no, thank God, meanness is not one of my sins.'[15]

As a young woman Janet Bean, the emigrant daughter of a small farmer from Scotland, had worked as a dairywoman on a large property, where she had met the governess employed on the property, Mary Roberts. They decide to run a farm together and after Mary Roberts had saved up £200, they rented Bower Farm on the Nepean. By the time *Myra* begins they own the farm and are known to the neighbours as 'the lady farmers'. The description of their 'masculine/feminine' roles, one exclusively engaged on household chores, the other on farm work, is so striking that it appears they were based on observation of a similar menage,

159

possibly a lesbian relationship. On one occasion when Janet Bean arrives home, she addresses her friend as 'Rabby woman...The lady with this somewhat masculine name saluted her ruddy cheek with a hearty smack of a kiss, very unconventional, but evidently sincere'.[16] The success of the women in running their farm places them in the forefront of the very capable female characters who form the backbone of all Louisa Atkinson's novels.

Another dominant woman enters the story with the arrival of Mrs Linklater from the farm next door, offering some of her daughter's clothes for Myra. At home is Mr Linklater

> trotting around the domestic precincts, in a state of active idleness, evidently awaiting orders, which were liberally given him in a preemptory tone, with a remark thrown in parenthetically that everything was at six and sevens when she, Mrs Linklater, turned her back, and the children would be brought to beggary if she were not slaving her fingers to the bones.[17]

Despite his subservience to his wife, Mr Linklater has a praiseworthy role in understanding and caring for one of the Linklater children, who has a physical disability. His actions are contrasted with those of his wife, who is unsympathetic to the child.

As a young child Myra joins the Linklaters' daughter Totty in taking lessons from a schoolmaster, Mr Dilk, at nearby Lellan Park. Dilk is typical of the schoolmasters Louisa had described in *Gertrude*. Near-sighted, unsuspicious and rather deaf, he had had 'several lampoons, parodies, and satires' published but he had no control of the unruly Lellan boys. Soon Myra and Totty are crying and unhappy but the fourth Lellan son, Kenard, a dreamy boy with an ambition to be a poet, befriends them and plucks them peaches from a tree. There is approval of these male/female roles. The

> miniature man and women fell into their natural places, he the protector and they the protected, admiring and devoted, ready to bestow their slices of cake or meadow flowers gathered by the road side, always so proud of him and his doings and sayings, and he so well content it should be so.[18]

At this early age Myra was already one of Louisa's heroines whose responsibility it was to improve the moral outlook of those around her. Due to Myra's influence

> in after life there was a refinement and purity about Kenard which distinguished him from his brothers, and proved a safeguard in many an hour of temptation. Gross and low pleasures had no temptation over him, but he did not know that his little playmate had fostered, if

not inspired, that higher inward life, which proved like a coat of mail in those dark hours of evil. It was not her influence only, but that study which she had taught him to love above all others—the Bible. Myra was one of those children whom the unseen influence from on high cultures and trains; simple, unconscious piety ripened and elevates the girl's mind and heart, as true religion always does.[19]

Myra is revealed in a flashback to England to be the child of a squire's daughter, Mary Ingleton, and her unworthy husband, Guy Kershaw, who covets her fortune. This is not the only unhappy marriage Louisa depicts in her novels. Her views would have been influenced by her experience of her mother's unhappy marriage to Barton and possibly may reflect Louisa's views on her sister Charlotte's marriage. She remarks:

There is nothing more melancholy than the binding together the dove and the vulture. Coarse, sinful, without one spark of nobleness about him, how could even his kindness not be revolting? Yet she loved him—yes, and even believed in him, long after every one else had seen him as he was; long after the heart-sad old squire had grown to answer demands upon his purse only for her sake, and the sake of her child; demands the proceeds of which never cheered her poverty; and all this time she wrote cheerful letters home to her father, and had no reproaches for Guy, her dear Guy still. God help the poor trusting heart of a woman in her bitter need.[20]

As Totty and Myra grow up the contrasts in their characters sharpen. While Mary Roberts had influenced Myra's education in a scholarly direction, Totty, left to a governess, had 'learnt to strum horribly on the piano and do wool work, and crochet, and to dance, and know the fashions, and a great many other wonderful things, which made her, at least to some eyes, quite a lady'. On Totty's seventeenth birthday, Myra helps Mrs Linklater to prepare for the party and before long brought 'order out of the confusion, and that lady's shot silk out of the drawers'. Meanwhile Totty spent her time dressing:

The low dress showed the plump white shoulders and round arms; but the march of gentility had added a huge bustle, they were fashionable then—which bordered on the ridiculous in some eyes, and helped to make a stronger contrast between Myra and her friend.[21]

Later Totty Linklater marries a rich Jewish storekeeper. Mrs Linklater is antagonistic towards Jews but succumbs to the 'clang of gold'.

The developing romance between Myra and Kenard Lellan is interrupted by the discovery of gold. Lellan and his four sons, including Kenard, leave for the goldfields, where Kenard falls out with his brothers when he refuses to join them in selling sly grog. With no income from this source he is seen at the goldfields 'seated under a tree, a little removed from the busy scene... penning notes of the diggings. He is prolonging life, rather than living, upon the pay of a correspondent to a country paper'.[22] As in *Cowanda*, life on the gold diggings is portrayed as inducing lawlessness and the breakdown of moral attitudes and also as an unlikely way of making a fortune.

The main character, Myra, has similar characteristics to other Atkinson heroines. She is a young girl whose actions and thoughts are dictated by Christian love and the dictates of the Bible and who influences those around her, particularly the man she marries, Kenard Lellan. By contrast her childhood friend, Totty Linklater, develops into a superficial young lady interested only in her appearance and her admirers.

The men include the pathetically dominated Mr Linklater, who has more genuine feelings than his wife but lacks the courage to stand up to her; Guy Kershaw, an unrelieved picture of a villian who marries an heiress, squanders her property, abandons his child, to reappear in later life an alcoholic to sponge on her; and Kenard Lellan, a rather ineffectual young man whose moral character, however, has been formed by the heroine Myra, so that he has the strength to resist temptation.

The descriptions of life in the country are the strongest aspects of the story. When the Nepean River overflows, 'surging, muddy waters, laden with a dirty froth and eddying straws and twigs', creep up the stairs at Bower Farm step by step until they reach the second storey. After the water subsides the ground floor is 'a sad sight...a thick slimy mud adhering to every object, chairs and sofas cased with it; window glass scattered everywhere, a drowned pig on the dining room table'. The occupants noted this scene before drawing the bars from the door and exploring the 'outer desolation'. 'Here was wreck and ruin, dead animals, broken or uprooted fruit trees, fences carried away.' Apart from the physical devastation the flood takes a toll on the inhabitants of the house: 'A week's rain in a country house betrays what inward resources its inmates have; no letters or papers come; there are no visitors, no riding, no walking; guns lie idle in their cases, and kangaroo dogs creep close to the fire and whine'.[23]

Material progress is apparent during the course of the twenty years which the story covers. Janet Bean's and Mary Roberts's home, originally a cottage, is replaced by a substantial two-storey house, although still furnished in a rather spartan way. The Linklaters' home, originally a complex of three unpretentious buildings forming three sides of a square, backed by stables and sheds, undergoes great changes. Louisa's account of these changes conveys a gently ironic and enchanting picture of the advance of gentility.

> There were indications not so much of increased wealth, though they were not wanting, but of the march of gentility; but if the kitchen revealed this, how much more the sitting-room in the other building, here were windows draped with leno and moreen, a mantelpiece groaning under the weight of blue and crimson shepherdesses and impossible turtledoves and cats, a handsome sideboard loaded with a heterogeneous collection of glass and china, with a centre piece of plaster-of-paris, in the form of a pottle-like basket, overflowing with gorgeous fruits, which a fertile imagination might name. But no one could do justice to the pictures adorning the papered walls,—they were unique. Oh those Chloes and Phillises of blushing beauty, and those tender swains with pipes. Oh those artless beauties crowning snowy lambs with roses—criticism forbear. The centre table showed crochet mats and a vase of flowers, they, at least, were beautiful to any eye, there was such a fine taste too in their arrangement and choice, which the rest of the room seemed to want, that they looked as if they had rather wandered in than belonged there.[24]

Another aspect typical of most of Louisa Atkinson's novels is the absence of clergymen and churches. The minority of characters who are depicted as living out Christian values, particularly the heroine, are shown as missionaries in a heathen land, their task being to spread knowledge of the Bible and Christian ideals.

With the publication of *Myra* in 1864 and a few further articles in 'A Voice From the Country' series in 1864 and 1865, Louisa's writing output tapered off. Some dramatic changes occurred in her life. By this time it is possible that she had met James Calvert; if so, she may at thirty or more have wanted to marry him. Her mother, by then in her late sixties, remained strongly against Louisa marrying. Her youngest daughter had been her companion and her pride for many years, particularly following the exclusion of Charlotte Elizabeth from the family, and the death of Emily. Apart from this selfish need for keeping Louisa, Charlotte Barton feared that with her poor health, a similar fate to her older sister would await Louisa should she bear a child. There is some evidence in the number of unhappy marriages Louisa includes in her novels that Charlotte Barton, following her stressful experience as the wife of George Barton, may have become antipathetic to the idea of marriage and may have influenced Louisa in this direction.

At about this time, probably in 1865, Charlotte Barton fell and broke her arm badly in several places. She was to remain an invalid until her death two years later and Louisa's life was almost entirely devoted to looking after her. They moved from Fernhurst back to Oldbury to live with Louisa's brother, James, also still unmarried.

13

The only one who behaved perfectly was Mr Calvert

If Louisa Atkinson and James Calvert had not met by 1865, the catalyst for the development of their friendship may have been a stirring article on explorer Ludwig Leichhardt's fate which Louisa wrote for the *Sydney Morning Herald*. By 1865 Leichhardt had been missing in some unknown part of the interior of Australia for seventeen years, his last letter having been written from the Darling Downs in south-east Queensland on 4 April 1848. He had set out with a party of six from a spot near the present-day town of Roma. On his third journey of exploration he intended to cross the continent from east to west and then follow the coast down to the Swan River settlement at Perth. In the years he had been missing there had been many searches for Leichhardt and his party, and many stories of his supposed fate, including reports of the existence of wild white men, possibly members of his party, living with Aboriginal tribes.

James Calvert, as a member of the Leichhardt's first and only successful journey of exploration, maintained a close interest in his leader's fate. In 1854 he wrote to the *Sydney Morning Herald* stating that he believed some of the party might still be alive, being kept captive by an Aboriginal tribe. In his letter, published under the heading 'Poor Leichhardt', he pleaded for 'a *really* well organised expedition' to search for 'one of the noblest and most distinguished travellers that ever went forth into the wilderness'. He called on the wealthy citizens of Sydney, 'ye merchants rolling in wealth' to 'think *once* again of poor Leichhardt'. Four years later he reiterated his view that Leichhardt might be still alive and hoping to be 'rescued and restored to civilization and his numerous friends'. Again he called on 'the rich merchants and squatters of the colony' to finance a search party.[1]

In the many years since his disappearance there had been

periods when Leichhardt's fate was almost forgotten, but interest in exploration in general quickened in 1860 when the Burke and Wills expedition left Melbourne intending to cross the continent from south to north. Newspaper reports of this expedition, appearing over more than a year, rekindled speculation about the fate of Leichhardt's party. Its dramatic conclusion, with Burke and Wills both dead and John King rescued after being fed and cared for by Aborigines for four months, revived hope for Leichhardt and his party. This was reinforced by news of a find by Victorian settler, Duncan McIntyre, who in 1863 made an overland journey from Victoria to western Queensland in search of land. Exploring further to the Gulf of Carpentaria he came to the Flinders River, where he discovered trees marked 'L.' and two old horses. When he reported these finds in Melbourne they were taken as evidence of Leichhardt's movements.[2]

Baron Ferdinand von Mueller, Leichhardt's German compatriot, took up this cause. Aware that many women held heroic notions of explorers, he proposed in a public lecture in Melbourne on 9 February 1865, entitled 'The Fate of Dr Leichhardt', the formation of a ladies' committee to help finance an expedition to search for the missing explorers.[3] His suggestion was taken up enthusiastically. A Ladies' Leichhardt Search Committee, consisting of two delegates each from the major churches, was formed to raise funds. Donations came from many sections of the community, some groups such as doctors setting up their own committees to raise funds.[4]

By this time Louisa knew Ferdinand von Mueller well by correspondence and admired his outstanding achievements as a botanist. With a long-standing interest in explorers, a desire to support von Mueller and, if by then she knew James Calvert, a personal interest in supporting his belief in Leichhardt's survival, Louisa wrote an article appealing to the women of New South Wales to support the search for the explorer. It was published in the *Sydny Morning Herald* and republished in the *Sydney Mail* under the heading, 'A Voice From the Country—Leichhardt'. 'Perhaps there are few subjects which awaken such lively interest in most minds as the explorations of unknown tracts of country,' she began. 'To many, the highly interesting lecture of Dr F. Mueller, delivered at Melbourne will be well known — in which that learned man, of whom the colonies may well be proud, brought forward the claims of Dr Leichhardt to our sympathies and exertions'.

In the article she dwelt particularly on the story of a man who had appeared at a station on the Balonne River two years previously claiming that he was a survivor of Leichhardt's expedition and

that he had escaped from an Aboriginal tribe leaving Leichhardt still a prisoner. Although this story might have been 'the
chimera of a disordered brain' or 'the fiction of an imposter', it
should be investigated. Louisa concluded her appeal to the women
of New South Wales:

> He *may* live—an old man, with white hair, with bent shoulders, daily
> more unfitted for the cruel slavery under savage man. He may have
> sunk to rest in the unknown wilderness. A mighty effort is making in
> Victoria to determine these doubts;—shall we not participate in so
> glorious and honourable a work? While the women of Victoria are
> collecting to fit out an expedition, shall their countrywomen here stand
> coldly aside? Surely not!⁵

The expedition financed as a result of von Mueller's appeal set
out in the middle of 1865 under the leadership of Duncan Mc-
Intyre. Unfortunately McIntyre died near Julia Creek in western
Queensland and without leadership the expedition broke up in
disorder. Although this effort to find Leichhardt came to nothing,
von Mueller maintained his interest in the search for many more
years. In 1871 in a letter to Louisa he still maintained his hope that
survivors would be found. He asked her to tell James Calvert, then
her husband, that a surveyor, Mr Birch, was to make a preliminary
search of the Thomson River in north-west Queensland 'to see if
the insane survivor of Leichhardt's party can not be brought to the
settlement'.⁶ The belief in Leichhardt's survival extended beyond
von Mueller. In 1871 a search by the Bulloo Native Mounted Police
in south-west Queensland returned with evidence that was believed for a time to have solved the mystery of Leichhardt's
disappearance.⁷

Louisa may have known and perhaps already loved James Calvert when she wrote her stirring appeal to the women of New
South Wales. If not, this article may have prompted the beginning
of their acquaintance. Perhaps James Calvert wrote to congratulate
her on her article.

James Snowden Calvert was in his late thirties at least when he
and Louisa met. He had the character of a gentle hero, a stoic
survivor of Leichhardt's first journey of exploration during which
he had suffered terrible injuries during an attack by Aborigines.
Unlike Leichhardt and some other members of the party, however,
he lacked the wish, or perhaps the drive, to capitalise on the great
experience of his youth. He appeared content to resume a comparatively obscure life, for some time in Sydney and then at Cavan in
the Yass district. In his quiet way he had achievements in public

life and in natural science, but they passed almost unnoticed. Throughout his life he remained a man of integrity and honour.

He was born on 13 July 1825 at Otley, in the West Riding of Yorkshire, one of seven children of William and Ann Calvert. His father was a leather manufacturer and may also have had farming interests, as on his marriage certificate James Calvert described his father as a grazier. The family lived for some time in Liverpool, where James first went to school, and then in Manchester and Birmingham, where he attended 'some of the best schools then known'. The family then lived for three years in London's West End before returning to Yorkshire. They were apparently well off, as James and his older brother William travelled widely on the Continent.[8]

The family wealth, if it still existed, was not called on when the two brothers decided to emigrate to Australia. They sailed in 1841 as steerage passengers on the *Sir Edward Paget*, arriving in Sydney on 14 February 1842, two of 248 bounty (assisted) migrants aboard. The few cabin passengers included Ludwig Leichhardt. Another steerage passenger was James Murphy, who became friendly with Leichhardt, as did the Calvert brothers, and whose young son John was to accompany Leichhardt on his expedition to Port Essington.

The Calvert brothers were described in their travel documents as natives of Ecorthy, their calling as farm labourers and their ages as 20 and 22—James Calvert was in fact only sixteen when he sailed from England. Their health was described as very good, their religion as Episcopalian. On arrival William was engaged by Bryan and Ward of George Street, Sydney at £1/10/0 per week and James by Mrs Broughton, also of George Street, at £25 per year.[9]

On the surface William and James Calvert seemed to be similar to the thousands of relatively unskilled bounty migrants who reached Australia during the years the scheme was in operation. However, while they may have been short of money, they had some prospects in Australia through an older sister, Harriett Amelia, born on 14 April 1816 at Otley. She was the second wife of Robert Dawson, sometime chief agent of the Australian Agricultural Company, for which he had established and administered a pastoral domain of over 400 000 hectares in the Port Stephens area in New South Wales.

By the time William and James Calvert arrived in Australia in 1842 the Dawsons were living for at least part of the year on their 40-hectare property at Redhead, south of Newcastle. Although engaged to work in Sydney, William and James Calvert were soon farming on this property and living either with the Dawson family in their weatherboard house or in a hut on Dawson's property.

In the latter part of 1842 Ludwig Leichhardt travelled to Newcastle, where he stayed with entomologist and entrepreneur Alexander Walker Scott. Two of Walker's daughters, Harriet and Helena, were to become famous as artists and naturalists. Helena Scott (1832–1910) is said to have been a lifelong friend of Louisa Atkinson's.[10] During his journeys south of Newcastle, Leichhardt, wanting to buy a horse, called at Robert Dawson's property at Redhead. During the visit he probably renewed acquaintance with his shipboard companions, the Calvert brothers.

A few days later he met the Calverts in the bush and they invited him to stay at their hut, situated 'in a romantic spot in a high-lying pocket' near the Valley of Palms. Already interested in the flora and fauna of Australia, James presented Leichhardt with a *Caprimulgus albogularis* (white-throated goat-sucker) for dissection, and probably expressed an interest in accompanying Leichhardt on his planned journeys of discovery. Before undertaking an exploratory journey, Leichhardt determined to travel through all the settled districts. He travelled in the Upper Hunter and Goulburn Valleys and through what was to become the New England district to Moreton Bay, then to the last outpost of settlement in the north, at Durundur, near the Glasshouse Mountains north of Brisbane. Leichhardt made his base at the Archer station for about nine months from July 1843, during which time he undertook many journeys acquiring knowledge of Australian plants and learning some bushcraft.[11]

There had been much talk of an expedition to explore a route to the north coast of Australia and Leichhardt seized upon the idea of undertaking it himself. He planned to travel through unexplored country across the north-east of Australia from the Darling Downs to the British settlement at Port Essington, east of the present day site of Darwin, a distance of some 5000 kilometres. When Leichhardt returned south to organise the expedition, James Calvert volunteered to become one of his exploring party. With little idea of the terrible hardships and dangers ahead and probably unable to contemplate how far and how long the party would be in unchartered bush, he joined at his own expense, providing his own equipment, clothing, provisions and horses.

The party consisted of Leichhardt together with Calvert; John Roper, 22, who had worked for Walker Scott at Ash Island but was then unemployed; John Murphy, 16, the son of one of Leichhardt's shipboard acquaintances; William Phillips, 44, a convicted attorney who had been transported for forgery; and an Aborigine from the Newcastle district, Harry Brown. They left Sydney on 13 August 1844 for Moreton Bay aboard the *Sovereign*.[12]

Donations flowed in from many supporters who were later to be honoured by having natural features named after them. In Brisbane the party was expanded to include Charley Fisher, an Aboriginal policeman from the Bathurst district, and Caleb, an American negro. On the Darling Downs two more joined the party—John Gilbert, a collector of specimens for the famous naturalist, John Gould, and Christopher Pemberton Hodgson, a young squatter. The party left the last outpost of settlement—Thomas Bell's Jimbour Station near the present day town of Dalby in Queensland—at the beginning of October 1844.

Food became a problem almost immediately, with many fewer native birds and animals being shot than Leichhardt had expected. He eventually decided that the party was too large and that Pemberton Hodgson and Caleb should return.[13] Pemberton Hodgson, although he had been used to a squatting life, wrote of the 'unparalleled hardships' of the journey to that early stage.[14]

As the expeditionary party continued north through what was later to be the state of Queensland, they came across a stream which Leichhardt named the Dawson River after Calvert's brother-in-law, who had supplied blood horses for the expedition. Following this stream, now believed to be Downfall Creek, a tributary of Juandah Creek which flows into the Dawson, they came across fertile country similar to the Darling Downs and Leichhardt gave to this area the name of 'Calvert's Plains'.[15] The Downfall Creek-Guluguba area south of the town of Wandoan (originally known as Juandah) is now a rich grain growing and mixed farming district.[16] Soon they were in the beautiful Dawson Valley later to become one of Queensland's richest districts. As they went they marked trees. A coolibah tree still standing in the main street of Taroom on the Leichhardt Highway between Miles and Banana is marked 'LL 1844'.

On 26 January 1845, north of the present day town of Emerald, Leichhardt and Calvert, travelling ahead of the rest of the party, became the first Europeans to see Peak Range with its remarkable conical and dome-shaped mountains. But by the end of the following day they had become lost, without water and suffering severely from thirst in the summer heat. The next morning they discovered their horses had strayed. Leichhardt was exhausted from diarrhoea, so Calvert had to set out to retrieve them. He walked for four hours in the hot sun, without water, before finding them. Both men were nearly dead from thirst when they eventually found the tracks of bullocks from their camp and found their way back. They had travelled for 32 hours in arid country entirely without water.[17] Calvert, described by Gilbert as having 'rather a weak frame' and 'withal of a weak constitution', was so changed that his companions scarcely knew him.

While still in area of Peak Range, Leichhardt on 5 February 1845 named a lofty peak shaped like the roof of a house 'Calvert's Peak'. Shortly after they met a tribe of Aborigines who were anxious to detain some of the party and offered to exchange two of the tribe for some of Leichhardt's men. This episode made such an impression on James Calvert that he attributed Leichhardt's eventual disappearance to his being held captive by an Aboriginal tribe.[18]

On 28 June 1845 in the southern part of Cape York Peninsula, west of the present day Dunbar station, after the party had camped for the night, they were attacked by Aborigines. During the encounter Gilbert was killed, Roper was pierced by six spears, Calvert by five, and both were beaten by waddies and womeras. Leichhardt and the remaining members of the party fought off the attackers with their guns.[19]

That Roper and Calvert escaped from death during the attack and during the critical next few days is amazing. One barbed spear had gone through Calvert's left testicle and penetrated his groin and a second struck his knee. His nose had been crushed by several severe blows from a waddi and his elbow and hand had been smashed. Roper had been injured in many places. One spear had pierced his cheek and eye and injured the optic nerve, another his left arm and another his loins, and he had also suffered a heavy blow on the shoulders. The agony of the wounded men as Leichhardt, who had some medical training, tried to extract the barbed spears is unimaginable. He had to force one spear through Roper's arm to break off the barb and cut another out of Calvert's groin. All of this had to be carried out in darkness. In fear of another attack, the camp fire had been put out.

It was clearly unsafe for the party to remain in the area, so two days after the attack, although Calvert and Roper were still in acute pain and danger of infection, the group moved on. Roper described his sufferings when he put his feet on the ground as having 'red hot pokers up both legs'. He suffered intense pain in the small of the back and was completely blind. In a letter written later to his brothers, Roper said of Calvert and himself:

poor Calvert was little better—any mortal with human feelings would have pitied us—skeletons—poor emaciated ghosts we were—a few miles ride would fatigue us and then bowed down on the pummels of our saddles we were indeed the picture of toil worn woe begone travellers—not able to wash myself I should have passed for a mulatto

170

3 weeks have I been without getting washed. My companions altho [sic] not wounded had quite enough to do (in this hot climate particularly so destroying to all energy) without bestowing much attention upon either me or Calvert not being able to work ourselves or watch our share devolved upon them.[20]

Amazingly, three weeks later James Calvert had recovered to the extent that he was able to resume his duties. Roper took much longer to recover, at one stage being so weak he had to be carried. But a few months later he was sufficiently recovered to discover a river, called the Roper after him. Their recovery, in a tropical climate where wounds could easily become infected and living on very basic rations, is a remarkable tribute to their stamina and stoicism.

The party spent many weeks struggling west across the Gulf country before crossing what was later to become the Queensland/ Northern Territory boundary. On 8 September the party reached a small river, of which Leichhardt wrote in his *Journal*: 'I named this river the "Calvert," in acknowledgement of the good services of Mr Calvert during our expedition, and which I feel much pleasure in recording.'[21]

Wandering among the lagoons and rugged stony ranges of Arnhem Land, the party became desperate for food and all suffered severely from prickly heat which made any movement painful. By the time they knew, through meeting Aborigines who understood English, that they were approaching Port Essington, Leichhardt wrote of their condition:

The least friction in consequence of riding, or of the rubbing of the stirrup leathers or of the trowsers, the pustules inflamed and formed into furuncles of long standing, giving great pain and crippling almost Calvert and myself, appearing at the joint of the knee, at the loins, buttocks, arms, the elbow. These boils appeared however particularly when the thunderstorms and rains set in, and that moisture is very probably the real cause.[22]

They reached the settlement at Port Essington on 17 December 1845, nearly fifteen months after they had left Jimbour station, north of Brisbane. During the few months they spent at the settlement waiting some means of transport to Sydney the party recovered from their ordeal. Leichhardt reported that Calvert, Roper and Phillips got very fat on the regular meals.[23]

The party had long since been given up as lost and it was not until 25 March 1846 that they made their unexpected and triumphant entry into Port Jackson aboard the *Heroine*. The death of the explorers had been so much accepted that Leichhardt's friend, Lt

Robert Lynd, had written an ode to his departed friend entitled 'Leichhardt's grave'. The ode was set to music by composer Isaac Nathan and was to have been performed at the Victoria Theatre in Pitt Street on the day that the 'lost' party reappeared in Sydney.[24] The explorers were given a triumphant welcome to Sydney and were feted at public receptions.

Though said by Gilbert to have a delicate constitution James Calvert recovered from the severe wounds he had sustained in the attack by Aborigines and from the desperate privations of the journey, although he bore the scars for the rest of his life and suffered greatly from arthritis and rheumatism.

When other members of the exploratory party criticised Leichhardt, Calvert remained loyal. Evidently loyalty was ingrained in him and he had no streak of meanness in his character. Leichhardt wrote that of all the members of the expedition, 'The only one who behaved perfectly, with few exceptions, was a young man, Mr Calvert, who came in the same boat with me from England'.[25] Leichhardt painted an endearing picture of the young Calvert. He was, he wrote, of a talkative nature, 'being full of jokes and stories, which, although old and sometimes quaint, are always pure'.

James Calvert's regard for Leichhardt remained with him all his life, despite incidents which could have turned him against him. According to Roper, he and Calvert had an agreement with Leichhardt to share equally in the profits of a book to be published by Leichhardt, but this sharing of money never occurred. After the triumphal return of the expedition, money was subscribed to a fund for the explorers. Again according to Roper the Committee which allocated the money was made up of '24 gents all friends of Dr Leichhardt's neither myself nor Calvert knowing any of them'. In the division of the money, Leichhardt received £1554 and Calvert and Roper £290 each with lesser amounts going to the other members. Roper thought the Committee should have taken more account of his loss of an eye and of 'Calvert's wounds'.[26]

Apart from the money they received from the fund, Calvert and Roper did not benefit from being members of an expedition which had discovered hundred of millions of hectares suitable for settlement and had created great enthusiasm among the whole population. When they attempted to obtain positions in the customs department in Newcastle and asked Leichhardt to use his influence to help them, he wrote to Sir William Macarthur, 'If there is a chance and if I can be of use, though Heaven knows how?—I shall do my best to serve them'. But this came to nothing.[27]

Following his return from the expedition to Port Essington in

James Calvert was only twenty when he was speared and attacked by waddis and womeras during the attack by Aborigines on Leichhardt's expedition to Port Essington. He never recovered completely from his wounds. (Janet Cosh)

1846, Calvert, still not twenty-one years old, may have returned to farming at Redhead for some time. When Leichhardt was planning his expedition to cross the continent from east to west he urged James Calvert to join him, 'he was very desirous that I should again accompany him', Calvert wrote.[28] Leichhardt discussed his plan to travel north-east of the route taken by the explorer Augustus Gregory with Calvert who, when searches for Leichhardt were being planned, said *'that was his favourite plan*; and this plan he freely discussed with me in *all* its bearings'. Calvert, still suffering the effects of his wounds, declined Leichhardt's invitation.

Following this James Calvert's movements are unknown. Possibly he farmed near the Balonne River or at some other place for some time, or he may have already moved to Sydney. He is recorded living at Astor House, Cumberland Street on Bunker's Hill at the Rocks in the 1850s. Through his interest in botany, which had developed on the Leichhardt expedition, he became friendly with many members of Sydney's scientific community, including Lieutenant Robert Lynd, Leichhardt's great friend and executor, William Woolls, William Sharp Macleay and the geologist Rev. W.B. Clarke. He was also in touch with Baron von Mueller in Melbourne.[29]

At some time in the 1850s James Calvert left Sydney to live at

Cavan, 25 kilometres from Yass, south of Sydney. A letter he wrote to the *Sydney Morning Herald* in November 1858 gave his address as Cavan and it is probable that he had been living at the historic Cavan station on the west bank of the Murrumbidgee for a few years before he was appointed a magistrate at Yass on 16 June 1859.[30] In 1866 Cavan, a property of 51 000 acres with a grazing capacity of 7000 sheep, was recorded as being occupied by Joseph Frederick Castle and James Calvert.[31] Castle was an absentee owner being principal of Calder House boarding school at Redfern until 1870.

Living with Calvert at Cavan was his nephew Joseph Robert Barrington Dawson. Joseph's father, Robert Dawson, who had by then been separated from his wife for many years, sold his Redhead property and left Australia to return to England. His wife, Calvert's sister Harriett, remained in Australia. It was apparently at the time of his father's departure that Joseph Dawson went to live near Yass with his uncle. Calvert's brother William was on a farm nearby.

At Cavan James Calvert developed his interest in collecting botanical specimens, and he experimented with new crops and animals. He was awarded a medal of honour for exhibits he sent to the first International Exhibition held in Paris in 1855. At the first International Exhibition held in London in 1862 he gained a bronze medal for botany and a silver medal for an exhibit of vegetable fibres, proposed as materials for paper-making.[32] He continued to win other medals at subsequent international exhibitions.

James Calvert had friends in the vicinity of Cavan. Near Yass was his friend and fellow explorer, Hamilton Hume, and across the Murrumbidgee River at Yeumberra was Charles Hall, with whom he had an early association through his brother-in-law, Robert Dawson. He also joined community organisations. In 1862 when the Yass Pastoral, Agricultural and Horticultural Association was formed, Calvert was elected one of the vice-presidents. The Society held its first show in March 1863. In 1867 he was appointed a sheep director under the *Diseases in Sheep Act 1866*.[33]

Calvert maintained his interest in the aftermath of the Port Essington expedition. In 1865 he wrote to the *Sydney Morning Herald* to correct a letter signed 'Warrego Squatter'. The letter stated that John Gilbert had been second-in-command of the Leichhardt expedition. In accordance with the agreement with Leichhardt that a joint book was to be written by Leichhardt, Roper and Calvert, Calvert claimed Leichhardt's account of the expedition as 'our book'. He advised 'Warrego Squatter' to read page 15 of *'our book'*:

Mr Gilbert went solely at his own expense, but not as one using any authority over the party. There are other errors about our journey in his [Warrego's] letter, too trifling for me to correct especially as he does not give his name. At any rate, after the answer he got from Dr Mueller, I should have thought in future he would have only written on what he thoroughly understood. As I have no desire to appear in your paper on *every* occasion offering.[34]

If Louisa Atkinson and James Calvert were acquainted during these years, their friendship must have developed by correspondence. Considering the distance between Fernhurst and Yass, they would have been able to meet only very infrequently. When Louisa moved back to Oldbury probably in the latter part of 1865, meetings would have been much more feasible.

14

The tale has been much admired

After her years of achievement in the late 1850s and early 1860s, Louisa Atkinson's health deteriorated. It appears that the tuberculosis, of which she had probably already suffered one bout, returned, making it impossible for her to continue the active life she had led previously. Early in 1865, when Rev. William Branwhite Clarke, the Anglican clergyman and geologist, one of the eminent scientists to whom William Woolls had introduced her, visited Louisa at Kurrajong, he found her an invalid. After the visit he wrote, 'I hope you are much better than when I saw you. The very hot day of Saturday was not favourable for invalids.'[1]

Coinciding with the collapse of Louisa's own health, her mother's decline into invalidity made increased demands on Louisa's strength. Charlotte had broken her arm badly in several places and dislocated her elbow. The fall seems also to have affected her spine. Louisa continued her literary and scientific work at a much reduced level most of her time for the next two years being occupied in looking after her mother. This took a toll of her constitution. William Woolls noted that 'the exertion of talking to her aged mother, who was exceedingly deaf, and the difficulty which she experienced in moving her when on her dying bed, were very prejudicial to one, who, even at that time, manifested symptoms of pulmonary consumption'.[2]

Fernhurst was sold when mother and daughter moved back to Oldbury to live with James, and the two women resumed their lives at their old home, with its many memories. It is likely that during this lengthy period, when both the state of her own health and the demands of caring for her mother prevented her from very much activity, Louisa wrote her next novel, *Tom Hellicar's Children*. Although not published until 1871,[3] the theme of the novel seems to be a product of this time.

Rev. William Branwhite Clarke, an eminent geologist and Anglican clergyman, was about 60 and renowned for his association with the discovery of gold in New South Wales when Louisa Atkinson met him. Under the influence of her friendship with him, she became increasingly interested in geology. (*Sydney Mail* 13 July 1872)

With her long life nearing its end, Charlotte Barton may have recalled and relived with her daughter the great battles she had had with executors, lawyers and the legal system so long ago. As a young child Louisa had experienced the constant litigation that had dominated the lives of herself and her sisters and brother. As an adult she would have understood more about the traumas of that time, and more of her mother's anxieties and feelings against the people she believed had planned to deprive her of her children.

Louisa transmuted these views and feelings in a striking way into a novel about three children who were separated from their mother and deprived of their inheritance through the conniving, ruthless and criminal actions of the executors of their father's will. Against the background of her own family's litigation and years of stress, many of the comments in *Tom Hellicar's Children* have heightened significance.

In the novel, to a constant backdrop of ostensibly caring remarks —'the children's interests should be strictly considered' and 'our duty to my brother's children must be considered', the executors, Tom Hellicar's brother, Richard, and cousin, Max Ibotson, a magistrate, deprive the widow and her children of their property, Biribang. When she first realises what is happening, allegedly in the 'children's interests', the widow Ruth Hellicar thinks:

This was the first time she had ever heard those interests brought forward in that shape; it seemed — perhaps it was her low spirits, she thought — but it seemed as if it made her children and herself into two parties, antagonistic to each other, and she pressed the sleeping head of her baby closer to her bosom, with a frightened desolate sensation that ended in an hysterical fit of tears and sobs.

This was the first time—but not the last; oh no, not the last—she was to hear it every day—to hear it when the sleek, fat cows *he* was so proud of were driven from the pastures at Biribang to be sold; to hear it when even his favourite riding horse was disposed of, and when she found in the papers an advertisement announcing the sale of his valuable library at an early day, then she interposed. 'I too' she said with decision, 'forbid the sale.'

'Madam,' returned Richard Hellicar coldly, 'our duty to my brother's children must be considered rather than an idle whim' . . .

'You mistake,' she interposed quickly, 'it is not an idle whim—my husband valued his books above every other thing—he spent much of his time among them; he had the choicest collection in the country almost—and I am sure his wishes were to preserve them for his sons.'

'I find no mention of this in the will.'

'Why should he mention what he could not doubt would be understood? I cannot have them sold.'

'Your opinion is not required: you have no power.' He scowled sternly upon her.

'I have no power,' she retorted, stung by his manner;' 'I *his* wife, and mother of his children.'

'More the pity, madam.'[4]

Ruth Hellicar's two older children, Richie and Jack, are sent by the executors to live in a nearby country town with a solicitor who undertakes their education, as the executors find this is a cheaper solution than sending them to boarding school. Ruth and her baby daughter, also named Ruth, are forced out of Biribang and accommodated in a small cottage on Richard Hellicar's property. She is forbidden to see her sons and when it is discovered that she has contacted them her daughter is taken from her and she is forced to leave the district.

Biribang is put in the hands of Tristam, a nephew of Richard Hellicar's wife, with the excuse that Ruth is 'totally unfit to manage it. The bare idea is preposterous. The sooner such scum settle to the bottom the better'[5]—a reference to Ruth Hellicar's employment as a needlewoman before her marriage. Richard Hellicar had always resented his brother's marriage at the advanced age of 47, as he had regarded himself for so long as heir to his brother's property and had speculated on the strength of this likely inheritance.

Certain similarities with Charlotte Barton's position are obvious. She had offered to manage Oldbury but her offer had been refused out of hand. An executor of her late husband's will, Alexander

Berry, from a first meeting, had considered her unsuitable to be the wife of his friend James Atkinson and later unsuitable to be the guardian of her own children. The correlation between the situations of Ruth Hellicar and Charlotte Barton is so striking in some respects, that one wonders why Louisa gave Ruth Hellicar a character that was the antithesis of her mother's. Charlotte Barton was a woman of strong character; Ruth Hellicar, by contrast, is a timid woman who passively accepts her fate.

In creating this character, Louisa seems to be expressing the view that her mother's reaction to the forces ranged against her, in her fight to keep her children, was an unusual and extraordinary response for a woman in that situation. By contrast most women, like Ruth Hellicar, would be overwhelmed by the power exercised by men of position. It is made clear that Ruth Hellicar had been kept ignorant of business and farming. Charlotte Barton's character was such that it would have been difficult to keep her ignorant of business matters and in fact she put up a feasible proposition for taking over the management of Oldbury after the death of her husband. She was in a similar situation, however, in being left by her trusting husband in the hands of incompatible, and as she saw it, scheming executors. In the novel Ruth Hellicar was:

> so helpless, and friendless, and simple; had been treated as a child, and petted and fondled, and kept ignorant of business, that from very habit she deferred and left things to them.
>
> The easy, book-loving, careless Tom Hellicar had left her to the care of those very men who, a few years before, had cursed her as an interloper and robber.[6]

The development of the story of *Tom Hellicar's Children* depends on Ruth Hellicar being so passive and dominated by the forces ranged against her that she accepts the parting from her children. Years pass as the children are deprived of proper schooling while their mother roams from one place to another taking housekeeping jobs to keep herself, eventually reaching Tasmania, where she vainly tries to get financial help from her brother, Nicholas Spiro, to mount a legal case to regain her children. Spiro's wife, Dorothy, is more in the mould of Charlotte Barton. She says of the executors of Tom Hellicar's will, 'I'd have clawed their eyes out afore they would have laid a finger on mine'.[7]

The main action of the story takes place at Mount Hellicar, the residence of Richard Hellicar, and in the neighbouring village where Richie and Jack Hellicar live with Heland, the solicitor who undertakes their education and later employs them as his clerks. The setting of the story resembles the Moss Vale and Sutton Forest district, with a village not too far removed from the large properties and a minister and his family at the nearby rectory. The role of religion differs from Louisa's earlier novels. In *Tom Hellicar's Children*, unlike her other novels where clergymen are either absent or portrayed as a hindrance to the development of true Christianity, Christian influence comes through a clergyman and his daughters. Rev. John Thorell's daughters, Caroline and Esther, who take over the teaching of Richard Hellicar's young children, and Ruth's young daughter are typical of Louisa's heroines in undertaking good works and exerting an uplifting influence.

The bush disaster or adventure, which is included in all Louisa Atkinson's novels, comes in *Tom Hellicar's Children* in the form of a wild bush ride. This episode, which pre-dated many similar bush epics by male writers, occurs when Jack Hellicar decides to break away from the tyranny of his life in Heland's office. He flees with a drover, Sam Feagan, later becoming a stock boy on a station in a remote mountain district, similar to the Abercrombie Range outstation portrayed in *Gertrude*. Jack has an adventurous life in the bush providing the opportunity for one of the most thrilling episodes in Louisa Atkinson's fiction. As the stockmen cull the stock horses, which have strayed among brumbies in the mountain fastness:

> Everywhere foremost in the raid was Jack Hellicar's daring among the daring, till at length he had singled out the black mare, and it became a combat between them. Away she bounded, lashing her sides flaked with white foam with her long tail, and took down a steep point bounding in mad springs over the detached boulders, and hard pressed by Jack on his excited steed. Steeper each minute grew the way. Cooeys of warning were uttered behind him, but he heeded them not—indeed to stop was impossible, even when a creek rushing in a narrow chasm revealed itself before him. The mare gave a mad plunge, fell into the water, struggled out, and staggered on her way, with a broken fore leg. Burdened by its rider, Jack's horse fell headlong, shooting him on to the opposite bank, and killing itself.[8]

Although Jack Hellicar survives the fall he finally dies from spinal injuries.

Another interesting aspect of the story are the portrayals of Richard Hellicar's wife, formerly Maud Tristam, who is abnormally proud of her English antecedents, and her equally high-born but ineffectual nephew, Tristam, who manages Biribang. In a similar way to the introduction of the 'new chum' in *Gertrude*, Louisa introduces the Tristams as English characters ripe for satire to entertain her readers. The Tristams make delightful reading.

Miss Tristam belonged to one of the high families, and an old family who could count their sires up to the days of King Arthur's round table at least. They might have grown a little seedy in these last times, but had no lack of pride; indeed that was like a good edifice, each generation adding a tier till it was approaching the altitude of Babel...the Tristams never married young, because they rarely met with any swain who could bear comparison with their genealogical roll, so that old maids multiplied...[9]

The younger Tristam is even more a figure of fun. After making a remark about the boredom of living at Biribang, which he has allowed to deteriorate into a place where rats infested the walls and wind whistled through broken windows, he 'opened his wide mouth to laugh at his own wit...it was one of his misfortunes that good things always suggested themselves after the right time has passed—what smart things, on his own authority, he would have said half an hour afterwards'.[10]

Apart from its humorous aspect, Maud Tristam's pride in her ancestry has a serious purpose. Her inordinate pride is contrasted with her neglect in giving love to her children, so that 'every child she had looked as if it had missed its birthright'. Her sons 'although duly reminded of their high descent, had a perverse love of low society, freckled faces and warty hands, and hair that would tumble over their faces and stick out at the back of their heads'. At school they were 'eclipsed by shopkeepers' sons'. An even worse blow to her pride is that her daughter, Missy, is mentally retarded. Deprived of a sympathetic upbringing Missy grows up 'turbulent and sullen'. The inclusion of Missy in *Tom Hellicar's Children*, a deaf child in *Gertrude* and the 'crooked, ill-favoured' child, Cyrus Linklater, in *Myra* are aspects of Louisa Atkinson's portrayal of normal life. They have an added interest in being the first portrayals of children with disabilities in Australian literature.

After Ruth Hellicar's children grow up and the eldest regains possession of Biribang, by then rundown and unproductive, she makes a reappearance at her old home. Under the name of Mary Chard she takes the position of housekeeper at the property, where, because of the ravages of time and care on her appearance, she is not recognised by her own children. Her final degradation, having suffered so much from being separated from her children, is that she expects so little. It is happiness to her to serve her own children as an anonymous housekeeper in her former home. In this Louisa Atkinson seems to be stating the view that this could have happened to her own mother if she had been a timid and submissive character, that only very unusual women were not impotent when faced with exploitation by men of power and influence.

The executors put the estate in the hands of an incompetent manager in the foolish Englishman Tristam and bled it of its money and productiveness. When the children reach 21 there is an enormous deficiency in the accounts. Although the executors of the Atkinson estate were cleared of Charlotte Barton's charges of mismanagement, there are similarities in this situation to that of the Atkinson family. In *Tom Hellicar's Children* Ruth Hellicar says the actions of the executors divided 'her children and herself into two parties, antagonistic to each other', an accurate assessment of the legal battles of the Atkinson children's childhood.

Apart from the death of young Jack Hellicar, *Tom Hellicar's Children* ends happily with Richie Hellicar marrying Essie Thorell, the clergyman's younger daughter, and the young Ruth Hellicar escaping from a planned marriage to the elderly, scheming Max Ibotson.

In addition to its intriguing parallels with Louisa Atkinson's family background, the more superficial aspects of *Tom Hellicar's Children* had great appeal for readers at the time. The satirical treatment of the Tristam family, Jack Hellicar's adventurous life on outback stations and the portrayal of small town life with its solicitor's office, doctor and clergyman are all examples of Louisa Atkinson's ability to depict realistically the life with which so many readers could identify.

When he sent her cheque for the serialisation of *Tom Hellicar's Children* in the *Sydney Mail*, the proprietor John Fairfax wrote, 'The tale has been much admired'.[11] He sent £23 in payment, based on a length of 23 newspaper columns, each of 200 lines. This was a payment of a little over a penny a line, the usual rate of payment for casual contributors.

During the time she was nursing her mother, Louisa had her own dealings with lawyers—much less stressful than those of her mother—but indicating that she was not like Ruth Hellicar, a woman shielded from business affairs. She apparently had become concerned about the investment of her small inheritance and corresponded with her solicitors, Fitzhardinge Son and Houston, about changing her money from bank shares to real estate. She wrote on 29 July 1867 instructing them to buy two stone houses in Short Street, Darlinghurst for £410. Unable to leave Oldbury herself because of flood rains and 'all the other horrors of winter', she instructed her solicitors to check that the houses were sound, that the title was good and that they were likely to continue to be lettable at the current rents of 14/- and 9/- per week respectively. Simultaneously she instructed that her shares be sold. Later that day, however, after receiving the mail and reading the financial news in the newspapers, she wrote another hurried letter counter-manding these instructions as she had read that 'the share market is much depressed'. She 'would not wish to sell her shares at a sacrifice', she wrote. This letter arrived in time to stop the sale of her bank shares and the purchase of the houses. A few days later she wrote:

> Thank you for your prompt & kind attention to my wishes. Your advice certainly appears just—I am rather at a loss with regard to my affairs but in the present depressed state of the share market will do nothing—as I must sell now at a loss—as regards the City Bank and very small profit on the Joint Stock Bank.
>
> Whenever I go to Sydney, not likely for some little time as Mama continues a confirmed invalid—I will call on you and be glad of your advice before taking any other steps in the matter.[12]

Charlotte Barton died at Oldbury on 10 October 1867. She was 71 years old. Although on her death certificate she was described as Charlotte Barton, the document contained no information about the whereabouts of George Barton, or whether he was dead or alive. Charlotte was buried at All Saints' graveyard at Sutton Forest in the family vault, where her first husband, James, her daughter Emily and Emily's baby son, Henry Warren, were buried. Louisa and her brother James undoubtedly attended the burial. Whether her remaining child, Charlotte McNeilly, also attended is un-known. There is some evidence in the memory of descendants that towards the end of Charlotte Barton's life, there was renewed contact between mother and daughter. In her old age Charlotte McNeilly's eldest child Flora told her descendants of visiting Old-bury in her youth, describing to them various aspects of the house.[13]

By the time of Charlotte Barton's death Flora was already mar-ried. On 24 April 1866, at the age of just under eighteen, Flora Charlotte McNeilly, married, with her father's consent, George Garlick, a teamster of Penrith at St Nicholas's Catholic Church, Penrith. At the time of the marriage she was living with her parents at Nattai near the Fitzroy iron mines. The first child of her large family, Emily Susan, was born near Blayney on 1 March 1868.

At the time of the marriage of her eldest child, Charlotte Mc-Neilly's child-bearing years were not finally over. On 20 April 1867 just a few months before Charlotte Barton's death, she gave birth to her last child, a daughter named Henrietta. Soon after Charlotte Barton's death, Charlotte and Thomas McNeilly moved with their family to Orange. There, with her child-bearing years behind her

183

This pastoral scene at the Canobolas Mountains, near Orange, painted by Charlotte Elizabeth McNeilly, is similar in style to scenes at Oldbury painted by members of the Atkinson family. It shows the influence of John Glover, who taught their mother when she was a young woman in London. (Charlotte Drevermann)

and possibly feeling relief at the break from the associations of her childhood and youth, Charlotte McNeilly began to use the talents that had been submerged under the demands of domestic life for twenty years. For some years Charlotte McNeilly ran a private school at Orange in a building at the corner of Sale and Byng Streets. She wrote letters to Sir Henry Parkes advocating universal education and she wrote at least one letter to the press. This letter published in 1905, in which she claimed that her father was the pioneer importer of Saxon sheep, contained valuable family information. She is said to have written articles for newspapers but, unfortunately, none of this writing has been discovered.[14]

As a child Charlotte McNeilly had the family talent for painting and in her mature years she developed this. At least two of her paintings have survived, perhaps others remain to be discovered. An expert opinion of one of her watercolours, a pastoral scene on a farm near the Canobolas Mountains near Orange, was that it is in the style of John Glover, an opinion given before it was known that her mother had trained under Glover. How well she had

184

learnt from her mother![15] Her other known painting is a water-colour of Holy Trinity Church, Orange, which she painted in 1868, very soon after her arrival in Orange. In recent years this painting has been reproduced on postcards. The original was presented to the Church on 17 August 1959 by a descendant and hangs in the rectory.[16]

Charlotte McNeilly is also believed to have executed two paintings of the Lucknow Mines, situated about ten kilometres east of Orange, for which she was paid £25. The paintings were sent to London and Paris to encourage investors to invest in the Lucknow Gold Mine, which was developed on the site of the Wentworth Diggings. The paintings have not been located.

15

Mr Calvert has as kind thoughtful ways as a woman and I want for nothing

Following her mother's death in 1867 Louisa Atkinson remained at Oldbury with her brother for well over a year. She renewed her bush excursions with Emma Selkirk, indicating that she had regained some strength. However, she was still suffering breathing problems and 'heart attacks',[1] so there was clearly some cause for concern. As she gradually regained her strength, she began to resume some of her activities in writing and plant collecting and debated whether to ignore her mother's advice not to marry. It was probably during this time that she worked on her great plan for an illustrated book on Australian natural history to be published overseas.

By the beginning of 1869 she had decided to marry James Calvert, 44, of Cavan. The marriage took place at Oldbury on 11 March 1869, soon after Louisa's thirty-fifth birthday.[2] Rev. Thomas Horton and Rev. James Hassall married the couple and the witnesses were Louisa's brother James, Rev. Horton's daughter, Sarah Annie Horton, and Dorothea D'ayrele Hussey, who had recently arrived to join the Horton household as governess in a school run at the rectory.

After their marriage Louisa and James Calvert went to live for a time at Calvert's property, Cavan. Two months after their marriage, they returned for a visit to Oldbury. In a letter to her former maid, Mary Kelly, written on 8 May 1869,[3] advising her of their plan to visit the following week arriving after a two days' journey, Louisa also gave news of her health and of their plans for buying another property:

> Your affectionate letter gave me pleasure—particularly as you were better—Re the 17th of this month Mr Calvert and I go down to Oldbury which we shall reach on the 19 about 5 o'clock—Will you,

my dear go over to Oldbury in the course of this day and get my room ready and be prepared yourself to stay—certainly for about a week—I should like you not to enter into any engagement till I have seen you as I have a plan that I think will be agreeable to all parties.—We are going on to Windsor to see a nice property offered us for purchase and I mean to try and go by Train from Mossvale—so you will see am better—my breathing is very well now and I have never been delirious—but the heart attacks are rarely more than a week apart and sometimes very bad—still I am much stronger and able to walk about a little—I do not do much and keep myself very quiet and am well taken care of—Mr Calvert has as kind thoughtful little ways as a woman and I want for nothing...[4]

During the week the Calverts spent at Oldbury, Louisa's brother James, 37, married Wollongong-born Sarah Annie Horton, 28, a daughter of the Sutton Forest Minister Rev. Thomas Horton, at All Saints' Church, Sutton Forest on 24 May 1869. The witnesses were Charlotte Horton and Edward Bell.[5]

After her brother's marriage Louisa and James Calvert returned to Cavan to live for some time. They were there in the winter of 1869, as in an article published the following May, Louisa refers to the forbidding, although beautiful, winter scene at Cavan, so different from Kurrajong. While there she wrote two articles about the Cavan area which appeared in the *Sydney Morning Herald* in her series, discontinued for so long, 'A Voice From the Country'. She had lost none of her sure touch for writing in an interesting way, combining anecdotal material and information on the animals, birds, plants and the geology of the district with striking descriptions of the scenery. The following describes the ranges of hills and mountains stretching to the south, which she saw as she rode across the Yass plains during a snow storm:

Standing on the high hills overlooking the valley of the Murrumbidgee, there rises before the observer range above range. High as this one may be, a yet higher gleams in the sun's rays; while the more distant outline can hardly be determined among the mass of black clouds. There was an old fairy tale in our nursery, years ago, of certain fair damsels who set off through the world to seek their fortunes, and entered a region of mountains, up which they were ever toiling without gaining the top. The old tale often recurred to the memory when among these hills, which gradually ascend till they assume the title of Australian Alps. Once a snow storm broke over the range while we crossed the Yass plains. Black and heavy gathered the clouds reft aside by the fierce winter winds, while the snow surged about like columns, and before an hour the whole scene was white, only broken by the heavy purple patches of shade on the mountain sides. With the withering wind, laden by sleet, sweeping over the fine plains, and the Alpine scene in the background stretching right away to Maneroo—how striking the contrast to the semi-tropical valleys of the Blue Mountains! It was hard to believe the distance was, comparatively, short between them—the palm and the ice-field.[6]

At Cavan, she wrote of the scenery about her, the bare hills, the outcrops of limestone forming ridges that stretched like stone walls across the paddocks, and a curious arch formed in the river bank by the wear of the river into the cliff at the neighbouring property, Taemas. As a 'plant hunter' she was excited by the very different physical appearance of the countryside compared with either Kurrajong or Sutton Forest, because it meant that she might find different plant varieties. She was not disappointed, for among the banksias, bursarias, casuarinas, appletree, box, black wattle and hollow flooded gums, so huge that 'half-a-dozen people could take shelter from a passing storm',[7] she found some ferns. Among them were *Nothochlaena clistone* and *chielanthes*, *Asplenium flabellifolium* (necklace fern) and—the most interesting—*Asplenium trichomanoides* (common maidenhair) and *Pteris longifolia*. The latter was a great find, as von Mueller later acknowledged. 'The locality for *P. longifolia* will be a new one', he wrote.[8] Among plants familiar to her from other areas she found some clematis and some 'very vivid-blossomed Grevilleas', later identified by William Woolls as *G. phylicoides* and *G. mucronulata*.

She wrote of the animals and birds native to the area—rock possums which made their homes in the caves in the hills, the hydromys or water rats with webbed feet which attacked poultry, the 'pretty' *Ornithorhynchus* (platypus), the musk duck and the echidna. A friend brought her an echidna, the largest she had ever seen. Wanting to move it she found its spines, 50 to 60 millimetres long, made this impossible but 'stratagem succeeded':

> Introducing the points of the fingers as nearly to the roots of the spines as could be, I gently tickled the thorny ball. Presently the spines collapsed and fell prone, the whole muscular system relaxed, and by the hind feet the animal was easily lifted out.

This method soon became unnecessary as 'Jack' became a friend.

> Jack submitted to be lifted where I liked, to be carried in the arms, patted and caressed. When I approached it uttered a low sound, lifted its head, licked my finger, and was on the alert. Lifted on to the ground, Jack slowly walked about licking the dew drops from the grass on the surface of the ground. The long tongue left a slimy track like a slug behind it. After a little while, Jack would return to me, lay its hard beak-like snout on my foot a few seconds in a caressing manner, and then walk away again, never trying to escape.[9]

Ignoring ants, insects and worms. Jack lived on bread and milk and honey and bees from a beehive, but his unnatural diet was fatal, 'illness overwhelmed the poor creature, and it died, quite missed, so familiar and affectionate were its ways, its appearance so singular and interesting'.

Louisa Calvert's other article about Cavan described a visit to the banks of the Murrumbidgee at the boundary of the Taemas run with Cavan station. There, rising from a ledge above the river she found a shale bank, four to six metres high, covered in shells 'not in ones, or twos, but by bushels'. She imagined the ocean rolling over them in the long distant past as she collected shells like cockles, spirals, trochus and bivalves. 'What a revel it was in fossils!' she wrote, 'the hand bathed and buried in shells—the difficulty not where to find specimens, but where to select'. Since Louisa's visit this wall of fossils, named 'Shearsby's wallpaper' after Alfred James Shearsby (1872–1962), who spent many years studying the geology of the district, has become a well known geological feature. It is now protected by a cyclone wire fence to stop eager geology students from chipping away at the remaining fossils.

As she collected fossils of shells from the limestone ridges on Cavan station Louisa regretted her meagre knowledge of geology:

> it was only as a collector of curiosities, not as one acquainted with geology, that these strange remains were examined. Some day I hope to submit the specimens in my possession to the inspection of the Rev. W.B. Clarke, whose opinion past experience enables me to feel will be given with a cheerfulness doubling the obligation.[10]

This article, 'After Shells in the Limestone' brought a letter to the editor headed 'Palaeontology' from S.H. Wintle of Eastbourne. He queried her statement that some of the shells she had found were like 'the muddy trochus in form'. 'To speak of the trochus as a "muddy" shell-fish is irregular,' he wrote, 'its habitat being on rocks...' It is interesting that Wintle regarded the author of the article as male. His letter continued with further information and elucidation concluding, 'these remarks are made in no captious spirit; but, as one who as a searcher for scientific truth is desirous of dispelling any erroneous conclusions.'[11]

In a following article, Louisa thanked Wintle for his letter, but, as on other occasions when she replied to correspondents, she was not daunted by criticism when it was unjustified. 'The name "muddy Trochus" has no reference to the habits of the shellfish,' she wrote, '...but it is in allusion to the dull suit of red or purple with which it is striped'. She quoted from 'a work on conchology, which I possess' and from a book by English nature writer Anne Pratt, in which the author referred to 'that very common shell, the muddy-red Trochus [Trochus ziziphinus]...'[12]

Not all of this article was about fossils. Another section was about insects which attack trees, particularly the coccus, which was destroying the *E. eugenoides* (blue gum) in the county of Camden, and the destruction of so many forests by farming practices. What conservationist today, after more than a century of further destruction of trees, could write more feelingly than Louisa Atkinson did in 1870 on this subject?

> That various causes are killing the forests of New South Wales every traveller well knows. For some years past the black-butts and flooded gums in the vicinity of Berrima have been dying, until now the 'floss' or treeless watersheds of that district are bordered by belts of dead timber. Even the woolly butts are now perishing, while in many localities miles of forest have died—apart from artificial means or ring-barking—that the ultimate consequence will be of a nature materially to affect those districts there can be no doubt. The immediate effect is to render them marshy and unfit for sheep pasturage. It would seem that the forests have acted as safety valves to carry off the superfluous moisture of the earth, and attract that of the atmosphere, thus forming a circulating system. The minor vegetation is undergoing a considerable change. Rushes and aquatic plants present themselves in erstwhile dry regions. In time, there is much reason to fear this excessive humidity will give place to the reverse; and, like treeless countries, we shall suffer from an arid climate and soil. But our wide forests render such a catastrophe a misfortune in the distance. Yet it would seem advisable to plant suitable trees largely year by year; for, while the woodman's axe can fell the growth of a century in an hour, the forest springs up but slowly....
>
> Persons having rich soil, particularly valleys, not over the coast ranges to the interior, would do well to plant the red cedar. What better legacy could be left than a hundred acres of cedar trees? or walnut nuts, which in a few years would yield an interest on the outlay in the shape of the yearly crop of nuts for sale.[13]

Soon after she wrote these articles Louisa left Cavan with her husband and it is likely this was her last visit to the property with its 'bright green lucerne paddocks' and summit 'crowned by masses of broken rock, interspersed with veins of quartz'.[14] At the end of 1870 Calvert's partner at Cavan, J.F. Castle, after a 30-year association with education in Sydney, sold his school in Sydney to retire and live at Cavan until his death in 1883. His manager, Frederic W. Roche, married Castle's daughter, Eliza Grace, their surnames being combined. Cavan remained in the Castle Roche family until the main block with its imposing sandstone homes-

tead, built in the early 1900s, was sold to the international newspaper and media proprietor, Rupert Murdoch. He remains the
owner, the Castle Roche family retaining Cavan West.

Louisa and James Calvert's idea of buying a property at Windsor
came to nothing, and while waiting for a suitable property they
moved to the Oldbury estate to live. With James Atkinson and his
wife occupying Oldbury, the Calverts went to live at a cottage on
the other side of Mt Gingenbullen, previously occupied by the
Oldbury overseer. Known as Swanton, it was a small, sparse
cottage of four rooms near the junction of Whites Creek and Medway Rivulet. Their stay there was longer than they originally intended, as although they bought a property called Winstead at
Nattai, it required much work before they could move in. Nattai,
about thirteen kilometres from Berrima, was in the same area as
the town of New Sheffield, the Fitzroy mines and Mittagong. The
bewilderment of names 'being further increased by the neighbourhood being called Nattai', wrote Louisa.[15]

Swanton was similarly situated to the overseer's cottage Louisa
had described in *Gertrude*:

> [The] cottage stood upon a level, a little way up the range, where the
> creek made a detour, and a long deep pool of water lay immediately
> before and below it, an Eucalyptus, dull blue stemmed, with leaves
> almost black, towered considerably more than a hundred feet in
> height close by the building, and a few lesser ones stood at the back,
> otherwise the slope was clear, till a thick belt of wattles shut in the top
> of the range...
>   Though the walls of the cottage were wooden it was superior to the
> ordinary huts; the windows were glazed, the door painted, the floors
> boarded, and the walls white-washed. The furniture was perfectly
> plain; a square cedar table, a few chairs, a colonial couch, with cushions
> and palliass, a lock up book case, with pigeon holes for papers; these
> were all in the sitting room...[16]

Sparse and small as Swanton was, Louisa made it into a pleasant
temporary home, not least by growing flowers and plants around
it. An old photograph of Swanton shows a small porch adorned
with climbing plants. She advised her readers to adorn their homes
in this way, after passing a free selector's cottage, from which the
sound of a flutina came to her, as she rode to the Fitzroy waterfalls:

> A simple musical instrument, and a plot of flowers—neither costly—
> how great a pleasure and charm they throw over the rudest dwelling,
> and how many an heartache may be thus dispelled and interest

awakened. I have seen a rough slab hut rendered quite an object of beauty, by having the common scarlet geranium trained against its walls; while a few saplings made into a rustic porch above an entrance, and clustered over with roses, turns a hovel into 'quite a nice little place,' in the eyes of passers-by and to the residents strengthens home love, cheers and animates dull hours, and often keeps the husband and father away from the public-house; a better and happier man as he cultivates a few flowers and vegetables. Many a cottage wife has said to me, 'A bit of garden's such company,' and in that wholesome society she has escaped idling from house to house gossiping.[17]

Both Louisa and James Calvert were interested in the cultivation and use of native plants and animals and in innovative farming and grazing practices. In articles written at Kurrajong, Louisa had advocated the use of native plants for medicinal and culinary uses and James Calvert had won a medal at the London International Exhibition of 1862 for his entry on the possible commercial cultivation of native flax.[18] In an article deploring the disappearance through senseless shooting of wallabies, 'now a tradition, or nearly so', Louisa advocated farming native birds and animals. 'Had the same zeal been expended in domesticating the native bustard, scrub turkey, emu, &c, that has been in wantonly destroying them, the result would have been to the credit, and not the disgrace, of the persons so employed', she wrote.[19]

At Swanton, however, James Calvert turned not to the cultivation of native animals but to imported angora goats, becoming an enthusiast for their qualities in producing angora wool and meat. Initially his interest seems to have come from Ferdinand von Mueller, who had begun a zoo in a section of the Botanic Gardens in Melbourne. There he kept, in addition to kangaroos and koalas, some angora goats he had imported, hoping they would form the nucleus of a new Australian industry. However, when Calvert asked von Mueller for some angoras he was unable to send him any. He apologised in a letter to Louisa:

I hope Mr Calvert will not be angry with me, for not doing more for him regarding the Angoras, wished by him. But I am almost powerless in this matter, for altho' I am Senior Vice President of the Acclimatisation Society since its existence, and altho' I hold free trade principles at the broadest base, the majority of my colleagues on the Acclim. Council want to retain the Angoras in Victoria, a very large sum of money having been spent on them by our Society, to import them. I sent on my own impulse a pair to Sir Will Denison the Governor-General about 12 years ago (before the Society existed) and from that pair is the flock now so much increased under Mr Black's care in your colony.[20]

James Calvert obtained some angoras from Black's flock, which had increased from a pair to 1400, to begin his breeding and later was to write engagingly about their characteristics. Eventually von Mueller was able to prevail upon the Acclimatisation Society to send a buck to Calvert, 'a beautiful animal, five months old; his wool hangs in ringlets about five inches long, just clearing the ground'.[21]

During this residence at Swanton James Calvert became favourably known in the district. He occasionally sat on the bench as a magistrate and when an election was to be held for State Parliament he was asked to stand as a candidate for the seat.[22] He was described as 'one of my most attached parishioners' by the Rev. J.H.L. Zillmann, who was stationed at All Saints' Church, Sutton Forest, for a brief period. He described Louisa as Calvert's 'amiable and highly-cultured wife' and he found Calvert to be a modest hero.

> Though Mr Calvert had shared with Leichhardt the hardships and privations of crossing Australia from east to west [sic], I never heard one word of brag from him. He never seemed to indulge in those sanguine expectations, so long rife among many, of Leichhardt ever turning up again in the resorts of civilisation.[23]

Zillmann was probably mistaken in thinking Calvert had given up hope of some trace of Leichhardt being found.

One day, soon after the outbreak of the Franco-Prussian War in August 1870, Mr Zillmann, who was of Prussian descent, met the Calverts driving in their buggy on the Moss Vale road. He was pleased to find Calvert was a great supporter of the German cause. This was not surprising as both Louisa and James Calvert had associations with Germans and Germany. Calvert had maintained his admiration for Ludwig Leichhardt and both had a friend in Ferdinand von Mueller. Louisa had made the heroine of her first novel a girl partly of German descent and she herself had studied the German language. She also maintained a correspondence with Caroline Fliedner, widow of Dr Theodore Fliedner, an evangelical clergyman of Kaiserswerth, near Dusseldorf. He was involved in prison reform and the care of prisoners after release, and the establishment of hospitals, orphanages and mental asylums for the poor, both in Germany and in cities of Europe and Asia. Louisa Calvert's particular interest in Fliedner was as founder in 1833 of an institute of deaconesses who undertook the staffing of his charitable institutions. This movement became known to the extent that the *Sydney Morning Herald* published an editorial on the work of the deaconesses in Europe and Asia. Louisa Calvert followed this with an article entitled 'Prussian Deaconesses', in which she quoted translations of parts of Dr Fliedner's works which had been sent to her by his widow. She ended the lengthy article with her own comment:

> Such, briefly, are the labours and rules of the Kaiserswerth Deaconesses. Many other like institutes have been founded in other places, not as offshoots of the mother-house, but under the auspices of other founders; and this truly noble work of charity, love, and mercy is spreading far and wide.[24]

It is not surprising to find this manifestation of Christianity appealing to Louisa Calvert, as it was in accord with her own intensely practical view of religion.

At Swanton, happily married, Louisa Calvert's spirits and health revived and she entered a period of great creative activity. She made many journeys in the district around Oldbury writing about the natural features and the plants she found for a new series of 'A Voice From the Country' in the *Sydney Morning Herald* (not all were published under this title, some had only the title of the article, a few were under the heading 'The Tourist'). She used the influx of visitors to the district following the opening of the railway from Picton to Mittagong and Moss Vale in 1867 as the rationale for her articles. Following the opening of the railway, the Moss Vale, Mittagong, Berrima and Sutton Forest district had become very popular as a holiday resort. Its popularity gained vice-regal endorsement when the Governor, the Earl of Belmont, rented Throsby Park, near Moss Vale, as a summer residence. Later Hillview, near Sutton Forest, was purchased as a vice-regal residence. Many well-to-do Sydney residents began to visit the district, some building their own holiday homes. Louisa began her first article on local places of interest:

> Strangers visiting the country are frequently at a great loss for information regarding objects worth seeing. Fine points of view and places of interest are thus either not known of, or not found, and much of the pleasure derivable from a few weeks' sojourn in a district is lost. It is therefore proposed to offer a few sketches of some of the principal sights of the districts of Berrima, Nattai, Sutton Forest, and the Sassafras, as the season is approaching when many Sydney families will begin to look around them and decide where they shall spend a few weeks in the country during the heat of summer. To such as choose either of the foregoing localities, such notices may prove acceptable.[25]

In her article on the Fitzroy iron mines, she publicised the amenities of the Mittagong Railway station, a 'neat structure, in the usual style'.

Recently hot coffee and tea are supplied at a moderate rate to travellers here, and it proves a great comfort, particularly in these times of night trains; in a cool—often severely cold—climate a cup of hot coffee has a reviving effect, and was really needed. Bread and butter sandwiches, cakes, &c, are also obtainable at the refreshment room.[26]

In the same article she noted 'Mr Wallis's pleasant establishment for boarders'.

Her articles retained the uniqueness and charm which had been the strength of her previous series written from Kurrajong. In subject they ranged over the vegetation, comments on geology and natural history, reminiscences of olden days, comments on farming practices, and some gentle advice or thoughts on life. She continued to make great botanical finds and reported these in her columns. In one article she revealed that she had collected 24 species of terrestrial orchids in the vicinity of Berrima alone and that she expected the gullies of the Sassafras would yield many more.[27] On another expedition she found, near New Sheffield on the tramway used for the Fitzroy iron works, 'tufts of Erechites Atkinsonia, a Kurrajong old friend. Specimens sent thence to Dr von Mueller were pronounced new to science, and named by that gentleman in compliment to the finder'.[28]

As she had done at Kurrajong, she sent plant specimens to William Woolls and through him to Ferdinand von Mueller. Acknowledging one parcel on 17 November 1870, William Woolls wrote from Parramatta:

My dear friend
It was only this day that I received the parcel of specimens which you so kindly sent me. On the other side you will find a list of the names, but I am not at all sure of the *Callistris*.
Mrs Woolls sends her love & hopes you are well. . .[29]

He listed the botanical names of 21 plants, including rutaceous shrubs, boronia, myrtle, heaths and wattles. He listed the pine he was unsure of as *Callistris australis*.

When von Mueller received the specimens he wrote with great enthusiasm to Louisa as she had discovered several of the plants in places where they had never been found before.

Not very long ago, dear Madam, I got the select plants, which you kindly sent thro our good Mr Woolls to me, and of which I now furnish

the names. Several give us *new localities*, and these will be quoted with the name of the accomplished finder...
1. Anthocercis albicans All. Cunningham
12. Choretrum lateriflorum R.Br.
5. Calycothrix tetragona Labill.
21. Mirbelia reticulata Sm.
10. Leptospermum parvifolium Smith
6. Logania floribunda Br.
7. Eriostemon (Phebalium) lepidotus Sprengel
13. Leptomeria acerba Br.
2. Philotheca Australis Rudge
11. Ionidium filiforme F.v.M.
16. Styphelia (Leucopogon) virgata Labill. also 15.
17. Styphelia (Leucopogon) ericoides Labill.
14. Epacris paludosa R.Br.
19. Callistris (of the section Frenela) of which I should be glad to see the fruit (& flowers)
3. Boronia polygalifolia Sm. var. trifoliolata
4. Boronia anemonifolia A. Cunningh.
9. Kunzea capitata Reichenbach
8. Kunzea parvifolia Schauer.
20. Acacia elongata Sieb.
18. a variety of Prostanthera incisa Sieber.[30]

This is the only letter from von Mueller to Louisa that has been discovered, but it is evidently part of a continuing correspondence as in the rest of the letter von Mueller ranged over a number of subjects discussed between them previously. He told Louisa when all his 'anxieties will have passed', he intended to work on grasses and rushes for Volume 6 of *Flora Australiensis* asking, 'If you could favour me with any of these plants, particularly rushes and serges, from your thus far unknown locality, you would be certain to add again to the material for the work'. He also asked her for seeds of *Atkinsonia ligustrina*, the parasitic shrub she had discovered and which von Mueller had named after her in his *Fragmenta* published in 1865, to send to Dr J.D. Hooker, Director of the Royal Botanic Gardens at Kew.

> Dr Hooker always asks me to send him seeds of Loranthaceae for cultivation at Kew. If you should pass the Atkinsonia in fruit at any time, pray bear kindly his request in remembrans [sic]. I believe that this beautiful & remarkable plant could be propagated from cuttings under a bill glass, if it were at Kew.
> With gratitude & best regards for you & Mr Calvert
> Ferd. von Mueller.

In a postscript to his letter is the first mention of the book Louisa had written and illustrated over the previous years on Australian

This is one of the illustrations prepared by Louisa Atkinson for her book on Australian birds and animals. (Mitchell Library, State Library of NSW. Calvert Sketches)

plants and animals. When she had completed this work, she sent the text and portfolio of illustrations to von Mueller, who had undertaken to have it published in Germany. He sent the material first to Karl August Moebius (1825–1908), a German zoologist. He also sent it to Dr Christian Ferdinand Friedrich von Krauss (1812–1890), a German botanist and zoologist, who had been employed at the Natural History Museum in Stuttgart from 1840.[31] Von Mueller wrote:

> The war has upset allmost all scientific literary work in Germany or at least brought it for a time to a stand still. So Prof. Moebius tells me by last mail. But your fine drawings are all safe and will probably be sent to Prof. Krauss in Stuttgart (a special friend of mine) for the Royal Museum there with a view of literary utilisation at the first favourable opportunity.[32]

Plate 6. *Aprosmictus kapulatus*

The illustrations of birds in this chapter are some of those which Louisa Atkinson prepared for a book on Australian birds and animals to be published in Germany.

Trichoglossus Swainsonii

In 1870 Baron Ferdinand von Mueller told Louisa publication had been delayed by the Franco-Prussian War. (Mitchell Library, State Library of NSW)

Plate 15 (Mitchell Library, State Library of NSW. Calvert Sketches)

Plate 22 (Mitchell Library, State Library of NSW. Calvert Sketches)

Had Louisa Atkinson lived and the book been published, it would have brought her international fame. Its chequered pre-publication history is evident from von Mueller's postscript, and from subsequent events. Unfortunately the project was to sink into oblivion following her death. Inquiries to the universities of Kiel and Stuttgart have not been successful in establishing what happened to this material. Some plates, presumably duplicates of ones sent overseas for this publication, are located among Louisa's manuscript material.

Although she regarded herself simply as a plant collector not a botanist, Louisa was confident enough of her own knowledge to query the work of botanists, including, on one occasion, 'that eminent botanist' Allan Cunningham. He and other botanists, she wrote, believed that *'Quintinis Sieberii'* grew only in the caudex of the tree fern or if in the ground that it had got there by its weight tearing away its fibrous roothold.

More recent botanists have repeated this opinion; but my own experience, as a plant-collector, leads me to form a different opinion, although it is very frequently found springing from the trunk of the tree fern, or as a parasite on rocks. The specimen seen at the Hanging Rock must have been miles from tree ferns, and in a position particularly barren and arid—in fact the last place where such a moisture-loving tree would be looked for.[33]

Apart from botanical discoveries, her articles contained much other interesting information. Some old stories reappeared. In 'The Fitzroy Waterfalls' there was the story of the two sawyers, originally told in 'Recollections of the Aborigines'. There was also the one about her father, lost in the Shoalhaven gorges, being saved from starvation by being fed on honey by his Aboriginal guide, Jim Vaughan, originally told in 'Incidents of Australian Travel'. She expressed again her sadness at the passing of the Aborigines.

Even then Jim Vaughan was a very old man. He could remember seeing the French ships off the mouth of the Shoalhaven River, and the terrible destruction among the native tribes by smallpox...

Poor creatures! with their sins and good qualities; friendships and hatreds, so quickly to have passed away! We may spare their memories a few minutes...[34]

There were echoes of the lawless days of Lynch and other bushranger gangs in several articles. In 'Hanging Rock on the Southern Road', she wrote:

The rock is seen to better advantage from the intervening trees having been felled in the days of the bushrangers, so that travellers might

have, at least, the satisfaction of seeing their foes before falling into
their power.
This was the watchtower of the bushrangers.[35]

In another article, she described a place, later part of the Cataract
coal mine, where bushrangers had lived. They had excavated a
coal seam about six metres above the floor of a natural cave on the
Medway River and secured it with a breastwork of stones.

> This was the residence of bushrangers years ago, and a most out of the
> way and safe retreat. However, they were captured, and though one
> would wonder how, as seated behind their rude fortifications they
> must have commanded the whole vale, and had the police in their
> power. It would seem that the smoke from their fire was detected, and
> their retreat thus discovered, while their very security had perhaps
> made them careless, or treachery may have assisted.[36]

'Climatic Influences on the Habits of Birds' is a particularly
interesting article as it gives the most information that is available
on Louisa's dissection of birds and animals. Referring to the
strange birds she observed in the Sutton Forest district, forced
there by the drought in 1869, she wrote of dissecting the 'darter of
the far North':

> Perched upon a tree above the water or floating on its surface, we
> found this awkward bird on the watch for fish, or frogs, the long
> slender neck protruded, the short tail spread, and the striped black and
> white plumage glittering in the sun. In two specimens which I have
> examined there were no nostrils. A long slit in the roof of the mouth
> communicates with the windpipe, and it may be that the bird, when
> diving, inflates the pouch beneath the lower mandible and can remain
> under water until this receptacle is exhausted. The first specimen
> examined was brought from the Balonne River, Queensland. They have
> been met with in the Flinders, and the Northern waters appear their
> proper *habitat*.[37]

She also dissected pelicans she found in the fresh water streams
near Berrima, not the species she had observed at St George's
Basin and Jervis Bay, but those of the Queensland Gulf country:

> Dissection proved the fitness of these birds for lengthy and continuous
> flight. Not only were the lungs and the air sacs large, and the bones
> marrowless, but the portions of the body, as the breast, which looked
> like flesh, when cut open, consisted of a mass of air sacs arranged like
> cells, and separated only by their membranes.[38]

She also described a bird brought to the neighbourhood during a
drought in April 1868, quoting from notes she had made at the
time she had examined it. Her description was very detailed: 'Eight

inches from top of head to point of bill; gape, two inches...', and ending, 'The specimen was a female. The stomach was filled with the remains of fish and beetles'.[39] As she did not find the bird in Gould's *Birds of Australia*, she believed it to be uncommon. In this article she also wrote of the absence or the falling away in numbers of many birds which had formerly visited the district in large flocks. She attributed this less to climatic influences than to 'the extensive killing of the forests', as the birds were mainly honey eaters. She noted the opposite phenomenon on the day following the wreck of the clipper *Walter Hood* on the New South Wales south coast,[40] 'a number of gulls alighted on the Medway— messengers of the fatal storm that had broken on the coast'.

There were delightful stories of the taming of native birds and animals 'even when fully grown' and the strong attachment they developed for their carers.

> So strong is this power of attachment in the kangaroo, for instance, that I have known a hand-reared and partly grown one fret to death during the temporary absence of the person who reared it, even though surrounded by other kind friends.[41]

She gave some hints on a suitable diet for wild birds and animals reared in a domestic environment—'as simple as possible'—and a warning 'never to give way to pettishness; one blow will sever the golden cord of confidence and be remembered as long as the little creature lives'.[42]

Without quoting more extensively, it is difficult to convey the range of information and anecdotes and the charm of presentation in her writing. It is matter for regret that at the time she had material published in the *Sydney Morning Herald* and the *Sydney Mail*, neither paper published illustrations. From the number of her illustrations and drawings that have survived it seems obvious that she instinctively illustrated her writing. Apart from some plates she prepared for her book on animals and plants to be published in Europe, she also prepared a portfolio of drawings of ferns intended to illustrate a publication on Australian ferns. Some other drawings that survive can be related to specific articles.

16

We will be most happy to see you and Mr Calvert

Early in March 1871 Louisa and James Calvert set out from Swanton on a journey south to the Monaro. With them in the wagon was an angora goat, a 'handsome pure buck', which Calvert was taking as a present to his friend Maurice Harnett at Rosebrook station, near Cooma.[1] It was a strenuous trip, 'days of bad roads' and 'nights at inferior inns', but they covered about 80 kilometres each day. Louisa described the trip in two articles, 'A Trip Southward' and 'A Trip to the Southward—Manaro, Molonglo, and the New Road', published in the *Sydney Morning Herald*.[2] Skirting Goulburn, which they glimpsed from Governor's Hill, they turned south travelling through Tarago to Boro, 'a tempting field for the naturalist'. The next day they drove over the Boro hills and descended to Deep Creek near Bungendore, where recent rains 'had reduced the Bungendore lane to a series of lagoons, filled with an ink-like fluid and mud'. But they had good horses, Calvert was a competent and 'cool' driver, and they got through safely. Beyond Queanbeyan Louisa discovered 'a Casuarina new to me' which she was later to discuss in letters to William Woolls and Ferdinand von Mueller.

Although she was to make some interesting botanical discoveries during the journey, the bare landscapes, stark hills and sparse settlement were alien to her. Throughout her articles she remarked on the absence of people and the widely separated farms. 'A great absence of life marked the greatest portion of the day's journey. Birds were few and excepting sheep, and their guardian men and dogs, we saw no animal life', she wrote.

Passing through Micalago station beyond the Burra Valley, with the Tinderry Mountains to the east, she wrote, '...anything more unlike the scenery about Sydney could not well be imagined. Bold grassy plains swelling away for miles, high abrupt mountains, lesser ranges dotted with trees, and scrubless; and here and there a homestead'.

As she travelled she used her copy of *Researches in the Southern Gold Fields of New South Wales*, written by her friend Rev. William B. Clarke,[3] as a guide. When she spoke to people of 'our valued and learned friend' twenty years after Clarke had made his trip, she was delighted 'to see the kindling eye and smile of kindly remembrances on many a face'.

After crossing the Bredbo River the Calverts reached their journey's end at the Numeralla River north of Cooma. Louisa remarked of the trip, 'Sheep-runs do not furnish a promising field for the botanical collector', but she was pleased to find some ferns, several plants of the ranunculus family and 'a *zieria* with a delightful perfume'.

Although she did not mention it in her article, the reason for the journey was to visit Maurice Harnett at Rosebrook, a large sheep and cattle property of over 6000 hectares, north of Cooma. Harnett like Calvert was an enthusiastic breeder of angora goats. His flock was descended from the first to be imported into New South Wales by Edward Riley of Raby, near Liverpool, but through inbreeding and the cold winter climate of the Monaro had lost the capacity to grow more than a thin coat of wool. Calvert presented Harnett with the buck he had brought, known as 'Little Hunter', and in return received a few does.[4] Apart from their interest in breeding angora goats, Harnett and Calvert were acquainted through Calvert's former partner J.F. Castle as several members of the Harnett family had attended Castle's school, Calder House.[5] Maurice Harnett had taken over Rosebrook after his father's death and in 1861 married Mary Ann (Minnie) Hensleigh. At the time the Calverts visited them, Minnie and Maurice Harnett had three children, Ernest, Sidney and Catherine.[6]

While at Rosebrook Louisa drew the homestead and when she returned home sent the sketches to Minnie Harnett. It is regrettable that these sketches have not been traced. Minnie Harnett later wrote to Louisa from Rosebrook:

My dear Mrs Calvert
...it was so good of you to send the sketches so soon, they are so nicely colored too, and are the admiration of many of our friends, especially Mr Dawson[7] who is an *artist* and of course understands when a drawing is properly done—I wish I could sketch as well. Mr Harnett intends having them framed as soon as possible.[8]
...'Little Hunter' as the children call him, is doing remarkably well, he has grown a good deal and appears very happy and contented in

the little paddock with the other goat, and the emus and kangaroos.

We were glad to hear that our little goats are doing so well and have become so quiet and tame.

Tell Mr Calvert we read his letter in the Herald about the goats with very great interest.

[Mr Harnett] and Mr Harkness are at present away on a trip, up the country, and I don't expect my husband home before Friday so we are almost quite alone only my sister & nephew, besides the children in the house. I do dislike Mr Harnett being absent from home so much as the house is so dull without him. I think you will succeed in getting the proper name of 'Our Little Orange Plant'.

If you intend visiting Gippsland next Spring; remember we will be most happy to see you and Mr Calvert on your trip. Come and stay with us as long as ever you can spare the time.

Make my kind regards to Mr Calvert & again thanking you most sincerely for the sketches of Rosebrook.[9]

When she returned home Louisa sent specimens of the plants she had found on this trip and around the Sutton Forest district to William Woolls and to Baron von Mueller. They included the 'interesting *Zieria*' from north of Cooma, a small orchid she had found near Berrima and seeds of the *Casuarina* from south of Queanbeyan. Louisa's find of the *Zieria* appears to be the first time this plant had been discovered on the Monaro. Woolls wrote to her:

> Your pretty little Rutaceous shrub is 'Zieria cytisoides', which Dr F. von Mueller proposed to regard as a variety of *Z. Smithii* (See his 'Plants Indigenous to the Colony of Victoria.' p. 229) but, subsequently, he must have altered his opinion, as it is described as a distinct species in the *Flora Australiensis* Vol. 1. p. 306.[10] Some years ago, I found it near Bent's Basin, but strange to say, I never succeeded in getting a second specimen. The flowers are generally white, but yours seems pinkish...
>
> I dare say your *Casuarina* is interesting. We have only three here, and there is a fourth very common on the banks of the Nepean. A small stunted variety of Swamp Oak grows near the Coast. Mrs Woolls sends her best love, and with our united kind regards to Mr Calvert.

William Woolls' letter continued with news of the crisis in von Mueller's professional career caused by a Commission of Inquiry into whether the two positions he held, as Director of the Botanic Gardens and Government Botanist, should be separated. 'I expect he will either retire, or get into a bad state of health, if the decision should be opposed to his views', Woolls wrote.[11]

A few days later Woolls wrote again, excited that the orchid Louisa had discovered near Berrima had been a very important find, being the first sighting of the plant since George Caley had discovered it early in the century:

> Your specimens arrived safely in Melbourne, and the Dr says he will write to you. The orchid turns out to be *Lyperanthus ellipticus* which no one has found since the days of Caley!! Could you favour me with a specimen or another drawing of it, for I forwarded both to Melbourne? The Dr is still annoyed by the Govt. Commission but I hope he will come out victorious. You will be pleased to hear the University of Gottingen has conferred on me the degrees of Ph.D. and M.L.A. I have not as yet received the diploma, but I expect to do so by the next mail.
>
> Mrs Woolls sends her best love, and with kind regards to Mr Calvert.[12]

Louisa wrote independently to von Mueller, enclosing seeds of the *Casuarina stricta* and some of the grasses and rushes he had asked her to collect for the next volume of the *Flora Australiensis*. It is an interesting letter, showing the professional way she approached the recording of her observations and the collecting of seeds and plants:

> Dear Dr Von Mueller
> During the 3rd week of May I forwarded a parcel of specimens to Dr Woolls which I hope have long since reached you—They were chiefly Ruses [rushes], Reeds and grasses—The enclosed seeds are Oaks No 1. from the dry sandy ranges above Queanbeyan towards Manero No 2 from the mountain Brook which takes its source in the lower spurs of the Alps—a cold locality. The oaks there exceed any swamp oaks I have seen elsewhere in height & girth—say 100 to 150 high and 12 feet circumference. They are luxuriant trees with the habit of growth of the Pines of Norway.
>
> No 1. is a tree about 20 feet high and 1 foot in diameter with drooping long foliage giving a soft round appearance to the tree—I send a rough outline of the general appearance of the trees—The seed vessels of this one are very large, I sent specimens in the parcel of plants forwarded in May. The wing when moistened becomes viscid and floats in water like threads but not further soluble—it has a slight resinous tast[e]—I had a number of young growing trees but the mice gnaw them wherever planted and destroy them—I am surprised to hear from Dr Woolls that he is only acquainted with 3 species of Casuarina I know of 6 if not seven and will endeavour to forward you specimens of all—No 3 is the seed of our common Forest oak—a round topped dull green tree found on ranges not so ornimental [sic] as No 1. The sketch of seed vessels may enable you to determine the species. The thread like foliage of No 1 is fully twice as thick as that of No 3 and twice as large—color a soft yellow green—Even from a distance a distinct tree—Did Mr Woolls ever send you the cone of a Pine from Mt Tomah? I only had the one I gave him.

My husband desires [me to send you] his kindest regards—he has received the 3 goats safe and well and is much pleased with them.[13]

Because of his association with the geology of the Monaro Rev. William Branwhite Clarke also received a letter from Louisa about the trip:

We have lately been to Maneroo, just a hurried trip, but very interesting to me and since our return I have been going through your Southern Goldfields with new interest.

At Codrington—the little plain beyond a deep creek probably Ryans, and before you cross Bredbo they have been digging copper in the mountains for 12 months, but some delay has occurred and the works are forsaken—we saw some specimens of that brassy looking one, green and blue copper.

A new road has been made from Tarago to the Deep Creek near Bungendore in a cutting. I observed that green earth-like substance which I sent you from Oldbury—Iron I think you told me.

There was no time on our journey to look for fossils or any of my hobby horses but it was very pleasant and we had fine weather.—The drawback was bad roads—still we travelled about 50 miles a day—my husband driving a pair of ponies in the waggon—There is really nothing to interest you worth troubling you with a letter for, only you and your valuable labours seem to be so connected with the whole district that it seems you have a right to know we had been there.

My husband joins in affectionate remembrances.[14]

At Swanton James Calvert continued breeding angora goats, which he believed had a great future. In a long letter published in the *Sydney Morning Herald* he gave details of his breeding programme, including the crossing of Tibetan and angora goats. He expressed enthusiasm about their wool yield and their possible use as meat and for boiling down as tallow. He defended them as quiet animals, painting a delightful picture of their qualities. His were anything but 'troublesome', he wrote, 'they are quiet, and very affectionate things'.

If one gets at all unwell it will stay about the house, and know a stranger immediately it sees one, at a considerable distance. Also, they are very curious; if I put up any additions to their house, a little pigstye, or anything of that kind, when they come home at night all of them will go and examine it, making a sharp, short, clear noise, sounds like puff, puff.[15]

He said he intended to offer his small clip for the season for sale at a Sydney auction room.

Louisa received some letters from old friends at Kurrajong. Mrs Comrie, the wife of James Comrie, of Northfield on Tabarag Ridge, in a very long letter gave her news of her friends in the district and referred to a recent series of articles on 'Windsor, Richmond, the two Kurrajongs and Mount Tomah' published in the *Town and Country Journal* by a writer called Winter.[16] She thought the articles were not badly written although 'the writer was so intensely charmed with the Kurrajong that his description was of the "coleur de rose" tint'. Mrs Comrie continued:

> We were sorry Mr Calvert had been such a sufferer & sincerely hope that his health is by this time restored. Sciatica, and rheumatism, or lumbago, are all most severe and unwelcome pains.
>
> The unusually moist state of the atmosphere for the greater part of the last 15 to 16 months has been sufficient of itself to account for these complaints and then I imagine that in his bush explorations etc. your husband has been often exposed to extremes of temperature. With domestic comforts around him now, there is every reason to hope for a favourable change.
>
> No doubt you have felt a sort of pleasure in repaying him in some measure for his care of you when you were so delicate. From no allusion being made to your own state of health, we draw the inference that you are stronger and trust that we have arrived at the right solution. We followed the little journeys described by 'L.C.' it was a pity that your time was so limited. I have also been reading every chapter of 'Tom Hellicar's Children' & just as I was getting curious to know the finale Chris left us & his 'Mail' is now sent to his new address. The fact of your writing these various articles goes to prove that you are not ill...
>
> I should like to see your pretty silky goats—we have noticed the articles in the papers respecting the rearing of the Angoras—I trust that Mr Calvert may succeed.
>
> Your little nephew[17] must be a source of great interest to you all. I am glad that he is a healthy child...Mrs Selkirk has not been on the Kurrajong since Charlotte's marriage[18] her home ties are many & urgent.[19]

Ominously Mrs Comrie's letter contained news of the deaths of several women and children, including that of Mrs William Lamrock following a difficult birth, and three young children in families known to Louisa.

Louisa also had a letter from her great friend Mrs Emma Selkirk, addressed to 'My dearest Dianella'. Emma Selkirk, accompanied by her son Henry and probably other children had visited Louisa at Oldbury on at least one occasion. However, the demands on her time were great with the care of her four children, Henry aged 14, Mary, 12, William, 9, and Robert, 6 in addition to older step-children. Apart from the words of a poem Emma Selkirk wrote about her friend, this letter is the only evidence remaining of the close friendship between these two women who shared such an enthusiasm for collecting plants.

I have heard your voice and heard of your 'being in the field again'—finding some orchid and doing other great things and I have done wonders—out done you and myself too for I have discovered—and brought some in triumph from quite close at home a veritable root of Gyrunogruman rutifolia, now is that not 'interesting', seeing it does not occur in Cumberland—I have got it and can produce it and it has put out three interesting little fronds since I got it. Harry[20] assures me that it grows under the terrace, that the rocks there resemble [those at?] the native dog caves—he & I are going there some day to look. It is years since he was there—but as soon as he saw my specimen he recognized it and remembered what we found in your dog caves—moreover I found a young vespertitionis! some young staghorns!! some dicksonias!!! and—nothing else in particular—talk of the Kurrajong it's easy to get ferns *there* no merit at all—bringing in a cartload but to find them here! [Richmond]—no wonder we come home in triumph even though our treasures are only 2 inches high—everyone says the Hills are so *unusually* lovely—happy they who get there I have not been up since December/69 and only for three days then after a year's absence—Mr Comrie is improving Northfield greatly we hear—planting tree ferns and oaks and doing great things . . . the children are all well—they are all growing up fast just now [but are] pigmies beside their great cousins—Alice Elder seven months older than my May who is just 12 is taller than myself and actually in effect a woman. Frank is taller than his father and has not a bit of stamina. It is alarming to see how these colonials grow up, don't fly at me please for using that word. You are no more colonial yourself than my children are who have both parents English—no but colonial [range high?] really as you used to do.

Now my dear Dianella—do please write to me & let me know from yourself that you are alive—& if you care to give me any hope from Germany—do

Hoping Mr Calvert is well
I am
With very much love
Affectionately yours
Emma Selkirk[21]

At about the time of the arrival of these letters Louisa Atkinson would have become aware that she was pregnant. She was 37, and with her history of frail health her pregnancy must have caused some foreboding to herself and her husband. Her botanical expeditions, no doubt, were suspended as she endeavoured to live a quiet life waiting for the birth of her child. Whether ill or well, however, her energy was always remarkable and it is impossible to imagine her idle. It is likely that she spent the latter part of 1871 writing her last novel, *Tressa's Resolve*, a long story encompassing three almost separate strands serialised in the *Sydney Mail* the following year.[22]

In her previous novels Louisa Atkinson had called on her family background, her own experiences and, particularly in *Tom Hellicar's Children*, her mother's epic struggles against lawyers and executors. In *Tressa's Resolve* for a part of the story set in the remote Queensland Gulf country she appears to have drawn on her husband's and her brother's experiences. There is no evidence that Louisa ever visited Queensland, although, as she took trips by sea to Wollongong and the Hunter, there is no reason why she might not also have visited coastal Queensland, at least. But while she loved travelling, it seems most improbable that she would have undertaken a journey over the vast distances of the Queensland interior. She had several sources of information on Queensland. Several times in her nature articles she mentions receiving specimens from a correspondent at the Balonne River in Queensland and there is a reference to the Burdekin River in 'Among the Murrumbidgee Limestones'.[23] Despite these references and the very vivid descriptions in *Tressa's Resolve*, there seems no doubt that her descriptions of the Queensland outback are based on her husband's recollections of the merciless nature of the country. She also had more recent information available from her brother's stories of his overlanding journey to the Flinders River in the Gulf country during the 1860s, twenty years after James Calvert had been there.

The Queensland strand of *Tressa's Resolve* develops with the arrival of Bessie Shelburne, a governess from England, to join her sister Tressa in Sydney. On board she had met the well-off Ross family who had been travelling overseas for two years in an effort to get their daughter, Adeline, to forget her suitor, Andrew Murray, a squatter in the remote Flinders River district in the Gulf of Carpentaria. When Murray meets them at the wharf, however, the family agrees to Adeline's marriage provided a female friend goes with her as, 'One of the great trials to women on these remote stations is that they are utterly out of the reach of womanly society or aid—ill or well they must look only to help from the men around them...'[24] Bessie Shelburne accompanies Adeline.

As they set out for Murray's station, the magnitude of the difficulties ahead of them gradually becomes apparent. Travelling north-west across Queensland from the port of Bowen and while still four days' ride from Murray's station they notice that the rivers are drying up. When they reach the station homestead, Adeline is shocked to find it consists of two rooms built from unhewn stone

211

interspersed with layers of mud. Not only is the accommodation primitive in the extreme, it is obvious that the station is badly run down. The wool on the sheep is matted by grass seeds, the clip is ruined by the delay in shearing during Murray's absence and the shearing team threatens violence if not paid extra to shear.

Adeline and Bessie have to exist on mutton, ration flour, milk-less tea and bad water. There is no water to wash their meagre supply of clothes, most having been left behind in their trunks at Bowen to be brought overland in the returning wool drays. In these conditions, Adeline's health declines rapidly. She becomes feverish and delirious and Andrew Murray becomes so despondent he is incapable of taking any decisions.

Bessie, one of the archetypal practical women of Louisa Atkinson's novels, takes charge of the situation. She decides that the 'offensive mud' they are drinking is killing Adeline and that they must travel in the relative cool of the night to reach fresh water at the next station, several days' ride away on the Plains of Promise.

'Do let us try,' pleaded Bessie.
Mr Murray looked wan with red, wild eyes, like a man who was suffering much.
'There is no water by the way,'
'Nor here; I feel certain this offensive mud we are using is poisoning her. If we travelled by night, and rested her under the scrub by day, we might yet reach water.'
'It would be best', he faltered. 'Do what you think well; I have no energy.'
'Go down to the lagoon and dig several little wells, at least six, and I will collect what water drains in, boil, and bottle it; and to-night we will start.' She spoke with some energy—it was needful; her companion looked fever-struck—he, too, might soon be past moving. They had delayed too long waiting his decision, she must now take command.[25]

Bessie fries a supply of lean, tough mutton, mixes a damper to cook on the hearth and walks to the lagoon with a bucket and pail to save any more water that may have leaked into the containers in the extreme heat. As they leave Bessie looks around at the 'Wide plains on all sides—dry, brown, grassless; everywhere the flickering air, now like a wide lake, dancing in the amber light'. In the distance whirlwinds dance in columns 'like weird spirits doomed to do penance for ever upon those arid tracks'.[26]

With Bessie in charge the three set off in the buggy, Adeline lying on a mattress in the back. They travel at night, directing their course by the planets 'over that pathless sand-ocean'. When they rest Bessie removes the canvas to get air to Adeline, continually fanning away mosquitoes and whispering words from the Bible, which she finds particularly rich in allusions to deserts.

In the distance they observe a fire where Aborigines had fired grass to windward. They have to harness up and continue through the suffocating smoke in an effort to get across the dry bed of a distant river, to form a barrier between them and the fire. At last they reach it and cross to the other side, where they make camp. Murray tries unsuccessfully to get water from the dry river bed and they have to share their little remaining water with the horses.

The travelling is in vain as the next day Adeline dies and Murray, mad with grief, is incapable of action. As they are completely without water, Bessie decides that they must press on, carrying Adeline's body in the buggy. Eventually they reach Sampsons' station, where there is water and a few cattle. The housekeeper looks after Bessie while she waits to get to Bowen to travel by ship to Sydney.

There is a happy ending to Bessie's epic of endurance and command. Although she returns to Sydney a shadow of her former self, she is soon cheered by the arrival of her suitor, Dr John Rosslyn. The Ross family show their appreciation for the help she gave to Adeline by recommending patients to Dr Rosslyn. He gradually builds up a practice in Sydney, enabling Bessie to look forward to the possibility of marriage within a year.

Louisa seems to have introduced this strand of the story because she wanted to convey to readers the dreadful sufferings that her husband and other explorers and pioneers had endured when they crossed the outback regions. That the one person who manages to overcome the daunting situation of illness, thirst, death and madness is a woman accords with the view evident in most of Louisa's previous novels, that women were the strong sex. Their inner resources, not least their religious faith, enable them to cope with crises and to remain steady and practical in adversity. Observing her mother's reaction to adversity during her childhood had an effect on Louisa which is obvious throughout her novels, but never more so than in Bessie's story.

The central figure in *Tressa's Resolve* is Tressa Shelburne, who is brought to Sydney by her wealthy aunt, Sarah Love, to live at Highlands, her mansion home overlooking Sydney Harbour. Tressa's role is to be a companion and to act as a buffer between Sarah Love and her relations in Sydney, whom she believes to have designs on her money. In England Tressa, the daughter of a painter who had died of consumption, had been a poorly paid under-teacher in a school. Tressa also has consumption, her cough, which she believed she had caught 'sitting in the cold music-room hearing the girls practise their pieces ready for the master', causing great concern after her arrival in Sydney.

The story of Tressa Shelburne takes place entirely in Sydney, particularly around the harbour. There are descriptions of ships sailing into port and departing, of rowing around Woolloomooloo Bay, of marine dealers' stores near the waterfront, and the waterfront itself. Train trips to Burwood and to Richmond, shopping in the city, and the operation of a women's refuge are woven into an involved story in which Tressa's other relatives, the Tinsley family, try to extract money from Sarah Love. Elizabeth Tinsley, Sarah Love's sister-in-law, has raised her family of two sons and three daughters in the constant expectation that they would soon inherit great wealth from their aunt. With these great expectations none of the children is trained for an occuption and all lead indolent lives, being supported by their mother, who runs a school for young ladies.

Early in the story Tressa is invited to the Tinsley home to meet her cousins. The gathering is held in a very small upstairs drawing room 'where much crochet eked out a want of furniture' and where the Tinsley family display 'little meannesses which are part of the daily life of those whose life is pretension'.[27] Their attempts at inveigling money from Sarah Love are recounted at first in an almost lighthearted way but it is soon obvious that one of the Tinsley sons, Gustavus, is in very deep trouble. Having embezzled money from his aunt to induce a suitor, Frank Fosbrook, to marry his sister Marion, Gustavus gambles at billiard saloons and gaming houses in a vain attempt to cover the cheque he has forged. He attends the wedding of his sister then walks through the dark city streets to the water's edge and next morning is found drowned.

Writing of Gustavus' mother, Louisa Atkinson said, 'Had she trained him to fear God, and pursue a life of honest industry, would she now be comparing [?contemplating] the pallid limbs of her firstborn son, hardly yet twenty-one?' The Fosbrooks are recalled from their honeymoon in Richmond to their cottage at Balmain. Fosbrook is no consolation to the bereaved family, being 'one of those men to whom anything of notoriety, and newspapers, and police, appear particularly galling; there was a disgrace to him in having a brother-in-law fished up out of oozy wharf mud, and examined by coroner and jury'.[28]

With Gustavus' suicide and Marion's unhappy marriage, the Tinsley family's pursuit of wealth is shown to have tragic results. There is part redemption for the family when the younger son, George, decides that 'the ruin of us all has been thinking we had fine prospects'. He takes a labouring job, starting at six in the morning, to Fosbrook's horror dressed in 'workman's dress', while he studies at night. After demonstrating his good intentions he is financed by his aunt to become a building contractor.

The third strand of the story involves the heroine, Tressa, and her cousion Tyrell Love. Like many others at the time, Tyrell deserts his former calling—as mate on a ship trading in the South Seas—and sets out with a rolled blue blanket, a quart pot and a tin pannikan hung from his waistband to select a block of land in the bush under the recently passed Act allowing free selection. Eventually he arrives at a picturesque valley with huge trees, creepers and tree ferns. Too inexperienced to realise the problems of clearing, he puts a deposit on 16 hectares at the Land Office and laboriously starts felling the huge trees singlehanded. His neighour warns him there is only 'work and ruin' ahead. Eventually Tyrell forfeits his selection and moves further out, but this time 'he did not sing on the way'.

In wooded ranges between the coast and Lake George he selects unoccupied open, forest country on which to run sheep. His life is hard as he erects a hut and sheep yard and encloses a few hectares for cultivation. Then he has to buy sheep, after which 'he was in no difficulty to count his shillings; pounds were few indeed'. He faces many privations—eating only corn-meal damper and potatoes and drinking only water, patching his old clothes and making his own boots.

Tyrell feels unable to declare his love for Tressa in case his aunt thinks he is after her money. At this low point in her life, Tressa decides

> I have thought much of life lately, its aims and and purposes... There does not seem to me that my future life is to have much happiness in it. I have chafed and struggled against this conviction until it has made me ill; but I feel differently now, and this is the resolve which has sprung out of much thought and prayer: From henceforth I will try to make each person I come in contact with a little happier and better. No life can be quite desolate which is devoted to the good of others. It is blessedness substituted for happiness.[29]

Through Tyrell's letters to his father Tressa comes to realise that Tyrell loves her, but she is happy to wait, 'My presence here is needed for aunt... This is the lot that the Lord has appointed me. I can wait his time'.[30] At this stage the book ends.

In Tressa there is a reminder of Louisa Atkinson's own life in her long wait before marrying James Calvert. She saw it her duty to look after her mother, as Tressa does her aunt. At the end there is a question mark over whether Tressa with her consumptive cough

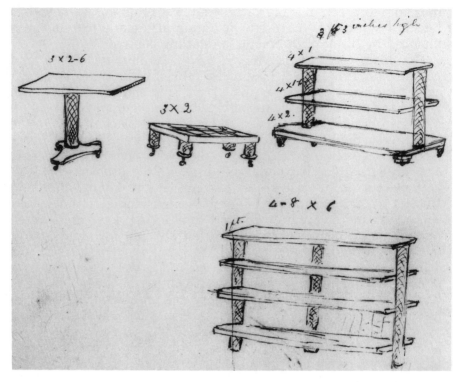

While waiting for the birth of her child, Louisa Calvert began a new series of articles for the *Sydney Mail* called 'The New Bush Home'. She also designed some furniture for her new home at Winstead, Nattai. (Mitchell Library, State Library of NSW. Calvert Sketchbook)

will live long enough to marry—Louisa Atkinson did, but her happiness was to last only a few years.

At the time she was writing *Tressa's Resolve*, Louisa received a letter from Robert Adams of Circular Quay, who described himself as a 'fellow literateur'. He had recently spent his silver wedding anniversary at Fernhurst, by this time being run as a boarding house or sanitorium by Mr and Mrs Peck. He enclosed a poem he had composed at Fernhurst which had been published in the *Sydney Mail* on 16 August 1871 and he expressed his best wishes to Louisa and the hope 'that you also may live thro' many happy years to celebrate *your* silver wedding'.[31]

As she waited for the birth of her child, Louisa experienced a period of great optimism and activity. Apart from writing *Tressa's Resolve*, she began a new series of articles for the *Sydney Mail* under the heading 'My First Bush Home'. Realising that she would be more restricted in her movements around the countryside after the

216

birth of her baby, she planned this new home-based series as a successor, possibly temporary, to 'A Voice From the Country' and similar articles.

In the first article 'The New Bush Home by a Country House Mother', which appeared in October 1871,[32] she gave hints on how to keep contented cows, methods of milking, how to keep a clean dairy, churn butter and make cheese. The second article contained hints on keeping fowls, ducks and turkeys plus a warning on the dangers of tiger snakes taking chickens and ducklings. Her article, like so many she had written previously, included a charming personal story which began with a comment on the prevalence of tiger snakes and the simultaneous disappearance of black and brown snakes. A naive neighbour attributed this to the black and brown snakes changing into tiger snakes. Louisa commented wryly, 'rather Darwinian, certainly'. After nine of her ducklings had disappeared she found a brood of chickens were disappearing one by one:

> presently the hen took to roosting, leaving the chickens on the henhouse floor. As they were only a few days old, and the weather chilly in the early spring, I went for a night or two after dark and lifted her down again to her brood. At length they were reduced to three. As usual, I had gone in the dark, not to disturb the fowls, and putting my hand in the usual place found the chicks were absent; so I carefully passed my hands, with extended fingers, round and about in vain, and rose to depart. In doing so a meandering ray of dim light caught my eye, just as much as a deep twilight made possible on a glossy surface—the mystery was explained—a snake was wriggling round my feet. To gain the door was the work of a minute, and call for help, while I prevented its escape. It was a tiger-snake, and the last three chicks of the brood were entire in its rapacious throat.[33]

In the third and last article, published two months before the birth of her baby, she described how to set up and keep a beehive. Such was her rapport with all living things that she was able to report that bees welcomed the approach of the person who fed them, crowding around 'buzzing gleefully'. She added, 'they remember such friends, even when summer's bright suns and prosperity make their help no longer needed, and will fly around them buzzing, while they have almost a perfect immunity from danger of stings'. She concluded this article with recipes for making mead and honey beer, remarking about the mead recipe that six months' fermentation would result in 'a pleasant, brisk drink', strong enough 'to produce intoxication with those easily affected'.[34]

This was her last published article. A few days later, on 12 February 1872, Louisa wrote to her friend Sarah Woolls, wife of William Woolls.

My dear Mrs Woolls
What a truly trying summer we have had, I hope it has not affected your health, few persons have been well—but I think the late rains have done good—particularly in those localities where the water is bad—our poor friend Mrs Selkirk writes doleful accounts of Richmond—and its stagnant lagoons. Will you tell Dr Woolls that we have been able to send the Baron the Tulus, the orchid and the frog [seed] he wished for but not the other specimens. I have not been botanising but at the new place may hope to do something—here we have to go miles before we can begin to search but there the botanising ground is all around us. I do hope when we are settled and have overcome the up-side-downness of a new place that you and Dr Woolls will be able to visit us—the climate and situation of Winstead are pleasant and there are wonderful gullies at the back with unknown treasures in them. It will certainly be 2 months before we can move; there is much to be done and we are having the cottage nearly doubled in size as it was not built for people who keep servants and so on—Mr Calvert is much from home as he has to keep an eye to his workmen and we will be quite glad when quietly settled down again—such separations break in upon home life so much.
Did I tell you that my Natural History has been removed from Kiel to Strasburg and placed in the Royal Museum there for publication. That is all I have heard of it for a long time since but if they are publishing the plates will take a long time—and it may not be completed for a year...
The school at the Parsonage goes on increasing but they do not speak as if it paid very well. Charles Hassal is staying there now but I have not seen him—The dear old lady is in Sydney, the last time I called her eye was very painful and she looked thin and worn. The district is likely to be disturbed by a double election. The people want my husband to come forward but I am grateful to say he has no ambition that way. These elections occasion so much bitterness and party spirit that I detest them. If possible little Berrima is more dull than ever—not advancing but not retrograding beyond the stagnation of poverty in the district—The disease has invaded the few vineyards and destroyed the grapes, so there will be no wine making; the crops I believe are pretty good—We do not farm—Have you read Miss Parks' Tale of "Fallen by the Way"? [published in *Sydney Mail* in 1871–72] we think it unnatural though clever and in the tension good—She appears to gather her estimate of character from books rather than life.
I hope that queer creature Miss Hussey or Mrs Brown will succeed in finding her husband and suffer no disappointments—it seems to have been an odd romantic affair.

This is another illustration Louisa Atkinson prepared for her book on Australian animals and birds to be published in Germany. The originals were sent to Germany but have never been located. (Mitchell Library, State Library of NSW. Calvert Sketchbook)

Please make our kind remembrances to Dr Woolls and accept my love for yourself.[35]

This is the last surviving letter of the few of Louisa's letters known to exist.

Phalangista Vulpina   Plate 29

220

Illustrations by Louisa Atkinson for her book on Australian birds and animals.
(Mitchell Library, State Library of NSW. Calvert Sketches)

17

She was cut down like a flower in the midst of her days

On 28 April 1872, while she was still recovering from the birth of a baby girl, Louisa Calvert looked out from her room at Swanton to see her husband's horse gallop into the yard riderless. Imagining James Calvert had been killed in a fall, Louisa suffered a heart attack and died suddenly. Soon after, her husband, who had fallen from his horse but was not injured, arrived home on foot to find his wife dead.[1]

Eighteen days before, on 10 April 1872, Louisa had given birth to a daughter, Louise Snowden Annie Calvert. Although her husband and friends must have had many anxious thoughts about the survival of a woman of 38 in frail health, in an era when the death of women in or soon after childbirth was common, Louisa had apparently weathered the worst of the ordeal. This must have given them the hope that, despite her delicate constitution, she would survive the birth of her daughter, but that was not to be.

Louisa was buried in the Atkinson family vault in All Saints' churchyard at Sutton Forest. The inscription on a plaque in the church reads in part, 'Distinguished as a botanist and authoress and well known for her charities to the poor she departed this life deeply regretted by all her friends, and leaving a baby 18 days old'.

Her sudden death cut short the life of a brilliant woman who had achieved so much and was to be so long remembered for her engaging, cheerful nature and personal magnetism. Her friends did not easily forget her. Fourteen years after her death her great friend William Woolls wrote to botanist Henry Deane, who had sent him a specimen of the plant named after Louisa, *Atkinsonia ligustrina*, 'I wish you had known Louisa Atkinson. She was an excellent creature and worthy to be had in remembrance'.[2] Henry Selkirk, the son of her closest friend, still remembered vividly his childhood friendship with her, more than 50 years after her death, when he was a man of about 70.

When Mary Wollstonecraft died at the same age as Louisa following the birth of a second daughter, Mary Godwin, an unsympathetic clergyman in the course of a diatribe againt her feminist ideas said, 'she died a death that strongly marked the distinction of the sexes, by pointing out the destiny of women, and the diseases to which they are liable'.[3] Louisa also was a victim of the 'destiny of women', her extraordinarily talented life, her vitality and good works, her achievements as a writer and naturalist, cut short by childbirth. At Kurrajong and following her marriage, she had experienced rejuvenations enabling her to regain her health despite 'much bodily pain and weakness'.[4] This time there was no recovery.

There was a deep sadness in her death at a time when she and her husband 'fondly hoped to enjoy many years of felicity in exerting themselves to discover the marvellous beauties of nature, and to advance the moral and material interests of Australia'.[5] There was deep irony in the death of a woman who loved children so much being deprived of the opportunity to raise and educate her own daughter.

Her life ended at a time when her greatest achievements could have been before her. Her work on the plants and animals of Australia and her beautiful and delicate drawings would surely have been published in Europe had she lived to follow its progress. A new and exciting field of plant collecting lay ahead in her projected trip to Gippsland and perhaps other trips to places of botanical interest. Her last novel, *Tressa's Resolve*, was published in the *Sydney Mail* after her death. At the top of the first chapter published on 31 August 1872, an editorial note referred to the articles and novels of 'this lamented authoress' and ended, 'The present tale, "Tressa's Resolve," we hope will be kindly criticised as a last production of an Australian authoress'.[6]

Louisa's baby daughter was cared for at Oldbury by her brother James J.O. Atkinson and his wife, Sarah Annie, by then the mother of two young sons, Horton William born in 1870 and Austin Waring in 1871. Another son, Tertius Trafford was born in 1873. Two others born in later years appear to have died as infants.

James Calvert moved from Swanton to Winstead at Nattai, the home he had been extending and renovating for his family, a move Louisa had looked forward to for so long. He appears to have suffered a deep depression following the loss of his wife of only three years. This, combined with his severe physical sufferings from the wounds he had suffered nearly 30 years before, caused

This locket contains photographs of Louisa Calvert (*above*) and (*right*) her grand-daughter, Janet Cosh. (Mitchell Library, State Library of NSW)

him to age prematurely. Now and then he emerged from his depression sufficiently to write letters for publication. In July 1872 he wrote to the *Sydney Morning Herald* of the use of gum leaves for medicinal purposes for both humans and animals, advocating particularly the leaves of the blue gum, a remedy first brought to his notice by his brother-in-law James.[7] Very occasionally—twice in 1874 and once in 1875—he sat on the Berrima bench, but an overwhelming sadness and inertia seems to have overtaken him.

When his daughter was about two he quarrelled with his brother-in-law and removed the child from Oldbury. Losing the will and perhaps the physical capacity to farm, he moved in about 1876 to Botany, then a small settlement on the southern outskirts of Sydney. There he lived almost as a recluse, his young daughter sharing his secluded life. She spent a lonely and unhappy child-

hood being brought up by housekeepers in their house in Botany Road.[8]

About 1880 James Calvert moved from Botany to a house he named 'Winstead' in Mount Vernon Street, Forest Lodge, near the home of his brother. William Calvert, at the age of 54 years in 1874, had married Eleanor Thatcher, a daughter of a farmer on an adjoining block at Cavan. They had two surviving children Harriette Amelia, named after the Calverts' sister, born in 1876, and William Snowden born in 1878. After leaving Cavan William Calvert had lived in the Picton district for some time, sitting occasionally on the Picton bench in 1874 and 1875, before moving to Forest Lodge.

James Calvert died on 22 July 1884 at the age of 57 years from 'acute choleraic diarrohea' and was buried in Rockwood Cemetery.[9] In an obituary the *Evening News* said he had felt the loss of

James Calvert suffered a deep depression after the death of his wife, Louisa, and became prematurely aged. He died at 58. (Mitchell Library, State Library of NSW)

his wife severely, 'and contemplated, should fortune favour him with means, to have republished her numerous Australian literary productions'. It appears that James Calvert's papers, including not only letters from his wife but from Ludwig Leichhardt and Ferdinand von Mueller, were burnt at his death. Any that may have survived his death disappeared when his brother's family died out. His brother died in 1895 and his nephew in 1896, aged eighteen.

In his will James Calvert, in the event of his daughter not surviving him, left his estate to his brother with provision for a legacy to his nephew Joseph Barrington Dawson, by then living in Queensland. He was the only surviving child of his sister Harriett Amelia Dawson, who had died at Parramatta in 1871. In the event of his brother's family not surviving him, he left two-thirds of his estate to his nephew and one-third to Charles Castle Hall of Yeumberra, the son of his old friend from his days at Cavan. As Louise Calvert survived her father the other provisions of the will did not come into effect. She was twelve at the time of her father's death and her father's solicitor, James Frederic Fitzhardinge, became her guardian.

Louise returned to live with her uncle at Oldbury, by then only a shadow of its former standing as a large grazing and farming property. It was being run as a dairy farm. James Atkinson's investment in the Fitzroy coal mine had been a financial disaster and he had also lost money in the collapse of a bank in which he was shareholder.[10] Louise found her uncle a kindly man but very quiet and melancholy; his wife had had a stroke and the family lived very much in seclusion.[11] The arrangement under which Louise lived at Oldbury lasted only a short time. Her uncle was killed in a fall from his horse at the age 53 years on 13 March 1885. Her guardian arranged for Louise to live at the rectory at Sutton Forest with the family of Rev. J.H. Mullens, who had been appointed Anglican minister there in 1883. According to her daughter, this was the best home Louise ever had. There being little money from her mother's and father's estate, she had to plan to support herself and as soon as she was old enough she entered Royal Prince Alfred Hospital, Sydney, to train as a nurse.

Some time after the death of James Atkinson, his widow and her sister, Charlotte Horton, prepared to sell Oldbury by auction. In preparation for this Louise Calvert was summoned from the Sutton Forest rectory to collect her mother's possessions, which had remained at Oldbury. At the age of about thirteen, having to walk a distance of some five kilometres each way and believing her eldest cousin was harassing her, she was able to take only what she could collect in a hurried visit and could carry back to Sutton Forest. This, in part, accounts for the scant and haphazard nature of the collection of letters, papers and drawings of Louisa Atkinson's that have survived. All her other possessions, including numerous cases of stuffed animals and birds, were burnt or destroyed preparatory to the auction of Oldbury on 26 November 1887.[12]

James Atkinson's third son, Tertius Trafford Atkinson[13] and probably the other sons, went to the King's School, Parramatta. Some time later Tertius and his eldest brother, Horton, having inherited a love of exploration from their father and grandfather, set out for the Victoria River in the Northern Territory. From there they traversed the whole of Western Australia on horseback, a journey of some years, while they explored the possibility of entering the cattle industry. Just before World War I Tertius Atkinson married Lilla Burnet, whom he had met at Shark Bay during the brothers' ride down the west coast. He served in World War I and after farming near Northam became a bank inspector at Bencubbin, Western Australia. He died in South Australia in 1949.[14]

After her training at the Royal Prince Alfred, Louise Calvert took a position at Weymouth House, Orange, as a children's nurse. In 1891, at the age of nearly nineteen, she wrote from there to Rev. William Woolls, by this time retired from his post as rural dean at St Peter's, Richmond, and living at Burwood. Louise sought information about her mother. Woolls replied:

> Your letter brings back to my mind the correspondence I used to have with your excellent mother when she resided at Kurrajong and used send me specimens of plants. She was beloved by all the people there...
>
> Your mother's great friend Mrs Selkirk is residing near Cooma, the sons are scattered over the colony. It was Mrs Selkirk who wrote the piece of poetry about your mother, commencing 'Have you seen—
>
> I find that like your poor mother, you are fond of 'nature's beauties'...
>
> Your poor mother was cut off in the midst of her days, but she did a great work in her short life, it is pleasing to think of the many good things she did for the children at Kurrajong, &, I may add for their parents also.[15]

A fortnight before his death at Burwood in 1893 Woolls wrote again to Louise Calvert sending her a copy of the poem 'Dianella' written 'to your mother' by Mrs Selkirk, 'a particular friend of "Dianella"'.[16]

Just before her marriage to Dr John I.C. Cosh in 1900, Louise Calvert called at the home of Dr Woolls's widow, Sarah Woolls, who wrote later saying she was sorry she had missed her. She had wished to ask 'for a likeness of "your dear mother" to lend to be copied' for a gift to the Botanical Museum. 'The only likeness I have of your mother is pasted inside the cover of a [?book] together with a sketch of her life written by her late husband. I never remember having seen more than the one taken', she wrote.[17] Like so much other material concerning Louisa Atkinson, this sketch of her life by her husband has not been located.

While she lived at Orange Louise Calvert apparently remained unaware of the fact that her aunt, Charlotte McNeilly, and her cousins were living there. After nearly twenty years of struggling in the Berrima district, the McNeilly family flourished after their move to Orange in the latter part of the 1860s. Charlotte ran a private school in the early years after the move there. She painted, and according to her daughter, Flora Garlick, was 'a frequent writer to journals and newspapers'.[18] None of this writing has been traced, but the impression remains that had Charlotte been freer of childbearing and household duties, she may have displayed talents similar to her youngest sister Louisa. In later years Charlotte McNeilly became a great advocate of temperance, forming the first temperance lodge in Orange.[19]

Thomas McNeilly, dealer, died on 31 July 1885 at the age of 68 and was buried in the Catholic section of the Orange cemetery. Charlotte survived him for many years. When she died in Orange on 17 March 1911, following a fall in which she injured her back, Charlotte McNeilly was described as 'a very old and much respected resident'. She was buried in the Anglican cemetery. Of her six children who had survived to adulthood, only three survived her—Mrs Flora Garlick of Molong, Alderman Edwin Thomas McNeilly of Orange and Mrs Eva Duke of Sydney. Her son, Edwin McNeilly, auctioneer and stock and station agent, had become one of Orange's most favoured sons. He was an alderman on Orange Town Council for 35 years and mayor for almost all of the period from 1910 to 1918. He like his mother was an active member of a Foresters (temperance) lodge and during World War I he was an ardent supporter of the war effort and conscription.

When Louisa Atkinson died, in a century when the achievements of women were rarely recorded in the press, the *Sydney Morning Herald* published a lengthy obituary praising her. She had been 'cut down like a flower in the midst of her days' the obituarist wrote. She was 'highly distinguished' for her 'literary and artistic attainments' and for her 'Christian principles and expansive charity'. Her novels exhibited 'many of the most striking features of colonial life' and her drawings displayed 'great natural talent, unaffected elegance, and extreme accuracy'.[20]

There were plans to commemorate her memory with an annual prize to be offered by the Horticultural Society for the best exhibition of native flowers at the Society's annual show. When this came to nothing, her great friend. William Woolls organised a commemorative service at St Peter's Church, Richmond. Though held two years after her death and eight years after she had left the district, many people attended to honour her memory and distinguished people who had been her friends subscribed to a memorial tablet, which was erected in the church. The inscription read in part, 'This tablet is erected by her friends to mark their respect for her pious labours and scientific researches during a residence of several years at the Kurrajong'.

In this present century, with her books out of print and the memory of her articles lost, Louisa Atkinson's achievements were noted only in very occasional articles. In 1911, writing in the *Sydney Morning Herald*, Mary Salmon said that many people still living at Kurrajong remembered her as their earliest teacher and as a woman who 'loved every living thing and taught others to do the same'.[21] Another article by Mary Salmon published in 1923 entitled 'An Early Australian Press Writer' praised the aspect of her achievements usually the least noted—that she was one of the first women journalists in Australia, certainly the first woman to have a long running series.of articles published in the metropolitan press. It was a remarkable achievement by an 'unknown girl' writing from an 'obscure locality'. Mary Salmon wrote 'In her early writings to the *Herald*, the knowledge she showed of natural science, which was then an unusual subject for a woman to explore, made her contributions of value and caused them to be regularly looked for and accepted'. She also quoted Louisa Atkinson directly, although the source of her information is not known: living at Kurrajong helped 'to make me a passionate lover of grand and beautiful scenery, and to develop a taste for observation of the flora and native animals, which so richly abound in the district'.[22] Apart from these widely-spaced articles, it is fortunate that Louisa Atkinson's life and achievements appealed so much to Margaret Swann that in 1928 she prepared an article on her life while there were still a few people alive who had known her.

In 1899, in a letter to the editor of the *Sydney Morning Herald*, Edward Stack had suggested that a memorial be erected in Louisa Atkinson's honour in the Botanical Gardens.[23] Nothing came of this suggestion, but in recent years she has been commemorated by a third plaque to add to those erected at the churches at Sutton Forest and Richmond. This plaque was erected in a bush setting at Powell Park, Kurrajong Heights, not far down the hill from the site of her former home at Fernhurst. It describes her as 'Botanist of the Kurrajong'.

Some of Louisa Atkinson's books and articles have in recent years become available for the first time for more than a century. Victor Crittenden of Canberra has published two collections of Louisa Atkinson's articles, *A Voice From the Country* and *Excursions From Berrima*, and two of her novels, *Tom Hellicar's Children* and *Myra*, and he has plans for publishing more of her writing. An occasional paper written by Elizabeth Lawson of the English Department, Australian Defence Forces Academy, published in 1988, *The Distant Sound of Native Voices*, examines Louisa Atkinson's writings on Aborigines. A booklet, *Louisa Atkinson of the Kurrajong*, issued in 1979 by the Kurrajong Heights Garden Club, describes her botanical work at Kurrajoing.

Though their sentiments are expressed in the forms of the nineteenth century, two poems written about Louisa Atkinson are recorded here because they express something of her nature and the effect of her personality on other people. William Woolls concluded his sermon after her death with this poem expressing 'the praises of her of whom Australia may justly be proud':

No more shall she that softly moved
Amidst the wilds she so much loved.
Descend the vale, or climb the height,
To bring new beauties to our sight.

No more shall fern or tender flower
Invite her to some lonely bower,
Where dripping rocks, with mosses green,
In native loveliness are seen.

No more shall creatures gay or rare,
Insects of earth, or birds of air,
Attract the mind which knew so well,
Of all their various ways to tell.

No more shall grateful voices raise
With her the song of prayer and praise,
In that loved spot where many a youth
Imbibed from her the words of truth.

No more shall she by grace allure
To godly thoughts the sick and poor.
And speak kind words of sympathy,
'To teach the sinner how to die.'

No more shall she with tender heart
Unselfishly her aid impart,
To feed the hungry as they stray
Along the steep and rugged way.

But still she lives to memory dear,
Still does her love of art appear,
Still may we trace the guileless mind
In all the works she left behind.

Though dead, she speaketh in the flowers,
That sparkle in the vernal showers,
And tell of one who loved to trace
The gorgeous tints of nature's face.

Yes, still she lives! her lasting fame
Shall dwell in ATKINSONIA'S name,
And long as Tomah loves to wear
Its leafy garlands—she is there!

She is not dead! Oh! do not weep,
Her's is a sweet untroubled sleep,
She rests on Jesu's breast above,
Enjoying his eternal love.

To Him who loved, to Him who died
For those who in His truth abide—
Lord of this earth and Heaven's High King,
May we, like her, our offerings bring.

When, having walked with Him below,
Where woods may wave or rivers flow
May we, in Canaan's better land,
Upon the Rock of Ages stand!

At the end of the poem, William Woolls added these notes:

The genus ATKINSONIA of the Loranthaceae or mistletoe family was
named by Baron F. von Mueller in honour of the late Mrs Calvert, then
Miss Atkinson, at the request of Dr Woolls, who collected specimens of
it near Mount Tomah. This shrub is very remarkable, for, although of
the mistletoe family, it is not PARASITICAL.
The last two verses were composed by the Rev. W.B. Clarke, M.A.,
F.G.S., the eminent geologist, who had a great respect for the piety and
ability of Mrs Calvert.[24]

The other poem was written by Louisa's great friend, Emma
Selkirk.[25] When William Woolls sent this copy of Emma Selkirk's
poem to Louisa's daughter, he wrote:

Your dear Mother is here called *'Dianella'*, a diminutive of *Diana*, 'the
Goddess'
The genus *Dianella* is of the Liliaceous order & contains a pretty plant
which grew near your Mother's at the Kurrajong.

Have you seen Dianella, the pride of the mountain?
    If not it is certainly time that you should:
She's the fay of the forest, the sylph of the fountain,
    The fairest of fairies that haunt the greenwood.
With eyes brightly beaming and silken hair streaming
    And cheeks glowing roselike in morning's pure air,
Where is the city belle, who with our Dianelle
    May for fresh beauty and sweetness compare?

Equipped for the chase it delights her to ramble
    Through wilds the rude footsteps of man never trod,
Over rocks where the wallaby boundeth to scramble
    To pools unprofaned by the fisherman's rod.
Deep, deep through the woodland shade presses our mountain maid
    Where the tall fern rears her feathery crest.

The brooklet she crosses to seek the green mosses
   And climbs the tall cliff to the wild pheasant's nest.

Behold her returning with sylvan spoils laden
   Of flower and insect and lichen and fern. .
Each creature that liveth is dear to this maiden
   Who loves the sweet lessons of nature to learn.
The hoarder of treasure, the votary of pleasure,
   May seek in the whirl of the city to dwell:
But let me be roaming from morning till gloaming
   Our mountain and valley with dear Dianelle.

Endnotes

1 Searching for Louisa Atkinson

1 James Jervis *A History of Berrima*, Berrima, 1962, p. 15
2 Letter from Janet Cosh, Moss Vale, undated (1988)
3 *Truth* 5 May 1918
4 Margaret Swann 'Mrs Meredith and Miss Atkinson, Writers and Naturalists', *RAHS Journal*, Vol. XV, Part 1, 1929
5 Margaret Swann gave her talk to the RAHS on 25 September 1928; it was published in 1929.
6 Information from Elizabeth Plimer; Dr Marjorie Jacobs, RAHS Archives Officer; Ellen Errey and Elizabeth Plimer *William Swann and Elizabeth Swann*, 1984
7 *Truth* 5 May 1918
8 Margaret Swann op. cit.
9 William Woolls *Sermon preached in St Peter's Church, Richmond, on Sunday, April 12th, 1874, by Rev, William Woolls, Ph.D., F.L.S., on the occasion of a tablet being placed in that church to the memory of the late Mrs Calvert*, Windsor, 1874
10 NLA MS3141 Berrima District Historical Society. Notes given to the Society by Janet Cosh.

2 Atkinson is as fat as a pig and as saucy as a New South Wales farmer

1 ML MSS 3849/1 Cosh and Atkinson. Notes by Louisa Calvert. 'He died in the prime of life when only 39 years of age from inflamation brought on by drinking impure water on the top of Razorback when heated.'
2 *Sydney Monitor* 3 May 1834
3 ML MSS 3849/1. 'It was during his last illness that I was born and probably he never saw me, as when carried into his room I cried and he ordered me to be removed.'
4 ML MSS 3849/1 op. cit.
5 HRA Vol. XII p. 502. Letter James Atkinson to Earl Bathurst, 22 August 1826
6 Although his pay of £80 a year was low compared with those in higher executive and clerical positions who earned up to £720 a year, surprisingly it was higher than the £60 he was to receive in New South Wales in the important position of Principal Clerk. I am indebted to Neil McCormick for this observation.
7 Alexander Berry *Reminiscences of Alexander Berry* Sydney, 1912, p. 172
8 ML MSS 315 Berry papers. Letter Wollstonecraft to Berry, 31 July 1820
9 Berry papers. Letter Edward Wollstonecraft, Sydney to Elizabeth Wollstonecraft, Greenwich, England, 9 June 1821
10 NSW Lands Department. Promise of grant 6 November 1823. The grant was dated 1 January 1831 but not finalised until 27 September 1839

11   Berry papers. Letters Edward Wollstonecraft to Alexander Berry, 4 October 1822; James Atkinson to Alexander Berry 25 October 1822
12   James Atkinson *An Account of the State of Agriculture and Grazing in New South Wales* London, 1826, p. 94
13   Berry papers. Letter Alexander Berry to Edward Wollstonecraft, 16 April 1827
14   *Australian* 27 January 1827

3   She must be mistress of her own actions

1   ML MSS 3849/1 Cosh and Atkinson. Notes by Louisa Calvert.
2   ibid.
3   ibid.
4   AONSW 7/3460 Supreme Court. Equity Proceedings. Statement by Charlotte Barton 18 March 1841
5   ibid.
6   'The purple beetle' in *A Mother's Offering to Her Children* Sydney, 1841 pp. 92–93, 95
7   Letter Harriet King to Phillip Parker King 5 August 1826, quoted in Dorothy Walsh (ed.) *The Admiral's Wife* Melbourne, Hawthorn Press, 1967, p. 31
8   AONSW 7/3460 op. cit.
9   ML A1976 CY904 King papers Vol. 1, p. 446. Letter 3 October 1826
10   Letter 31 January 1827 quoted in Walsh op. cit. p. 55
11   Berry Papers, Berry to Edward Wollstonecraft 16 April 1827
12   ibid. 22 April 1827
13   Letter October 1827 quoted in Walsh op. cit. p. 74
14   'The History of the Swallows' in *A Mother's Offering* op. cit. pp. 85–8, 89
15   James Jervis 'The Journals of William Edward Riley' (3 September 1830), *RAHS Journal* Vol. XXXII, Part IV, 1946
16   *Australian* 20 June 1827
17   *Sydney Monitor* 3 May 1834
18   *Sydney Gazette* 3 May 1834
19   Norton papers ML A5328–2
20   ML MSS 3849/1
21   AONSW 7/3460

4   A widow lady and her family, who had suffered much, took refuge at her cattle station

1   'Recollections of the Aborigines', AVC *Sydney Morning Herald* 22 September 1863
2   *Sydney Gazette* 11 April 1836
3   James Jervis, *A History of the Berrima District 1798–1961* p. 36
4   In the 1837 Convict Muster, sixteen convicts were listed as assigned to George Barton, most of them at Sutton Forest (for Oldbury), the remainder at Berrima (for his own farm at Belanglo).
5   *Sydney Herald* 11 February 1836. I am indebted to Marcie Muir for alerting me to an account of this episode in *Push from the Bush*.
6   AONSW marriage licences; marriage certificate 349/20/1836
7   AONSW 7/3459, 60. The executors received £1100 from Barton in rent for Oldbury and Galgal for the period 1 April 1836 to 1 January 1839
8   *Sydney Herald* 15 August 1836
9   AONSW 7/3460
10   AONSW 7/3459 23 November 1841

11 AONSW 7/3460 1 June 1839
12 ibid. 26 October 1839
13 AONSW 7/3459
14 AONSW 7/3460 26 October 1838
15 ibid. 28 October 1839
16 'Incidents of Australian Travel', AVC *Sydney Morning Herald* 9 November 1863
17 'Recollections of the Aborigines', AVC *Sydney Morning Herald* 22 September 1863
18 'Extraordinary sounds' in *A Mother's Offering to Her Children* pp. 15, 17, 19
19 ibid. p. 9
20 AONSW 7/3459. This debt was still unpaid on 18 November 1841, when Charlotte Barton referred it to the executors.
21 Thomas Bott Humphery, later lessor of Oldbury
22 ML Uncat. MSS 511 Maddrell papers. Berry to Coghill 24 December 1839
23 AONSW 7/3461 op. cit.
24 N. Clout 'Genesis of the Clout family', n.p., n.d.
25 'Anecdotes of the Aborigines of New South Wales' in *A Mother's Offering to Her Children* pp. 203–04

5   I am totally averse to having any connection with such a notable she dragon
1   Dora Montefiore *From a Victorian to a Modern* London, 1927, pp. 30–31
2   AONSW 7/3459 Supreme Court Equity Proceedings. 6 July 1841
3   AONSW 7/3459, n.d.
4   AONSW 7/3459 (Charlotte Barton's petition) 1 September 1840
5   AONSW 7/3459, 21 November 1840
6   AONSW 7/3461, 6 March 1841
7   AONSW 7/3461, 29 May 1841
8   AONSW 7/3461, n.d.
9   AONSW 7/3460, 18 March 1841
10 AONSW 7/3459, 7 June 1841
11 AONSW 7/3459, 7 June 1841
12 AONSW 7/3460, 9 July 1841
13 AONSW 7/3460, 9 July 1841
14 AONSW 7/3459, 21 October 1842. The £1000 was paid before the Chief Justice's report in 1843.
15 AONSW 5/4497 Master in Equity Order book January 1841–May 1846. Entry book of orders and decrees. 9 July 1841; AONSW 7/3460, 9 July 1841
16 AONSW 2/3964 Supreme Court Equity. Minutes of Proceedings in Equity. 7 January 1842; *Sydney Herald* 8 January 1842
17 AONSW 7/3461, 10 July 1841
18 AONSW 7/3460, 18 November 1842
19 AONSW 7/3460, 9 July 1841
20 Maddrell papers op. cit. Berry to Coghill, 25 January 1842
21 AONSW 5/4497 op. cit. 15 April 1842
22 Maddrell papers op. cit. Berry to Coghill 14 July 1842
23 ibid. Berry to Coghill 5 August 1842
24 AONSW 5/4497 op. cit. 27 June 1843
25 ibid. 25 October 1843
26 AONSW 5/4497 op. cit. 9, 20 February 1846
27 *Sydney Mail* 8 June 1861
28 ibid. 6 July 1861

29   ibid. 13 July 1861
30   *Tom Hellicar's Children* p. 6 (serialised in *Sydney Mail* in 1871. Also published in book form by Mulini Press, Canberra 1983)
31   ibid. p. 2

6   She does not appear to have received any instruction after her twelfth year
1   William Woolls *Sermon* op. cit. p. 7
2   *Sydney Morning Herald* 20 December 1842
3   *Colonial Observer* 9 December 1841
4   *Sydney Herald* 27 June 1842
5   *Sydney Morning Herald* 20 December 1842
6   Elizabeth Windshuttle 'Educating the Daughters of the Ruling Class in Colonial New South Wales 1788–1850' in *Melbourne Studies in Education 1980* p. 120
7   *Gertrude* p. 85
8   ibid. p. 128
9   ibid. p. 156
10   *Cowanda* p. 36
11   *Tressa's Resolve* in *Sydney Mail* 31 August 1872
12   *Gertrude* p. 122
13   ibid. p. 125
14   *Tressa's Resolve, Sydney Mail* 12 October 1872
15   ibid. 30 November 1872
16   *Debatable Ground, Sydney Mail* 30 March 1861
17   Marcie Muir *Charlotte Barton: Australia's First Children's Author* Sydney, 1980
18   *Sydney Gazette* 23 December 1841
19   *Sydney Herald* 27 December 1841
20   Brenda Niall *Through the Looking-Glass. Children's Fiction 1830–1980* Melbourne, 1988, p. 58
21   'Anecdotes of the Aborigines of New South Wales' in *A Mother's Offering* pp. 205–07

7   The glass was broken in many places, and the walls cracked and damp-stained
1   *Cowanda* p. 69
2   AONSW 7/3459 Letter Charlotte Barton 10 June 1848
3   *Gertrude* p. 45
4   'Ovaology', AVC, *SM* 6 April 1861
5   'January', AVC, *SMH* 1 March 1860
6   'Balonne Lizard', AVC, *SMH* 14 July 1864
7   NLA MS 3141; interview Essie Whiteman, Springwood NSW
8   AONSW 2/4150 Equity Court cases and matters for hearing 1841–86; *SMH* 6 March 1844
9   AONSW 7/3459 5 March 1844
10   Essie Whiteman interview
11   NSW Births, Deaths and Marriages, Marriage McNeilly/Atkinson No. 1013, Vol. 95/1847; interview Janet Cosh
12   NSW Births, Deaths and Marriages Death McNeilly 13867/1885. Although Thomas McNeilly's death certificate gives his age at marriage as 28, it also states that he was 68 when he died in 1885, which would make his age at marriage 30.
13   *Gertrude* p. 48

14   ibid. p. 50
15   NSW Lands Department Parish of Berrima Lot 154, 37 acres, 156, 40 acres grants by purchase
16   There were many cases of stuffed birds and animals at Oldbury but they were burnt when the home was vacated by the Atkinson family in 1887. Information from Janet Cosh.
17   ML A4496 Manuscript material. Ch. 16 'A Rambling Paper on Zoology'
18   ibid.
19   AONSW 7/3461, 6 April 1853
20   James Johnson Warren was a farmer in the Berrima district at the time of his marriage, probably on leased land. Later he bought two forty-acre blocks, Portions 51 and 52, Parish of Belanglo, Co. Camden. NSW Lands Department records
21   NLA MS 3141
22   ML MSS 3849/1
23   'After Shells in the Limestone', AVC, *SMH* 24 May 1870
24   *Bathurst Free Press* 14 January 1854
25   ibid. 4, 25 February 1854
26   *Bathurst Free Press* 4, 11 March 1854; *SMH* 8, 15 March 1854
27   C.A. Henderson 'Sydney to Homebush, 1855' *RAHS Journal* Vol. VIII, 1923, pp. 355, 357

8   The sketch for October will appear in our next number
1   R.B. Walker The *Newspaper Press in New South Wales 1803–1920* Sydney, 1976, p. 226
2   *Illustrated Sydney News* 15 August 1853
3   ibid.
4   *Australian Encyclopaedia* Vol. 1 p. 251
5   Some botanical names used by Louisa Atkinson have since changed but others she used were mistranscribed from her handwriting.
6   *Illustrated Sydney News* 3 December 1853
7   ibid. 7 January 1854
8   ibid. 22 October 1853
9   ibid. 26 November 1853
10   ibid. 4 February 1854
11   William Woolls *Sermon...op. cit.* p. 7
12   *Gertrude* pp. 176–78
13   *Illustrated Sydney News* 14 April 1855
14   ibid. 12 May 1855
15   ibid. 16 September 1865
16   The pseudonym 'An Australian Lady' is not recorded as being used by any other writer apart from Louisa Atkinson.
17   F.C. Brewer The *Music and Drama in New South Wales* Sydney, 1892; information from Ken Snell, Melbourne
18   Eric Irvin *Australian Melodrama. Eighty years of Popular Theatre* Sydney, 1981; information from Ken Snell

9   Her Women were recognisably like Australian girls of today
1   Blanche Mitchell *The Diary of Blanche Mitchell* Sydney, 1980 p. 25. I am grateful to Victor Crittenden for telling me about this reference to Louisa Atkinson.
2   *Gertrude* p. 2

3   *SMH* 3 June 1857; also 10 December 1857
4   *Windsor Review* 1 July 1857; also August 1857. Also reviewed in *Goulburn Chronicle* 6 May 1857. The *Windsor Review* was published by J.R. Clarke, publisher of *Gertrude* and *Cowanda*.
5   G.B. Barton *Literature in New South Wales* Sydney, 1866, pp. 111–12
6   *SMH* 10 December 1857
7   *Gertrude* p. 2
8   ibid. p. 14
9   ibid. p. 35
10   ibid. p. 38
11   ibid. p. 52
12   ibid. p. 9
13   ibid. p. 101
14   ibid. p. 66
15   ibid. p. 91
16   ibid. pp. 103–04
17   ibid. p. 53
18   ibid. p. 32
19   ibid pp. 29–30
20   Miles Franklin *Laughter Not For a Cage* Sydney, 1956, p. 30
21   James Backhouse *Extracts From the Letters of James Backhouse* London, 1841
22   *Empire* 22 September 1859
23   *Cowanda* p. 103
24   ibid. p. 33
25   G.B. Barton, op. cit. p. 113

10   Every step reveals some new treasure to the lover of nature
1   'June', AVC, *SM* 21 July 1860
2   'July', AVC, *SM* 4 August 1860
3   'January', AVC, *SMH* 1 March 1860
4   'Scraps', AVC, *SMH* 8 August 1862
5   'Wiseman's Ferry', AVC, *SMH* 5 January 1864
6   'Botanical Ramblings', AVC, *SMH* 2 September 1862
7   'Ferns and Their Haunts', AVC, *SMH* 12 February 1863
8   'Flying Fox Hunting in the Blue Mountains' *SMH* 26 April 1860
9   'March', AVC, *SMH* 6 April 1860
10   'The Kurrajong Waterfalls', AVC, *SM* 18 August 1860
11   'Ovaology', AVC, *SM* 6 April 1861
12   'August', AVC, *SM* 22 September 1860
13   'Burrolow', AVC, *SM* 27 October 1860
14   'Tabarag', AVC, *SM* 29 December 1860
15   *Horticultural Magazine* March 1868
16   'Cabbage-Tree Hollow and the Valley of the Grose', AVC, *SM* 12 January 1861
17   'Mount Tomah', AVC, *SM* 2 February 1861
18   'The Grose River', AVC, *SMH* 10 April 1861
19   'Mount Tomah' op. cit.
20   'The Ranges of the Grose', AVC, *SMH* 30 January 1862
21   'Springwood', AVC, *SMH* 20 March 1862. Louisa Atkinson calls this article 'Springwood'. It refers to North Springwood and Springwood Creek, which flows north to the Grose River.
22   'Wiseman's Ferry', AVC, *SMH* 5 January 1864

23 'Ovaology', AVC, *SM* 6 April 1861
24 'A Winter's Garland', AVC, *SM* 6 July 1861
25 'Fitzroy Iron Mines' *SMH* 9 November 1870
26 'A Peep Into the Herb Doctor's Basket', AVC, *SMH* 10 June 1862
27 'Botanical Ramblings', AVC, *SMH* 2 September 1862
28 'Scraps', AVC, *SMH* 8 August 1862
29 'Orchidaceae', AVC, *SMH* 23 October 1862
30 W. Woolls *A Contribution to the Flora of Australia* Sydney, 1867, p. 178, quoting Louisa Atkinson
31 'Insects and Insect Feeders', AVC, *SMH* 2 May 1863
32 *SMH* 12 February 1862
33 'Orchidaceae' op. cit.
34 ML A4496 newspaper cuttings; *SMH* December 1862
35 'Ferns and Their Haunts', AVC, *SMH* 12 February 1863
36 *SMH* 16 November 1863
37 'Botanical Ramblings' op. cit.
38 'Stray Notes', AVC, *SMH* 25 October 1864
39 'Reptilia', AVC, *SM* 11 May 1861
40 *SMH* 20 September 1870
41 'Botanical Ramblings', op. cit.

11 ***Atkinsonia ligustrina* will ever remain a living monument of her exertions**
1   Rev. William Woolls *Sermon Preached at St Peter's Church, Richmond* 12 April 1874
2   Sir James Fairfax 'Some Recollections of Old Sydney' *RAHS Journal* vol. 5, Part 1, 1919
3   William Woolls 'Kurrajong and Tomah' *Sydney Morning Herald* 14 March 1861
4   Ferdinand von Mueller *Fragmenta Phytographiae Australiae* Vol. V, p. 34; Woolls op. cit. *Sydney Morning Herald* 14 March 1861; Louisa Atkinson 'Mount Tomah' op. cit.
5   Both quotes from Woolls *The Plants of New South Wales* p. 63
6   William Woolls 'Curiosities of Australian Vegetation' *SMH* 13 July 1872
7   F. von Mueller *Fragmenta* ... Vol. V, 1865, p. 88
8   ibid. Vol. VIII, 1873, pp. 52–53
9   William Woolls *SMH* 14 March 1861
10 ML MSS 3849/2
11 ibid.
12 William Woolls 'Kurrajong and Mount Tomah' *A Contribution to the Flora of Australia* op. cit.
13 NLA MS3148 Lionel Gilbert 'Botanical Investigations in New South Wales 1811–1880' PhD thesis University of New England, 1971; for example George Bentham *Flora Australiensis* Vol. 3, pp. 387–78 and pp. 658–89
14 *Australian Dictionary of Biography* Vol. 2 p. 182
15 Displayed at Macleay Museum, University of Sydney
16 Johann Ludwig (Louis) Gerard Krefft (1830–1881), zoologist, German-born curator of the Australian Museum, Sydney
17 Henry Halloran (1811–1893) public servant and poet
18 ML A4496 Calvert correspondence
19 *Horticultural Magazine* February 1864
20 ibid. April 1864
21 ibid. July 1864 pp. 173–34; August pp. 193–34; October pp. 239–40
22 ibid. February 1865 p. 29

23 ML A4496 Calvert correspondence
24 William Woolls 'Curiosities of Australian Vegetation' *SM* 13 July 1872
25 William Woolls *Sermon* p. 11
26 Information from Janet Cosh
27 'A Ride to the Fitzroy Mines', AVC, *SMH* 4 June 1863
28 'A Summer Picture', AVC, *SMH* 2 July 1863
29 'Recollections of the Aborigines', AVC, *SM* 12, 19, 26 September 1863; *SMH* 22, 25, 28 September 1863
30 *SM* 12 September 1863
31 ibid. 19 September 1863
32 ibid. 26 September 1863. Elizabeth Lawson in *Louisa Atkinson: The Distant Sound of Native Voices* Canberra, June 1989, discusses Louisa's writings on Aborigines in much greater depth.
33 'Incidents of Australian Travel', AVC, *SMH* 9 November 1863

12 Meanness is not one of my sins
1   *SM* 30 March–7 September 1861
2   The varied spelling of names could be due to carelessness on the author's part. My opinion is that they were mistakes made by the compositors in setting type from the handwritten copy. Some examples in *Debatable Ground* are Cursen/Curten and Shenstone/Thurston
3   *Debatable Ground, SM*, Chapter I, 30 March 1861
4   ibid. Ch. IX, 18 May 1861
5   ibid. Ch. XVIII, 20 July 1861
6   ibid.
7   ibid.
8   ibid. Ch. XXII, 17 August 1861
9   ibid. Ch. XIV, 22 June 1861. This chapter, entitled 'Lost' had some resemblance to a draft chapter called 'Lost!' in Atkinson MS. material ML A4496.
10 ibid. Ch. XXII, 17 August 1861
11 ibid. Chapter XXV, 7 September 1861
12 *SM* 27 February–23 April 1864
13 Among the misprinted names in *Myra* are Lellan/Sellan and Juan/Jann.
14 ML A4496 Calvert correspondence
15 *Myra SM* Ch. I, 27 February 1864
16 ibid.
17 ibid. Ch. II, 5 March 1864
18 ibid.
19 ibid.
20 ibid. Ch. III, 12 March 1864
21 ibid. Ch. IV, 12 March 1864
22 ibid. Ch. X, 16 April 1864
23 ibid. Ch. VIII, 2 April 1864
24 ibid. Ch. IV, 12 March 1864

13 The only who behaved perfectly was Mr Calvert
1   *SMH* 30 March 1854; *SMH* 18 November 1858
2   'Mr. McIntyre's Journey Across Australia...' *Proceedings of the Royal Geographical Society* 12 June 1865; *SMH* 11 July 1865
3   F. von Mueller 'The Fate of Dr Leichhardt and a Proposed New Search for His Party' reprinted from *Australasian* 18 February 1865

4 *Argus* 14, 25 April 1865
5 'Leichhardt', AVC, *SM* 6 May 1865; *SMH* 1 May 1865
6 ML A4496 von Mueller to Louisa Calvert 31 January 1871
7 *SM* 15 April 1871
8 J.H. Heaton *Australian Dictionary of Dates and Men of the Time* Sydney,1879
9 AONSW Reel No. 1347. Arrivals of bounty migrants *Sir Edward Paget* 14 February 1842
10 D.J. and S.G.M. Carr (eds) *People and Plants in Australia* Sydney, 1981, p. 326
11 M. Aurousseau (ed.) *The Letters of F.W. Ludwig Leichhardt*, Cambridge, 1986; information from Dr L.A. Dawson
12 *SMH* 14 August 1844
13 *SMH* 12 December 1844. Letter from L. Leichhardt at Dried Beef Creek written 3 November 1844
14 C. Pemberton Hodgson *Reminiscences of Australia, with Hints on the Squatter's Life* London, 1846
15 Information from Dr L.A. Dawson; Ludwig Leichhardt *Journal of an Overland Expedition in Australia* London, 1847
16 Gwen Fox (comp.) *Pioneers of the Taroom and Wandoan District* Taroom, 1959
17 L. Leichhardt op. cit.
18 *SMH* 30 March 1854
19 L. Leichhardt op. cit.
20 ML MSS 939 Roper family. John Roper to William and Charles Roper, 18 August 1846
21 L. Leichhardt op. cit.
22 ibid.
23 E.M. Webster *An Explorer at Rest. Ludwig Leichhardt at Port Essington and on the Homeward Voyage 1845–1846* Melbourne, 1986, pp. 25–26
24 *Truth* 9 February 1908
25 Ludwig Leichhardt *Dr Ludwig Leichhardt's Letters From Australia During the Years March 23, 1842, to April 3, 1848* Melbourne, 1944. L. Leichhardt to brother-in-law from *Heroine* 24 January 1846
26 ML MSS 939
27 ML A2992 Macarthur Papers 1844–5 Vol. 96 p. 7
28 *SMH* 18 November 1858
29 *Truth* 9 February 1908
30 *SMH* 18 November 1858; NSW *Government Gazette* 1859, No. 114
31 *Bailliere's Gazeteer of New South Wales* 1866
32 J.G. Knight (comp.) *The Australasian Colonies at the International Exhibition, London, 1862,* Melbourne, 1865
33 *Yass Courier* 4 January 1862; 6 April 1867
34 *SMH* 27 July 1865

14 The tale has been much admired
1 ML A4496 Letter W.B. Clarke to Louisa Atkinson 13 January 1865
2 W. Woolls *Sermon* op. cit. p. 7
3 Serialised in *SM* beginning 4 March 1871
4 *Tom Hellicar's Children* p. 2
5 ibid. p. 9
6 ibid. p. 14
7 ibid. p. 37
8 ibid. pp. 69–70
9 ibid. p. 8

10   ibid. pp. 47–48
11   ML A4496 Letter John Fairfax to Louisa Calvert, 7 July 1871
12   ML A4496 Letters Louisa Atkinson to Fitzhardinge, 29 July 1867; 29 July 1867 (another); 31 July 1867
13   Information from Enid Canning, Georges Hall, NSW
14   Information from Essie Whiteman, Springwood, NSW; *Truth* 5 May 1918; *Evening News* 27 July 1905
15   Tim Fisher, Australian National Gallery, commented that the painting was in the style of Glover. At that time I had not discovered that Charlotte Barton had trained under Glover. I am grateful to Charlotte Drevermann for lending me this painting to have it copied.
16   Information from Essie Whiteman. I am grateful to Essie Whiteman for giving me a copy of this painting.

15   Mr Calvert has as kind thoughtful ways as a woman and I want for nothing

1   ML A4496 Letter from Louisa Calvert to Mary Kelly 8 May 1869
2   ibid. Marriage certificate transcription
3   ML A4496. The letter is dated 8 May 1868 but this appears to be a mistake, as it is signed Louisa Calvert. The date is wrongly recorded in the index to ML A4496 as 8 November 1868.
4   ML A4496. Letter to Mary Kelly op. cit.
5   ML A4496 Marriage certificate transcription
6   'Among the Murrumbidgee Limestones', AVC, *SMH* 11 May 1870
7   ibid.
8   ibid.
9   ibid.
10   'After Shells in the Limestone', AVC, *SMH* 24 May 1870
11   *SMH* 27 May 1870
12   'Climatic Influences on the Habits of Birds', AVC, *SMH* 16 June 1870
13   'After Shells in the Limestone' op. cit.
14   ibid.
15   'Fitzroy Iron Mines' *SMH* 9 November 1870
16   *Gertrude* pp. 38–39
17   'The Fitzroy Waterfalls' *SMH* 2 January 1871
18   'A Trip to the Southward—Manaro, Molonglo, and the New South Road' *SMH* 29 May 1871
19   'The Wallaby Rocks' *SMH* 20 September 1870
20   ML A4496 Letter von Mueller to Louisa Calvert 31 January 1871
21   *SM* 1 April 1871
22   ML A4496 Letter from Louisa Calvert to Mrs Woolls
23   J.H.L. Zillmann *Career of a Cornstalk* Sydney, 1914 pp. 37–38; *Truth* 7 April 1918
24   'The Prussian Deaconesses' *SMH* 7 July 1870
25   'The Wallaby Rocks' op. cit.
26   'Fitzroy Iron Mines' op. cit.
27   'The Wallaby Rocks' op. cit.
28   'Fitzroy Iron Mines' op. cit.
29   ML A4496 Letter from W. Woolls to Louisa Calvert, 17 November 1870
30   ibid. Letter from F. von Mueller to Louisa Calvert, 31 January 1871
31   I am indebted to Mrs Doris Sinkora, National Herbarium of Victoria, and a member of an international committee collecting the correspondence of F. von Mueller for the information on Professors Moebius and Krauss.

32 ML A4496. Letter F. von Mueller op. cit.
33 'Hanging Rock on the Southern Road' SMH 3 February 1871.
34 'The Fitzroy Waterfalls' op. cit.
35 'Hanging Rock on the Southern Road' op. cit.
36 'The Cataract Coal Mine' *SMH* 6 October 1870
37 'Climatic Influences on the Habits of Birds' op. cit.
38 ibid.
39 ibid.
40 The *Walter Hood* was wrecked at Wreck Bay on 26 April 1870.
41 'The Wallaby Rocks' op. cit.
42 ibid.

16 We will be most happy to see you and Mr Calvert
1 'A Trip to the Southward–Manaro, Molonglo and the New Road' *SMH* 29 May 1871
2 *SMH* 15, 29 May 1871
3 William Branwhite Clarke *Researches in the Southern Gold Fields of New South Wales*, published in 1860 describing a journey made in 1851.
4 *SM* 1 April 1871
5 Testimonial by his former pupils at Calder House to J.F. Castle in possession of Mrs Helen Castle Roche, Cavan West
6 Information from Mrs Kathleen Cape, Rose Bay, NSW and Mrs Judy Bartram, Neutral Bay, NSW
7 Robert Dawson, Police Magistrate at Cooma, was a brother-in-law of Maurice Harnett, and also educated at Calder House. He was not related to James Calvert's brother-in-law, Robert Dawson of the Australian Agricultural Company.
8 Mrs Kathleen Cape, a grand-daughter of Minnie and Maurice Harnett, has been unable to trace these sketches.
9 ML A4496 Mrs Minnie Harnett to Mrs Calvert, 19 April 1871
10 *Flora Australiensis*—'Zieria cytisoides. A much branched shrub, hoary all over...' It had been found by Caley in the mountains, near Bathurst by Fraser and A. Cunningham, by Huegal and F. Mueller at Twofold Bay and at Castle Creek by Leichhardt.
11 ML A4496 William Woolls to Mrs Calvert, 15 March 1871
12 ibid. 20 March 1871
13 National Herbarium of Victoria, undated letter [?May/June 1871] Lousia Calvert to F. von Mueller
14 ML A4496 Louisa Calvert to Rev. W.B. Clarke, undated [April/May 1871]
15 *SMH* 14 April 1871
16 *Town and Country Journal* 13 May, 3 June 1871. These articles seem to be the basis for the claim that Louisa Atkinson wrote for the *Town and Country Journal*.
17 Horton William Atkinson, born to Louisa's brother James John Oldbury Atkinson and Sarah Horton in 1870.
18 Charlotte Ann Eliza Selkirk, born in 1844 to John and Sarah Selkirk, Emma Selkirk's step-daughter, married William Henry Bowman on 21 December 1869 at St Peter's Anglican Church, Richmond.
19 ML A4496 Mrs Comrie to Mrs Calvert 30 June 1871
20 Henry Selkirk, born in 1857 to Emma and John Selkirk, was employed in the NSW Lands Department for nearly 50 years, and was a Councillor of the Royal Australian Historical Society. He died in 1930.

21 ML A4496 Emma Selkirk to 'Dianella', 14 July [1871]
22 *SM* 31 August–7 December 1872
23 'Balonne Lizard', AVC, *SMH* 14 July 1864; 'Among the Murrumbidgee Limestones' *SMH* 11 May 1870
24 *Tressa's Resolve SM* 19 October 1872
25 ibid. 7 December 1872
26 ibid.
27 ibid. 14 September 1872
28 ibid. 30 November 1872
29 ibid. 30 November 1872
30 ibid. 7 December 1872
31 ML A4496 Robert Adams to Mrs Calvert, 8 September 1871
32 *SM* 21 October 1871
33 ibid. 2 December 1871
34 ibid. 10 February 1872
35 ML A4496 Louisa Calvert to Mrs Sarah Woolls

17 She was cut down like a flower in the midst of her days

 1 Information from Janet Cosh, Moss Vale, NSW. Louisa Calvert's death certificate (1872/3219) states the cause of death as 'heart disease'.
 2 NLA MS610 Deane papers, Series 4 14/228
 3 Rev. Richard Polwhele in Gary Kelly (ed.) *Mary, a Fiction and the Wrongs of Woman* London, 1976, p. vii
 4 W. Woolls *Sermon* op. cit. p. 13
 5 ibid. p. 8
 6 *SM* 31 August 1872
 7 *SM* 9 July 1872
 8 Information from Janet Cosh; *Sands Directory* shows J.S. Calvert living at Botany in 1877 and 1879
 9 Death certificate James S. Calvert. Obituaries were published in the *London Times* 15 September 1884 and Sydney *Evening News* 24 July 1884
10 Information from J.B. Atkinson, Bentley, WA
11 Information from Janet Cosh
12 ibid.
13 Tertius Trafford Atkinson's second name seems to be a link back to the Trafford family of Lancashire who employed Charlotte Barton (then Charlotte Waring) as a governess and with whom she remained friendly.
14 Information from J.B. Atkinson
15 ML A4496 William Woolls to Louisa Calvert, 17 March 1891
16 ibid. 1 March 1893
17 ibid. Mrs S.E. Woolls to Louise Calvert, 2 July 1900. This book with James Calvert's memoir of his wife has not been found.
18 *Truth* 5 May 1918
19 Undated cutting [1911], unnamed paper, in possession of Enid Canning, Georges Hall, NSW
20 *SMH* 2 May 1872
21 *SMH* 8 March 1911
22 *SMH* 1 January 1923
23 *SMH* 17 March 1899
24 W. Woolls *Sermon...*op. cit.
25 ML A4496 William Woolls to Louise Calvert, 1 March 1893

Bibliography

Works by Louisa Atkinson

Novels

Gertrude, the Emigrant: A Tale of Colonial Life by an Australian lady, Sydney, J.R. Clarke, 1857

Cowanda, the Veteran's Grant Sydney, J.R. Clarke, 1859

Debatable Ground, or the Carlillawarra Claimants serialised *Sydney Mail* 1861

Myra serialised *Sydney Mail* 1864; published book form Canberra, Mulini Press, 1989

Tom Hellicar's Children serialised *Sydney Mail* 1871; published book form Canberra, Mulini Press, 1983

Tressa's Resolve serialised *Sydney Mail* 1872

Articles

A Voice From the Country Canberra, Mulini Press, 1978 [selected articles from 'A Voice From the Country' series]

Excursions from Berrima and a Trip to Manaro and Molonglo in the 1870s Canberra, Mulini Press, 1980 [selected articles]

In *Illustrated Sydney News*
'Notes of the Months. October'; plus drawing of magpies. 15 October 1853
'The Burning Forest. A Sketch of Australian Bushlife.' 22 October 1853
'The Native Arts. No. 1'; plus drawing of scene. 26 November 1853
'Notes of the Months. December'; plus drawing of 'The Sparrow-Hawk of the Colonists'. 3 December 1853. Drawing repeated 2 June 1855; 16 November 1865
'Notes of the Months. January'; plus drawing of possums. 7 January 1854
'The Native Arts. No. 2'. 4 February 1854
Drawing of koala with unsigned note, 4 February 1854, repeated 26 May 1855; 16 September 1865
Drawing of 'The flying squirrel and the ring-tailed opossum' with unsigned note. 4 February 1854, repeated 12 May 1855; 16 September 1865
Drawing 'Razor Back on the Goulburn Road', 18 February 1854
'A Peep at a Coal Mine'; plus drawing of 'Mount Keira Coal Mine, near Wollongong', 14 April 1855; 'Sheep Washing' plus drawing, 15 October 1864
(Several other unsigned articles and drawings of animals and birds published in the *Illustrated Sydney News* in 1854–55 are probably by Louisa Atkinson.)

In *Sydney Morning Herald* and *Sydney Mail*
'January' [includes February], AVC, *SMH*, 1 March 1860

246

'March', AVC, *SMH* 6 April 1860
'Flying Fox Hunting in the Blue Mountains' *SMH* 26 April 1860
'April', AVC, *SMH* 15 May 1860
'May', AVC, *SMH* 5 June 1860
'June', AVC, *SM* 21 July 1860
'July', AVC, *SM* 4 August 1860
'The Kurrajong Waterfalls', AVC, *SMH* 9 August 1860; *SM* 18 August 1860
'August', AVC, *SMH* 10 September 1860; *SM* 22 September 1860
'Burrolow', AVC, *SMH* 19 October 1860; *SM* 27 October 1860
'Tabarag', AVC, *SM* 29 December 1860
'Cabbage-tree Hollow, and the Valley of the Grose', AVC, *SMH* 7 January 1861;
    SM 12 January 1860
'Mount Tomah', AVC, *SMH* 28 January 1861; *SM* 2 February 1861
'Ovaology', AVC, *SMH* 11 March 1861; *SM* 6 April 1861
'The Grose River', AVC, *SMH* 10 April 1861; *SM* 20 April 1861
'Reptilia', AVC, *SMH* 1 May 1861; *SM* 11 May 1861
'A Winter's Garland', AVC, *SMH* 2 July 1861; *SM* 6 July 1861
'Antechinus. Bees', AVC, *SMH* 30 July 1861; *SM* 3 August 1861
'A Night Adventure in the Bush', AVC, *SMH* 22 October 1861
'The Ranges of the Grose', AVC, *SMH* 30 January 1862
'Springwood', AVC, *SMH* 20 March 1862
'A Peep Into the Herb Doctor's Basket', AVC, *SMH* 10 June 1862
'Scraps', AVC, *SMH* 8 August 1862
'Botanical Ramblings', AVC, *SMH* 2 September 1862
'Orchidaceae', AVC, *SMH* 23 October 1862
'Epacrideae', AVC, *SMH* 2 January 1863
'Ferns and Their Haunts', AVC, *SMH* 12 February 1863
'Insects and Insect Feeders', AVC, *SMH* 2 May 1863
'A Ride to the Fitzroy Mines', AVC, *SMH* 4 June 1863
'A Summer Picture' and 'A Winter's Picture in the Tablelands of the South', AVC,
    SMH 2 July 1863
'Recollections of the Aborigines', AVC, *SM* 12 September 1863; *SMH* 22 September 1863
'Recollections of the Aborigines (continued)', AVC *SM* 19 September 1863; *SMH* 25 September 1863
'Recollections of the Aborigines (concluded)' *SM* 26 September 1863; *SMH* 28 September 1863
'Wiseman's Ferry', AVC, *SMH* 5 January 1864
'Balonne Lizard', AVC, *SMH* 14 July 1864
'Stray Notes', AVC, *SMH* 25 October 1864
'Spiders etc.', AVC, *SMH* 2 February 1865; *SM* 4 February 1865
'Leichhardt', AVC, *SMH* 2 May 1865; *SM* 6 May 1865
'Among the Murrumbidgee Limestones', AVC, *SMH* 11 May 1870
'After Shells in the Limestone', AVC, *SMH* 24 May 1870
'Climatic Influences on the Habits of Birds', AVC, *SMH* 16 June 1870
'The Prussian Deaconesses', *SMH* 7 July 1870
'The Wallaby Rocks' *SMH* 24 September 1870
'The Cataract Coal Mine' *SMH* 5 October 1870
'Fitzroy Iron Mines' *SMH* 9 November 1870
'The Fitzroy Waterfalls' *SMH* 2 January 1871; same 'The Tourist' *SM* 7 January
    1871
'Hanging Rock on the Great Southern Road' *SMH* 3 February 1871; same 'The
    Tourist' *SM* 11 February 1871

'A Trip Southward' *SMH* 15 May 1871
'A Trip to the Southward—Manaro, Molonglo, and the New Road' *SMH* 29 May 1871
'The New Bush Home' by a country housemother. No. I, *SM* 21 October 1871
—— No. II, *SM* 2 December 1871
—— [No. III], *SM* 10 February 1872

In *Horticultural Magazine*
'Ferns—Growing and Dried', July 1864
'Ferns of the Kurrajong' (Second paper), August 1864
'Ferns of the Kurrajong' (Third paper), October 1864
(It is possible that more articles by Louisa Atkinson will be discovered in the newspapers and periodicals of the 1850s–1860s.)

Lyrics

'Cooey' Melbourne, Sydney, John Davis, 185?
'The Light From the Mountain', Melbourne, Edward Arnold, 185?

Manuscript material

ML A4496 Calvert correspondence includes correspondence; drafts of some articles arranged as a book only a fragment of which exists—'Recollections of the Hunter District'; Chapter 16 'A Rambling Paper on Zoology. Animals'; 'A Second Paper on Zoology. Birds, Reptiles'; Chapter 18 'Phytological Sketches'; Chapter 22 'A Night Adventure in the Bush' (printed in AVC series, 22 October 1861); Chapter 23 'Lost!'; news cuttings; copies of marriage certificates
ML A4497 Press cuttings of some AVC articles
ML A4498 Ferns (about 40 watercolours of ferns, apparently intended as illustrations for a book on Australian ferns)
ML A4499 Calvert sketchbook. Sketches and watercolours of Oldbury, birds, plants and butterflies, practice drawings
ML A4500 Calvert sketchbook. Watercolours, sketches of scenes etc.
ML A4501 Sketches—Calvert and others. Includes five specimen plates for book on Australian animals and birds to be published in Germany
ML MSS 3849/1 Notes by Louisa Calvert
ML MSS 3849/2 Copies of presentation books
ML Uncatalogued material. Includes sketches, watercolours. Pic. Acc. 4928
Macleay Museum University of Sydney, Note Louisa Atkinson to William S. Macleay
National Herbarium, Melbourne, Letter to F. von Mueller

Manuscripts, unpublished material

Ancher, Edward A. 'Index to Drama and Music in New South Wales by F.C. Brewer', 1922. Typescript NLA
Barker, Thomas Papers NLA MS 3602
Berrima District Historical Society. Notes given to the Society by Janet Cosh. ML MS 3141
Berry Papers ML MSS 315
Clout, Rev. N. 'Genesis of the Clout family' (typescript in possession of James Fellows)

Cosh and Atkinson ML MSS 3849 1–2
Forde, J.M. 'Old Sydney' NLA MS 3487
Gilbert, Lionel 'Botanical Investigations in New South Wales 1811–1880', PhD thesis, University of New England, 1971, NLA MS 3148
Hunt collection, MS 'Australian Botanists Biographical and Bibliographic Papers', Australian Academy of Science, c. 1964
King papers ML A1976 CY904 Vol. I
Macarthur Papers ML A2992 1844–50 Vol. 96
Maddrell Papers ML Uncat. MSS 511
Norton, James Papers ML A5328–2; A5427–2; A5375 1–2
Roper family 1842–68, ML MSS 939

Official records

AONSW 4/5667 Bench books, Berrima Court of Petty Sessions, 2 September 1833–27 July 1836
AONSW Reel 664, Bench books, Sutton Forest Court of Petty Sessions, AO Reel 664
AONSW Reel 2560 Colonial Secretary. Index to land grants and leases 1792–1865
AONSW Passenger lists
AONSW 4/6529 Parramatta Gaol Entrance Books
AONSW 5/7646 Henry Selkirk papers
AONSW 4/4018 Shipping Lists Convict ships
AONSW 2/4150 Supreme Court. Causes and matters for hearing in Equity 1844–46
AONSW 7/3459–61, Supreme Court, Equity Proceedings
AONSW 2/3964 Supreme Court. Equity Proceedings in Court 1841–46
AONSW 5/4496 Supreme Court. Master in Equity Order Book July 1831– August 1839; 5/4497 January 1841–May 1845; 5/4498 May 1845–May 1847; 5/4499 1847–50
HRA Series 1, Vols X, XI, XII, XVI, XVII
ML B773 Bench books Berrima Court of Petty Sessions, 3 April 2826–2 April 1827
NSW Births, Deaths and Marriages records
NSW Census 1828
NSW General return of convicts 1837
NSW Government Gazettes
NSW Lands Department. Grants and purchases; parish maps
NSW Supreme Court. Wills

Books, pamphlets

Atkinson, James *An Account of the State of Agriculture and Grazing in New South Wales* London, J. Cross, 1826; facsimile edition, introduction by Brian H. Fletcher, Sydney, Sydney University Press, 1975
Atkinson, James *On the Expediency and Necessity of Encouraging Distilling and Brewing From Grain in New South Wales* 2nd ed:, Sydney, 1829
Australian Council of National Trusts *Historic Homesteads of Australia* North Melbourne, Vic., Cassell Australia Ltd, 1969
Aurousseau, M. (ed.) *The Letters of F.W. Ludwig Leichhardt* The Hakluyt Society and Cambridge University Press, 1986
Bailliere's Gazetteer of New South Wales 1866
Barnhart, John Hendley (comp.) *Biographical Notes upon Botanists* Boston, G.K. Hall and Co., 1965

[Barton, Charlotte] *A Mother's Offering to Her Children* by 'A lady long resident in New South Wales' Sydney, G.W. Evans, 1841; another edition introduction by Rosemary Wighton, Adelaide, 1978
Barton, George Burnett *Literature of New South Wales* Sydney, Government Printer, 1866
Bentham, George *Flora Australiensis: a Description of the Plants of the Australian Territory* London, Lovell Reeve and Co., 7 vols. 1863–78
Berry, Alexander *Reminiscences of Alexander Berry* Sydney, Angus and Robertson, 1912
Bodkin, Frances *Encyclopaedia Botanica* North Ryde, NSW, Angus and Robertson, 1986
Brabazon's NSW General Town Directory 1843
Brewer, F.C. *The Drama and Music in New South Wales*, Sydney, Government Printer, 1892
Budawang Committee *Fitzroy Falls and Beyond* Budawang Committee, 1988
Burfitt, Charles E. *History of the Founding of the Wool Industry of Australia* Sydney, F.W. White, 1907
Carr, D.J. and S.G.M. (eds) *People and Plants in Australia* Sydney, Academic Press, 1981
Cavanough, Jane, Prell, Anthea & North, Tim *Gardens of the Southern Highlands NSW 1828–1988*, [Sydney?], *The Australian Garden Journal*, 1988
Chisholm, Alec H. (ed.) *Australian Encyclopaedia*, Sydney, Angus and Robertson, 1958
—— *Strange journey, the Adventures of Ludwig Leichhardt and John Gilbert* Adelaide, Rigby, 1973
Collier, James *The Pastoral Age in Australia* London, Whitcombe and Tombs, 1911
Desmond, Ray *Dictionary of British and Irish Botanists and Horticulturalists* London, Taylor and Francis, 1977
Eldershaw, Flora (ed.) *The Peaceful Army 1788–1938*, Sydney, Women's Executive Committee and Advisory Council of Australia's 150th Anniversary celebrations, 1938
Else-Mitchell, R. *Early Industries in the Mittagong district*, Berrima District Historical Society, 1974
Eslick, Christine, Hughes, Joy and Jack, R. Ian *Bibliography of NSW Local Histories* Kensington, NSW, NSW University Press, 1987
Flexner, Eleanor *Mary Wollstonecraft* New York, Coward, McCann and Geoghegan, 1972
Fox, Gwen (comp.) *Pioneers of the Taroom and Wandoan District* Taroom Shire Council, 1959
Franklin, Miles *Laughter, Not for a Cage* Sydney, Angus and Robertson, 1956
Gilbert, Lionel *William Woolls 1814–1893 A Most Useful Colonist* Canberra, Mulini Press, 1985
Gledhill, P.W. *St Peter's Church of England, Richmond. 1810–1941*, 1941
Gould, John *The Mammals of Australia* with modern notes by Joan M. Dixon, South Melbourne, Vic., Macmillan, 1983
Grainger, Elena *The Remarkable Reverend Clarke* Melbourne, Oxford University Press, 1982
Hall, Norman *Botanists of Australian Acacias* Canberra, CSIRO, 1984
—— *Botanists of the Eucalypts* Canberra, CSIRO, 1978
Heaton, J. Henniker *Australian Dictionary of Dates and Men of the Time* Sydney, George Robertson, 1879
Hergenhan, Laurie *The Penguin New Literary History of Australia* Ringwood, Vic., Penguin Books, 1988

Bibliography

Hodgson, C. Pemberton *Reminiscences of Australia, With Hints on the Squatter's Life* London, W.N. Wright, 1846

Irvin, Eric *Australian Melodrama, Eighty Years of Popular Theatre* Sydney, Hale and Iremonger, 1981

Jack, R. Logan *Northernmost Australia* London, Simpkin, Marshall, Hamilton, Kent, 1911

Jervis, James *A History of the Berrima District 1798–1961* Berrima County Council, 1962; another edition 1798–1973

'Juvenal, Pindar' *The Van Diemen's Land Warriors, or the Heroes of Cornwall; a Satire in Three Cantos* Hobart, Colonial Times Office, 1827

Keay, John *Explorers Extraordinary* London, John Murray/BBC, 1985

Knight, J.G. (comp.) *The Australasian Colonies at the International Exhibition, London, 1862* Melbourne, Government Printer, 1865

Kynaston, Edward *A Man on Edge. A Life of Baron Sir Ferdinand von Mueller* Ringwood, Vic., Penguin, 1981

Lawson, Elizabeth *The Distant Sound of Native Voices* Occasional Paper No. 15, Canberra, English Department, University College, ADFA, June 1989

Lee, Sidney (ed.) *Dictionary of National Biography* London, Smith Elder, 1899

Leichhardt, Ludwig, assisted by Capt P.P. King *Journal of an Overland Expedition in Australia* London, T. & W. Boone, 1847

Maclehose, James *Picture of Sydney and Strangers' Guide to N.S.W. 1839* facs. ed. Sydney, John Ferguson, 1977

Mennell, Philip *Dictionary of Australasian Biography* London, Hutchinson, 1892

Mitchell, Blanche *Blanche, An Australian Diary 1858–1861. The Diary of Blanche Mitchell With Notes by Edna Hickson* Sydney, John Ferguson, 1980

Miller, E. Morris *Australian Literature From its Beginnings to 1935* Carlton, Vic., Melbourne University Press, 1940

Montefiore, Dora B. *From a Victorian to a Modern* London, E. Archer, 1927

Mount Tomah Society *The Mount Tomah Book*, 2nd ed. Sydney, The Mount Tomah Society and the Royal Botanic Gardens, 1987

Moyle, Ann *A Bright and Savage Land*, Sydney, Collins, 1986

Moyle, Ann Mozley (ed.) *Scientists in Nineteenth Century Australia. A Documentary History* Melbourne, Cassell Australia, 1976

Mueller, Ferdinand von *Fragmenta Phytographiae Australiae* Melbourne, Government Printer, 1858

Muir, Marcie *Charlotte Barton: Australia's First Children's Author* Sydney, Wentworth Books, 1980

Niall, Brenda *Australia Through the Looking-Glass* Melbourne University Press, 1984

Oakes, Archdeacon G.S. *Pioneers of Bathurst /Kelso and Bush Memories of the West*

Perry, T.M. *Australia's First Frontier* Melbourne University Press, 1963

Pike, Douglas (ed.) *Australian Dictionary of Biography* Melbourne University Press, 1966

Politzer, L.L. (ed.) *Dr Ludwig Leichhardt's Letters From Australia During the Years March 23, 1842, to April 3, 1848* Melbourne, Pan Publishers, 1944

Pratt, Anne *Haunts of the Wildflower* London, Routledge, Warne and Routledge, 1863

Proceedings of the Royal Geographical Society 1865

Ransom, W.S. (ed.) *Australian National Dictionary* Melbourne, Oxford University Press, 1988

Roderick, Colin *Leichhardt, the Dauntless Explorer* Sydney, Angus and Robertson, 1988

Roxburgh, Rachel *Early Colonial Houses of New South Wales* Sydney, Ure Smith, 1974

—— *Historic Homesteads of New South Wales* North Melbourne, Cassell, 1969
Serle, Percival *Dictionary of Australian Biography* Sydney, Angus and Robertson, 1949
Shepherd, T.W. *Catalogue of Plants Cultivated at the Darling Nursery, Sydney, NSW* Sydney, W. and F. Ford, 1851
Silken Whispers from Sutton Forest, Sydney, Anglican Press, 1959
Smail, J.M. *Louisa Atkinson of the Kurrajong,* J.M. Smail, Kurrajong Heights, NSW, Kurrajong Heights Garden Club, 1984
Spender, Dale *Two Centuries of Australian Women Writers* London, Pandora, 1988
—— *Women of Ideas and What Men Have Done to Them* London, Ark Paperbacks, 1983
Stanbury, Peter and Julian Holland *Mr Macleay's Celebrated Cabinet* Sydney, The Macleay Museum 1988
Therry, Sir Roger *Reminiscences of Thirty Years' Residence in New South Wales* London, Sampson, Low, 1863
Thompson, M.M.H. *William Woolls, a Man of Parramatta* Sydney, Hale and Iremonger, 1986
Tindale, Norman B. *Aboriginal Tribes of Australia* Canberra, 1974
Tomalin, Claire *The Life and Death of Mary Wollstonecraft* London, Weidenfeld and Nicholson, 1974
Toy, Ann et al. *Hearth and Home. Women's Decorative Arts and Crafts 1800–1930* Glebe, NSW, Historic Houses Trust of NSW, 1988
Walsh, Dorothy (ed.) *The Admiral's Wife* Melbourne, The Hawthorn Press, 1967
Walker, R.C. *Works on New South Wales* Sydney, Government Printer, 1878
Webb, Vivienne *Kurrajong. An Early History* Sydney, Vivienne Webb, 1980
Webster, E.M. *An Explorer at Rest Ludwig Leichhardt at Port Essington and on the Homeward Voyage 1845–1846* Carlton, Vic., Melbourne University Press, 1986
—— *Whirlwinds in the Plains* Carlton, Vic. Melbourne University Press, 1980
Wells, William Henry *A Geographical Dictionary or Gazetteer of the Australian Colonies* Sydney, W. & F. Ford, 1848
Wilde, William, Hooton, Joy and Andrews, Barry *The Oxford Companion to Australian Literature,* Carlton, Vic., Melbourne University Press, 1985
Wollstonecraft, Mary *Vindication of the Rights of Woman* 2nd ed., London, J. Johnson, 1792; another Brody, Miriam Krammick (ed.) Middlesex, England, Penguin, 1975
Woolls, William *A Contribution to the Flora of Australia* Sydney, F. White, 1867
—— *Lectures on the Vegetable Kingdom* Sydney, C.E. Fuller, 1879
—— *The Plants of New South Wales* Sydney, Government Printer, 1885
—— *Sermon Preached in St Peter's Church, Richmond...April 12, 1874...on the occasion of a tablet...placed...to the memory of the late Mrs. Calvert* Windsor, NSW, B. Isaacs [printer], 1874
Wrightson, S.O. *Notes on Early History of Berrima* 1977 (pamphlet)
Zillmann, J.H.L. *Career of a Cornstalk* Sydney, 1914

Articles

Atkinson, James 'Remarks on Saxon Sheep Farming' *Australian Quarterly Journal of Theology, Literature and Science* C.P.N. Wilton (ed.), Sydney, 1828
Cambage, R.H. 'Exploration between the Wingecarribee, Shoalhaven, Macquarie and Murrumbidgee Rivers' *RAHS Journal and Proceedings* Part V, 1921
Fairfax, J. 'Some Recollections of Old Sydney' *RAHS Journal* Vol. V, Part 1, 1919
Gilbert, L. 'Plants, Politics, Personalities in Nineteenth Century New South Wales' *RAHS Journal* Vol. 56, Part 1, March 1970

Henderson, C.A. 'Recollections of Mr. C.A. Henderson. Sydney to Homebush, 1855' *RAHS Journal* Vol. VIII, 1923

Hendy-Pooley, Grace 'Early History of Bathurst and Surroundings' *RAHS Journal* Vol. 1, Part II, 1905

Jervis, James 'Berry, the Laird of Shoalhaven' *RAHS Journal* Vol. XXVII. Part I, 1941

—— 'Fitzroy Falls' *RAHS Journal* Vol. 29, 1943

—— 'Illawarra: a Century of History 1788–1888' *RAHS Journal* Vol. XXXIII, 1942, Part VI

—— 'The Journals of William Edward Riley' *RAHS Journal and Proceedings* Vol. XXXII, Part IV, 1946

—— 'Kangaroo Valley—some notes on its history' *RAHS Journal* Vol. XXXVI, Part II, 1950

—— 'Settlement in the Marulan-Bungonia district' *RAHS Journal* Vol. XXXII, Part II, 1946

——'Some notes on Kangaroo Valley' *RAHS Journal*, Vol. XXXVI, part II, 1950

—— 'The Wingecarribee and Southern Highlands district' *RAHS Journal* Vol. XXIII. Part IV, 1937

Jose, Arthur 'The Van Diemen's Land Warriors' *RAHS Journal* Vol. XIV, Part IV, 1928

Lawson, Elizabeth 'Louisa Atkinson, Naturalist and Novelist' in Adelaide, Debra *A Bright and Fiery Troop. Australian Women Writers of the Nineteenth Century* Ringwood, Vic., Penguin Books, 1988

Mueller F. von 'The fate of Dr Leichhardt and a proposed new search for his party', delivered at St George's Hall, Melbourne, 9 February 1865. Reprinted from the *Australasian* 18 February 1865

Prior, James 'Literary Lady Who Never Went to School' *Sun* 21 January 1986

Reeve, G. 'Richmond native. The Late Henry Selkirk' *Windsor and Richmond Gazette* 4 July 1930

Roxburgh, Rachel 'The Meryla Pass' *RAHS Journal* Vol. 66, Part 4, March 1981

Rudduck, Loma 'A Woman and her Book' *RAHS Jounral* Vol. 48, Part 4, 1962

Salmon, Mary 'Australian Pioneers. Literary Woman' *Sydney Morning Herald* 8 March 1911

—— 'An Early Australian Press Writer' *SMH* 1 January 1923

Swann, Margaret 'Mrs. Meredith and Miss Atkinson, Writers and Naturalists' *RAHS Journal* Vol. XV, Part 1, 1929

Windschuttle, Elizabeth 'Educating the Daughters of the Ruling Class in Colonial New South Wales 1788–1850' *Melbourne Studies in Education* (ed.) Stephen Murray-Smith, Carlton, Vic., Melbourne University Press, 1980

Woolls, William 'Curiosities of Australian Vegetation' *Sydney Mail* 13 July 1872

Wymark, Marjorie 'Pioneer Women' *Country Woman* July 1969

'First of the Native-born—a Woman in Australian History' *Australian Woman's Mirror* 1 March 1950

'Henry Selkirk' *RAHS Journal* Vol. XVI, 1930

'The late Mrs Calvert' (Obituary) *SMH* 2 May 1872

'The late Mrs J.S. Calvert' *Town and Country Journal* 30 November 1878

'Oldbury Farm' *Australian Women's Weekly* 14 October 1964

'Our First Woman Novelist. Work of Caroline Atkinson' by H.M. *Melbourne Age* 25 October 1947

Index